American Diplomatic History
Since 1890

GOLDENTREE BIBLIOGRAPHIES
In American History
under the series editorship of
Arthur S. Link

American Diplomatic History Since 1890

compiled by

Wilton B. Fowler
University of Washington

AHM Publishing Corporation
Northbrook, Illinois 60062

ISBN: 0-88295-544-6

Library of Congress Card Number: 74-76971

PRINTED IN THE UNITED STATES OF AMERICA

715

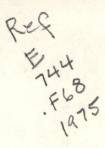

Contents

Editor's Foreword

GOLDENTREE BIBLIOGRAPHIES IN AMERICAN HISTORY are designed to provide students, teachers, and librarians with ready and reliable guides to the literature of American History in all its remarkable scope and variety. Volumes in the series cover comprehensively the major periods in American history, while additional volumes are devoted to all important subjects.

Goldentree Bibliographies attempt to steer a middle course between the brief list of references provided in the average textbook and the long bibliography in which significant items are often lost in the sheer number of titles listed. Each bibliography is, therefore, selective, with the sole criterion for choice being the significance—and not the age—of any particular work. The result is bibliographies of all works, including journal articles and doctoral dissertations, that are still useful, without bias in favor of any particular historiographical school.

Each compiler is a scholar long associated, both in research and teaching, with the period or subject of his volume. All compilers have not only striven to accomplish the objective of this series but have also cheerfully adhered to a general style and format. However, each compiler has been free to define his field, make his own selections, and work out internal organization as the unique demands of his period or subject have seemed to dictate.

The single great objective of *Goldentree Bibliographies in American History* will have been achieved if these volumes help researchers and students to find their way to the significant literature of American history.

Arthur S. Link

Preface

In compiling this bibliography, I have benefited from suggestions made by the following friends and associates: Thomas A. Bailey, Arthur S. Link, J. Kenneth McDonald, Gaddis Smith, David F. Trask, and Samuel F. Wells, Jr. I thank them, but I also absolve them of responsibility for the finished product. The scheme of organization and the final choice of items for inclusion are mine.

My intention has been to select approximately 2,500 titles (a) which cover the important topics in the diplomatic history of the United States since 1890, and (b) which are available to the user of a college or university library. Because doctoral dissertations are now readily accessible (on microfilm or by interlibrary loan), and because so much of recent scholarship is contained in them, I have incorporated quite a few of them in this listing. No doubt some items have been omitted which should not have been, but I trust that the number is small.

Wilton B. Fowler

Abbreviations

Ag Hist	Agricultural History
Am Econ Rev	American Economic Review
Am Hist Rev	American Historical Review
Am J Int Law	American Journal of International Law
Am Pol Sci Rev	American Political Science Review
Am Q	American Quarterly
Ann Am Acad Pol Soc Sci	Annals, American Academy of Political and Social Science
Bus Hist Rev	Business History Review
Can Hist Rev	Canadian Historical Review
Cath Hist Rev	Catholic Historical Review
Econ Hist Rev	Economic History Review
For Aff	Foreign Affairs
His Am Hist Rev	Hispanic American Historical Review
Int Aff	International Affairs (London)
Int-Am Econ Aff	Inter-American Economic Affairs
Int Jour	International Journal
Int Organ	International Organization
J Am Hist	Journal of American History
J Am Stud	Journal of American Studies
J Confl Res	Journal of Conflict Resolution
J Econ Hist	Journal of Economic History
J Hist Ideas	Journal of the History of Ideas
J Interam Stud	Journal of Interamerican Studies and World Affairs
J Latin Am Stud	Journal of Latin American Studies
J Mod Hist	Journal of Modern History
J Neg Hist	Journal of Negro History
J Pol	Journal of Politics
J Pol Econ	Journal of Political Economy
J S Hist	Journal of Southern History
Jour Q	Journalism Quarterly
Mid-Am	Mid-America
Mil Aff	Military Affairs
Miss Val Hist Rev	Mississippi Valley Historical Review
N Eng Q	New England Quarterly
Pac Hist Rev	Pacific Historical Review
Pol Sci Q	Political Science Quarterly
Proc Acad Pol Sci	Proceedings, Academy of Political Science
Proc Am Philos Soc	Proceedings, American Philosophical Society
Proc Mass Hist Soc	Proceedings, Massachusetts Historical Society
Pub Am Jew Hist Soc	Publications, American Jewish Historical Society

ABBREVIATIONS

Pub Opin Q	Public Opinion Quarterly
Rec Am Cath Hist Soc	Records, American Catholic Historical Society
Rev Pol	Review of Politics
Rocky Mtn Soc Sci J	Rocky Mountain Social Science Journal
S Atl Q	South Atlantic Quarterly
Sci Soc	Science and Society
Soc Stud	Social Studies
Va Q Rev	Virginia Quarterly Review
W Pol Q	Western Political Quarterly
Wor Pol	World Politics

NOTE: Cross-references are to item numbers. Items marked by a dagger (†) are available in paperback edition at the time this bibliography goes to press. The publisher and compiler invite suggestions for additions to future editions of the bibliography.

I. General References

1. Bibliographies, Guides, Historiography

1 *America: History and Life.* Santa Barbara, Cal., 1964-   . Abstracts relating to American history.

2 *American Historical Review.* Each issue contains an extensive list of articles in other periodicals.

3 BEMIS, Samuel Flagg, and Grace Gardner GRIFFIN, eds. *Guide to the Diplomatic History of the United States, 1775-1921.* Washington, 1935.

4 CONOVER, Helen F. *A Guide to Bibliographic Tools for Research in Foreign Affairs.* 2d ed. Washington, 1958.

5 Council on Foreign Relations. *Foreign Affairs Bibliography.* 4 vols. New York, 1933-1964.

6 Council on Foreign Relations. *The Foreign Affairs 50-Year Bibliography: New Evaluations of Significant Books on International Relations 1920-1970.* Ed. Bryan Dexter *et al.* New York, 1972.

7 DECONDE, Alexander. *New Interpretations in American Foreign Policy.* Washington, 1961. Historiographical pamphlet.

8 DENNIS, Donnie Lee. "A History of American Diplomatic History." Doctoral dissertation, University of California, Santa Barbara, 1971.

9 DOENECKE, Justus D. *The Literature of Isolationism: A Guide to Non-Interventionist Scholarship, 1930-1972.* Colorado Springs, Colo., 1972.

10 *Dissertation Abstracts: A Guide to Dissertations and Monographs Available in Microfilm.* Ann Arbor, Mich., 1952-

11 EVANS, Laurence. "The Dangers of Diplomatic History." *The State of American History.* Ed. Herbert J. Bass. Chicago, 1970.

12 *Foreign Affairs.* Each quarterly issue evaluates recent books.

12-A GRIFFIN, Grace Gardner, *et al. Writings on American History, 1902-* Washington, 1905-

13 HANDLIN, Oscar, *et al. Harvard Guide to American History.* Cambridge, Mass., 1954.†

14 HOWE, G. F., *et al. The American Historical Association's Guide to Historical Literature.* New York, 1960.

15 MCCORMICK, Thomas J. "The State of American Diplomatic History." *The State of American History.* Ed. Herbert J. Bass. Chicago, 1970.

16 MAY, Ernest R. "The Decline of Diplomatic History." *American History: Retrospect and Prospect.* Ed. George Athan Billias and Gerald N. Grob. New York, 1971.

17 MUGRIDGE, Donald H., and Blanche P. McCRUM. *A Guide to the Study of the United States of America.* Washington, 1960.

18 NEU, Charles E. "The Changing Interpretive Structure of American Foreign Policy." *Twentieth-Century American Foreign Policy.* See 64.

19 SCHMECKEBIER, Laurence F., and Roy B. EASTIN, eds. *Government Publications and Their Use.* 2d ed. Washington, 1961.

20 TRASK, David F. "Writings on American Foreign Relations: 1957 to the Present." *Twentieth-Century American Foreign Policy.* See 64.

21 TRASK, David F., Michael C. MEYER, and Roger R. TRASK, comps. and eds. *A Bibliography of United States-Latin American Relations Since 1810: A Selected List of Eleven Thousand Published References.* Lincoln, Nebr., 1968.

2. Documents

22 BARTLETT, Ruhl J., ed. *The Record of American Diplomacy.* 4th ed. New York, 1964.

23 CHALLENER, Richard D., ed. *From Isolation to Containment, 1921-1952. Three Decades of American Foreign Policy from Harding to Truman.* New York, 1970.†

24 Council on Foreign Relations. *Documents on American Foreign Relations.* New York, 1953-   . Annual.

25 Council on Foreign Relations. *The United States in World Affairs.* New York, 1931-   . Annual survey. Recent vols. ed. Richard P. Stebbins.

26 FERRELL, Robert H., ed. *America as a World Power, 1872-1945.* Columbia, S.C., 1971.†

27 GRAEBNER, Norman A., ed. *Ideas and Diplomacy: Readings in the Intellectual Tradition of American Foreign Policy.* New York, 1964.

28 HACKWORTH, Green H. *Digest of International Law.* 8 vols. Washington, 1940-1944.

29 ISRAEL, Fred L., ed. *Major Peace Treaties of Modern History, 1648-1967.* 4 vols. New York, 1967.

30 LINK, Arthur S., and William M. LEARY, Jr., eds. *The Diplomacy of World Power: The United States, 1889-1920.* New York, 1970.†

31 MOORE, John Bassett. *A Digest of International Law.* 8 vols. Washington, 1906.

32 MOORE, John Bassett. *History and Digest of International Arbitrations.* 6 vols. Washington, 1898.

33   RAPPAPORT, Armin, ed. *Sources in American Diplomacy.* New York, 1966.†

34   Royal Institute of International Affairs. *Documents on International Affairs.* London, 1928-   . Annual.

35   Royal Institute of International Affairs. *Survey of International Affairs.* London, 1925-   . Annual survey with supplementary topical volumes.

36   SCHLESINGER, Arthur M., Jr., ed. *The Dynamics of World Power: A Documentary History of U.S. Foreign Policy, 1945-1973.* 5 vols. New York, 1973.

37   SMITH, Daniel M., ed. *Major Problems in American Diplomatic History: Documents and Readings.* Boston, 1964.

37-A *Treaties and Alliances of the World: An International Survey Covering Treaties in Force and Communities of States.* New York, 1968.

38   United States Department of State. *A Decade of American Foreign Policy: Basic Documents, 1941-1949.* Washington, 1950.

39   United States Department of State. *American Foreign Policy, 1950-1955: Basic Documents.* 2 vols. Washington, 1957.

40   United States Department of State. *American Foreign Policy: Current Documents.* Washington, 1959-   . Annual, covering years since 1956.

41   United States Department of State. *Department of State Bulletin.* Weekly since 1939. Contains public policy statements and other current material.

42   United States Department of State. *Papers Relating to the Foreign Relations of the United States, 1861-*   . Washington, 1862-   . Diplomatic documents; the most important single source for the American diplomatic historian; more than 200 volumes published.

43   United States Department of State. *U.S. Treaties and Other International Agreements, 1950-*   . Washington, 1952-   .

44   United States General Services Administration. *Weekly Compilation of Presidential Documents.* Washington, 1965-   .

45   WHITEMAN, Marjorie M. *Digest of International Law.* 14 vols. Washington, 1963-1970.

46   WILLIAMS, William A., ed. *The Shaping of American Diplomacy: Readings and Documents in American Foreign Relations, 1750-1955.* Chicago, 1956.†

47   World Peace Foundation. *Documents on American Foreign Relations.* New York, 1939-1952. Annual. For continuatior see 24.

3. Syntheses and Broad Interpretations

48   ADLER, Selig. *The Isolationist Impulse: Its Twentieth-Century Reaction.* New York, 1957.†

49 AMBROSE, Stephen E. *Rise to Globalism; American Foreign Policy 1938-1970.* Baltimore, 1971.†

50 ANDERSON, George L., ed. *Issues and Conflicts: Studies in Twentieth Century American Diplomacy.* Lawrence, Kan., 1959.

51 BAILEY, Thomas A. "America's Emergence as a World Power: The Myth and the Verity." *Pac Hist Rev,* XXX (1961), 1-16.

52 BAILEY, Thomas A. *A Diplomatic History of the American People.* 8th ed. New York, 1969. 9th ed. forthcoming.

53 BAILEY, Thomas A. *Essays Diplomatic and Undiplomatic of Thomas A. Bailey.* Ed. Alexander DeConde and Armin Rappaport. New York, 1969.

54 BAILEY, Thomas A. "The Mythmakers of American History." *J Am Hist,* LV (1968), 5-21.

55 BARNET, Richard J. *Roots of War.* New York, 1972. Principal focus on World War II and after.

56 BARTLETT, Ruhl J. *Policy and Power: Two Centuries of American Foreign Relations.* New York, 1963.†

57 BEARD, Charles A., and George H. E. SMITH. *The Idea of National Interest: An Analytical Study in American Foreign Policy.* New York, 1934.†

58 BELOFF, Max. "American Foreign Policy and World Power: 1871-1956." *British Essays in American History.* Ed. H. C. Allen and C. P. Hill. New York, 1957.

59 BEMIS, Samuel Flagg. *American Foreign Policy and the Blessings of Liberty, and Other Essays.* New Haven, Conn., 1962.

60 BEMIS, Samuel Flagg, ed. *The American Secretaries of State and Their Diplomacy.* 10 vols. New York, 1927-1929. Covers Secretaries to 1925. See 79 for continuation.

61 BEMIS, Samuel Flagg. *A Diplomatic History of the United States.* 5th ed. New York, 1965.

62 BEMIS, Samuel Flagg. "The Shifting Strategy of American Defense and Diplomacy." *Va Q Rev,* XXIV (1948), 321-335.

63 BLAKE, Nelson M., and Oscar T. BARCK, Jr. *The United States in Its World Relations.* New York, 1960.

64 BRAEMAN, John, Robert H. BREMNER, and David BRODY, eds. *Twentieth-Century American Foreign Policy.* Columbus, Ohio, 1971.

65 CARLETON, William G. *The Revolution in American Foreign Policy: Its Global Range.* 2d ed. New York, 1967.†

66 COLE, Wayne S. *An Interpretive History of American Foreign Relations.* Rev. ed. Homewood, Ill., 1973.†

67 COMBS, Jerald A., ed. *Nationalist, Realist, and Radical: Three Views of American Diplomacy.* New York, 1972.† Readings.

68 CRAIG, Gordon A., and Felix GILBERT, eds. *The Diplomats, 1919-1939.* Princeton, N.J., 1953.†

69   CURRENT, Richard N. "The United States and 'Collective Security': Notes on the History of an Idea." *Isolation and Security.* See 72.

70   DAVIDS, Jules. *America and the World of Our Time.* New York, 1960.

71   DECONDE, Alexander. *A History of American Foreign Policy.* 2d ed. New York, 1971.

72   DECONDE, Alexander, ed. *Isolation and Security: Ideas and Interests in Twentieth-Century American Foreign Policy.* Durham, N.C., 1957.

73   DECONDE, Alexander. "On Twentieth-Century Isolationism." *Isolation and Security.* See 72.

74   DULLES, Foster Rhea. *America's Rise to World Power, 1898-1954.* New York, 1955.†

75   DUROSELLE, Jean-Baptiste. *From Wilson to Roosevelt: Foreign Policy of the United States, 1913-1945.* Cambridge, Mass., 1963.†

76   EKIRCH, Arthur A., Jr. *Ideas, Ideals, and American Diplomacy: A History of Their Growth and Interaction.* New York, 1966.

77   FENSTERWALD, Bernard, Jr. "The Anatomy of American 'Isolationism' and Expansionism." *J Confl Res*, II (1958), 111-139, 280-309.

78   FERRELL, Robert H. *American Diplomacy: A History.* 2d ed. New York, 1969.

79   FERRELL, Robert H., and Samuel Flagg BEMIS, eds. *The American Secretaries of State and Their Diplomacy.* 8 vols. New York, 1964-1972. Continuation of item 60. Covers Secretaries from 1925 to 1961.

80   FONTAINE, André. *A History of the Cold War: From the October Revolution to the Korean War, 1917-1960.* Trans. D. D. Paige. London, 1968.

81   Foreign Policy Association. *A Cartoon History of U.S. Foreign Policy Since World War I.* Intro. by Richard Rovere. New York, 1967.

82   GARDNER, Lloyd C., Walter F. LAFEBER, and Thomas J. MCCORMICK. *Creation of the American Empire: U.S. Diplomatic History.* Chicago, 1973.

83   GRAEBNER, Norman A., ed. *An Uncertain Tradition: American Secretaries of State in the Twentieth Century.* New York, 1961.

84   HALLE, Louis J. *Dream and Reality: Aspects of American Foreign Policy.* New York, 1959.

85   HENKIN, Louis. *Foreign Affairs and the Constitution.* Mineola, N.Y., 1972.

86   HOLT, W. Stull. *Historical Scholarship in the United States and Other Essays.* Seattle, 1967. Includes three essays on foreign policy.

87   JULIEN, Claude. *America's Empire.* New York, 1971.

88   KALLINA, Edmund Frank, Jr. "A Conservative Criticism of American Foreign Policy: The Publications and Careers of Louis J. Halle, George F. Kennan, and Charles Burton Marshall, 1950-1968." Doctoral dissertation, Northwestern University, 1970.

89   KENNAN, George F. *American Diplomacy, 1900-1950.* Chicago, 1951.†

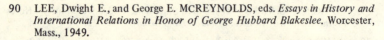

90   LEE, Dwight E., and George E. MCREYNOLDS, eds. *Essays in History and International Relations in Honor of George Hubbard Blakeslee*. Worcester, Mass., 1949.

91   LEFEVER, Ernest W. *Ethics and United States Foreign Policy*. New York, 1957.

92   LEFEVER, Ernest W. *Ethics and World Politics*. Baltimore, 1972. Includes observations on the Vietnam War.

93   LENS, Sidney. *The Forging of the American Empire*. New York, 1971.

94   LEOPOLD, Richard W. "The Emergence of America as a World Power: Some Second Thoughts." *Change and Continuity in Twentieth Century America*. Ed. John Braeman, Robert H. Bremner, and Everett Walters. Columbus, Ohio, 1964.

95   LEOPOLD, Richard W. *The Growth of American Foreign Policy*. New York, 1962.

96   LEUCHTENBURG, William E., ed. *The Unfinished Century; America Since 1900*. Boston, 1973. Sections on foreign policy by Samuel F. Wells, Jr., Robert H. Ferrell, and David F. Trask.

97   MAGDOFF, Harry. *The Age of Imperialism*. New York, 1969.

98   MIDDLETON, Drew. *Retreat from Victory: A Critical Appraisal of American Foreign and Military Policy from 1920 to the 1970s*. New York, 1973.

99   MORGENTHAU, Hans J. *In Defense of the National Interest: A Critical Examination of American Foreign Policy*. New York, 1951.

100   NEARING, Scott, and Joseph FREEMAN. *Dollar Diplomacy: A Study in American Imperialism*. New York, 1925.

101   NORTHEDGE, F. S., and M. J. GRIEVE. *A Hundred Years of International Relations*. New York, 1972.

102   O'CONNOR, Raymond G. *Force & Diplomacy: Essays Military and Diplomatic*. Coral Gables, Fla., 1972. Ranges over topics from the 1920's through the 1960's.

103   OGLE, Arthur Harrison, Jr. "Nationalism and American Foreign Policy, 1898-1920: A Series of Case Studies on the Influence of an Idea." Doctoral dissertation, University of Virginia, 1971.

104   OSGOOD, Robert E. *Ideals and Self-Interest in America's Foreign Relations: The Great Transformation of the Twentieth Century*. Chicago, 1953.†

105   PRATT, Julius W. *A History of United States Foreign Policy*. 3d ed. Englewood Cliffs, N.J., 1972.

106   SCHOLES, Walter V., ed. *United States Diplomatic History: Readings for the Twentieth Century*. Boston, 1973.†

107   SMITH, Daniel M. *The American Diplomatic Experience*. Boston, 1972.†

108   STRAUSS, W. Patrick. *Isolation and Involvement: An Interpretive History of American Diplomacy*. Waltham, Mass., 1972.

109   SWOMLEY, John M., Jr. *The American Empire: The Political Ethics of Twentieth-Century Conquest*. New York, 1970.† Largely post-1939.

110 TANNENBAUM, Frank. *The American Tradition in Foreign Policy.* Norman, Okla., 1955.

111 THOMPSON, Kenneth W. "Isolationism and Collective Security: The Uses and Limits of Two Theories of International Relations." *Isolation and Security.* See 72.

112 TRASK, David F. *Victory Without Peace: American Foreign Relations in the Twentieth Century.* New York, 1968.†

113 VAN ALSTYNE, Richard W. *American Crisis Diplomacy: The Quest for Collective Security, 1918-1952.* Stanford, Cal., 1952.

114 WEINBERG, Albert K. "The Historical Meaning of the American Doctrine of Isolation." *Proc Am Philos Soc,* XXXIV (1940), 539-547.

115 WEINBERG, Albert K. *Manifest Destiny.* Baltimore, 1935.†

116 WESTON, Rubin Francis. *Racism in U.S. Imperialism: The Influence of Racial Assumptions on American Foreign Policy, 1893-1946.* Columbia, S.C., 1972.

117 WEYL, Walter E. *American World Policies.* New York, 1917. New ed., intro. by Wilton B. Fowler. Seattle, 1973.

118 WILLIAMS, William A. *The Tragedy of American Diplomacy.* 2d ed. Cleveland, 1962.†

119 WOODWARD, C. Vann. "The Age of Reinterpretation." *Am Hist Rev,* LXVI (1960), 1-19. Reprint. *The Age of Reinterpretation.* Washington, 1961.† Free security thesis.

120 ZEVIN, Robert. "An Interpretation of American Imperialism." *J Econ Hist,* XXXII (1972), 316-360. Covers the twentieth century.

4. *Surveys of Long-term Relationships with Other Nations*

Canada and Great Britain

121 ALLEN, Harry C. *Great Britain and the United States: A History of Anglo-American Relations (1783-1952).* New York, 1955.

122 BREBNER, John Bartlet. *North Atlantic Triangle: The Interplay of Canada, the United States, and Great Britain.* New Haven, Conn., 1945.

123 BRINTON, Crane. *The United States and Britain.* Rev. ed. Cambridge, Mass., 1948.

124 BROWN, Robert Craig. "Canada in North America." *Twentieth-Century American Foreign Policy.* See 64. Canada and the United States since 1898.

125 CAMPBELL, A. E. "The United States and Great Britain: Uneasy Allies." *Twentieth-Century American Foreign Policy.* See 64.

126 CLARK, William. *Less Than Kin: A Study of Anglo-American Relations.* Boston, 1958.

127 CORBETT, Percy E. *The Settlement of Canadian-American Disputes.* New Haven, Conn., 1937.

128 CRAIG, Gerald M. *The United States and Canada.* Cambridge, Mass., 1968.

129 DAVIS, Forrest. *The Atlantic System: The Story of Anglo-American Control of the Seas.* New York, 1941.

130 KEENLEYSIDE, Hugh L., and Gerald S. BROWN. *Canada and the United States: Some Aspects of Their Historical Relations.* 2d ed. New York, 1952.

131 MCINNIS, Edgar W. *The Unguarded Frontier: A History of Canadian-American Relations.* Garden City, N.Y., 1942.

132 NICHOLAS, Herbert. *Britain and the U.S.A.* Baltimore, 1963.

133 PELLING, Henry. *America and the British Left: From Bright to Bevan.* New York, 1957.

134 RUSSETT, Bruce M. *Community and Contention: Britain and America in the Twentieth Century.* Cambridge, Mass., 1963. A theoretical analysis.

135 SHOTWELL, James T., ed. *The Relations of Canada and the United States.* 25 vols. New Haven, Conn., 1937-1945.

136 SWANSON, Roger Frank. "The United States Canadiana Constellation, I: Washington, D.C." *Int J*, XXVII (1972), 185-223.

137 SWANSON, Roger Frank. "The United States Canadiana Constellation, II: Canada." *Int J*, XXVIII (1973), 325-367.

138 TANSILL, Charles C. *America and the Fight for Irish Freedom, 1866-1922.* New York, 1957.

139 TURNER, Arthur Campbell. *The Unique Partnership: Britain and the United States.* New York, 1971.

140 WATT, D. C. "America and the British Foreign-Policy-Making Elite, from Joseph Chamberlain to Anthony Eden, 1895-1956." *Personalities and Policies: Studies in the Formulation of British Foreign Policy in the Twentieth Century.* London, 1965.

141 WILLOUGHBY, William R. *The St. Lawrence Seaway: A Study in Politics and Diplomacy.* Madison, Wis., 1961.

142 WILSON, Robert R., *et al. Canada-United States Treaty Relations.* Durham, N.C., 1963.

Europe and Russia

143 BAILEY, Thomas A. *America Faces Russia: Russian-American Relations from Early Times to Our Day*, Ithaca, N.Y., 1950.

144 BLUMENTHAL, Henry. *France and the United States: Their Diplomatic Relations, 1789-1914.* Chapel Hill, N.C., 1970.

145 BRINTON, Crane. *The Americans and the French.* Cambridge, Mass., 1968.

146 DECONDE, Alexander. *Half Bitter, Half Sweet: An Excursion into Italian-American History.* New York, 1971.

147 DULLES, Foster Rhea. *The Road to Teheran: The Story of Russia and America, 1781-1943.* Princeton, N.J., 1944.

148 FILENE, Peter G. *Americans and the Soviet Experiment, 1917-1933.* Cambridge, Mass., 1967.

149 FOGDALL, S. J. M. P. *Danish-American Diplomacy, 1776-1920.* Iowa City, Iowa, 1922.

150 HARRIMAN, W. Averell. *America and Russia in a Changing World: A Half Century of Personal Observation.* Garden City, N.Y., 1971.

151 HUGHES, H. Stuart. *The United States and Italy.* Cambridge, Mass., 1953.

152 JENSEN, Oliver O., ed. *America and Russia.* New York, 1962.

153 KEIM, Jeannette L. *Forty Years of German-American Political Relations.* Philadelphia, 1919.

154 KENNAN, George F. *Russia and the West Under Lenin and Stalin.* Boston, 1961.†

155 LASERSON, Max M. *The American Impact on Russia: Diplomatic and Ideological, 1784-1917.* New York, 1950.

156 LOVENSTEIN, Meno. *American Opinion of Soviet Russia.* Washington, 1941.

157 MCKAY, Donald C. *The United States and France.* Cambridge, Mass., 1951.

158 MAJOR, Mark Imre. "American-Hungarian Relations 1918-1944." Doctoral dissertation, Texas Christian University, 1972.

159 MEIER, Heinz K. *Friendship Under Stress: U.S.-Swiss Relations 1900-1950.* Bern, 1970.

160 SCOTT, F. D. *The United States and Scandinavia.* Cambridge, Mass., 1950.

161 WHITE, Elizabeth B. *American Opinion of France: From Lafayette to Poincaré.* New York, 1927.

162 WILLIAMS, William A. *American-Russian Relations, 1781-1941.* New York, 1952.

Africa and the Middle East

162-A BADEAU, John S. *The American Approach to the Arab World.* New York, 1968.

163 BEECHER, Lloyd Nelson, Jr. "The State Department and Liberia, 1908-1941: A Heterogeneous Record." Doctoral dissertation, University of Georgia, 1971.

164 BIXLER, Raymond W. *The Foreign Policy of the United States in Liberia.* New York, 1957.

165 DENOVO, John A. *American Interests and Policies in the Middle East, 1900-1939.* Minneapolis, 1963.

166 DENOVO, John A. "American Relations with the Middle East: Some Unfinished Business." *Issues and Conflicts.* See 50.

167 GALLAGHER, Charles F. *The United States and North Africa: Morocco, Algeria, and Tunisia.* Cambridge, Mass., 1963.

168 GORDON, Leland J. *American Relations with Turkey, 1830-1930: An Economic Interpretation.* Philadelphia, 1932.

169 GRABILL, Joseph L. *Protestant Diplomacy and the Near East: Missionary Influence on American Policy, 1810-1927.* Minneapolis, 1971.

170 HALL, Luella J. *The United States and Morocco 1776-1956.* Metuchen, N.J., 1971.

171 HUREWITZ, Jacob C., ed. *Diplomacy in the Near and Middle East: A Documentary Record.* 2 vols. Princeton, N.J., 1956.

172 HUREWITZ, Jacob C. *The Struggle for Palestine.* New York, 1950. Covers period 1936-1950.

173 LENCZOWSKI, George. *Russia and the West in Iran, 1918-1948.* Ithaca, N.Y., 1949.

174 MANUEL, Frank E. *The Realities of American-Palestine Relations.* Washington, 1949.

175 POLK, William R. *The United States and the Arab World.* Rev. ed. Cambridge, Mass., 1969.

176 SAFRAN, Nadav. *The United States and Israel.* Cambridge, Mass., 1963.

177 SCOTT, William Randolph. "A Study of Afro-American and Ethiopian Relations: 1896-1941." Doctoral dissertation, Princeton University, 1971.

178 SPEISER, Ephraim A. *The United States and the Near East.* Cambridge, Mass., 1950.

179 STOCKING, George W. *Middle East Oil: A Study in Political and Economic Controversy.* Nashville, 1970. Includes the historical background of the several concessions.

180 THOMAS, Lewis V., and Richard N. FRYE. *The United States and Turkey and Iran.* Cambridge, Mass., 1951.

181 TRASK, Roger R. *The United States Response to Turkish Nationalism and Reform, 1914-1939.* Minneapolis, 1971.

182 WALT, Joseph William. "Saudi Arabia and the Americans: 1928-1951." Doctoral dissertation, Northwestern University, 1960.

183 YESELSON, Abraham. *United States-Persian Diplomatic Relations, 1883-1921.* New Brunswick, N.J., 1956.

Asia and the Pacific

184 BATTISTINI, Lawrence H. *The United States and Asia.* New York, 1955.

185 BORG, Dorothy, ed. *Historians and American Far Eastern Policy.* New York, 1966. A pamphlet of six essays.

186 BROWN, W. Norman. *The United States and India, Pakistan, Bangladesh.* 3d. ed. Cambridge, Mass., 1972.

187   CLYDE, Paul H., ed. *United States Policy Toward China: Diplomatic and Public Documents, 1838-1939.* Durham, N.C., 1940.

188   COHEN, Warren I. *America's Response to China: An Interpretive History of Sino-American Relations.* New York, 1971.† Coverage through 1950.

189   COHEN, Warren I. "From Contempt to Containment: Cycles in American Attitudes Toward China." *Twentieth-Century American Foreign Policy.* See 64.

190   DAVIES, John Paton, Jr. *Dragon by the Tail: American, British, Japanese, and Russian Encounters with China and One Another.* New York, 1972. The author was a participant in some of the encounters.

191   DENNETT, Tyler. *Americans in Eastern Asia.* New York, 1922.

192   DULLES, Foster Rhea. *America in the Pacific: A Century of Expansion.* Boston, 1932.

193   DULLES, Foster Rhea. *China and America: The Story of Their Relations Since 1784.* Princeton, N.J., 1946.

194   DULLES, Foster Rhea. *Forty Years of American-Japanese Relations.* New York, 1937.

195   FAIRBANK, John K. *The United States and China.* Rev. ed. Cambridge, Mass., 1971.†

196   FISHEL, Wesley R. *The End of Extraterritoriality in China.* Berkeley, Cal., 1952.

197   GOULD, James W. *The United States and Malaysia.* Cambridge, Mass., 1969.

198   GRATTAN, C. Hartley. *The United States and the Southwest Pacific.* Cambridge, Mass., 1961.

199   GRISWOLD, A. Whitney. *The Far Eastern Policy of the United States.* New York, 1938.†

200   GRUNDER, Garel A., and William E. LIVEZEY. *The Philippines and the United States.* Norman, Okla., 1951.

201   IRIYE, Akira. *Across the Pacific: An Inner History of American-East Asian Relations.* New York, 1967.

202   ISAACS, H. R. *Scratches on Our Minds: The American Image of China and India.* New York, 1958.

203   KAMIKAWA, Hikomatsu, ed. *Japan-American Diplomatic Relations in the Meiji-Taisho Era.* Trans. Kimura Michiko. Tokyo, 1958.

204   KATTENBURG, Paul M. "Viet Nam and U.S. Diplomacy, 1940-1970." *Orbis*, XV (1972), 818-841.

205   LATOURETTE, Kenneth Scott. *A History of Christian Missions in China.* New York, 1929.

206   LEVI, Werner. *American-Australian Relations.* Minneapolis, 1947.

207   LIU, K. C. *Americans and Chinese: A Historical Essay and a Bibliography.* Cambridge, Mass., 1963.

208 McGOVERN, James R. "American Christian Missions to Japan, 1918-1941." Doctoral dissertation, University of Pennsylvania, 1957.

209 MAY, Ernest R., and James C. THOMSON, Jr., eds. *American-East Asian Relations: A Survey*. Cambridge, Mass., 1972. Essays by seventeen specialists.

210 NEUMANN, William L. *America Encounters Japan: From Perry to MacArthur*. Baltimore, 1963.

211 NEUMANN, William L. "Determinism, Destiny and Myth in the American Image of China." *Issues and Conflicts*. See 50.

212 POMEROY, Earl S. "American Policy Respecting the Marshalls, Carolines, and Marianas, 1898-1941." *Pac Hist Rev*, XVII (1948), 43-53.

213 POMEROY, Earl S. *Pacific Outpost: American Strategy in Guam and Micronesia*. Stanford, Cal., 1951.

214 REESE, Trevor R. *Australia, New Zealand, and the United States: A Survey of International Relations, 1941-1968*. New York, 1969.

215 REISCHAUER, Edwin O. *The United States and Japan*. Rev. ed. Cambridge, Mass., 1965.

216 SCHWANTES, Robert S. *Japanese and Americans: A Century of Cultural Relations*. New York, 1955.

217 SMITH, Michael John. "Henry L. Stimson and the Philippines." Doctoral dissertation, Indiana University, 1970.

218 SPENCE, Jonathan. *To Change China: Western Advisers in China 1620-1960*. Boston, 1969.

219 STEMEN, John Roger. "The Diplomacy of the Immigration Issue: A Study in Japanese-American Relations, 1894-1941." Doctoral dissertation, Indiana University, 1960.

219-A TOLLEY, Kemp. *Yangtze Patrol: The U.S. Navy in China*. Annapolis, Md., 1971. Covers 1853-1942.

220 TOMPKINS, Pauline. *American-Russian Relations in the Far East*. New York, 1949.

221 TUPPER, Eleanor R., and George E. McREYNOLDS. *Japan in American Public Opinion*. New York, 1937.

222 VARG, Paul A. *Missionaries, Chinese and Diplomats: The American Protestant Missionary Movement in China, 1890-1952*. Princeton, N.J., 1958.

Latin America

223 ATKINS, G. Pope, and Larman C. WILSON. *The United States and the Trujillo Regime*. New Brunswick, N.J., 1972. Discusses 1900-1970; focuses on 1930-1961.

224 BEMIS, Samuel Flagg. *The Latin American Policy of the United States*. New York, 1943.†

225 BERNSTEIN, Marvin D., ed. *Foreign Investment in Latin America: Cases and Attitudes.* New York, 1966.†

226 BLENDON, Edith M. J. "Venezuela and the United States, 1928-1948: The Impact of Venezuelan Nationalism." Doctoral dissertation, University of Maryland, 1971.

227 CALLCOTT, Wilfred Hardy. *The Western Hemisphere; Its Influence on United States Policies to the End of World War II.* Austin, Tex., 1968.

228 CAREY, James C. *Peru and the United States, 1900-1962.* Notre Dame, Ind., 1964.

229 CLINE, Howard F. *The United States and Mexico.* Rev. ed. Cambridge, Mass., 1963.†

230 CONNELL-SMITH, Gordon. "The United States and the Caribbean: Colonial Patterns, Old and New." *J Latin Am Stud*, IV (1972), 113-122. A review article.

231 COOLEY, John Andrew. "The United States and the Panama Canal, 1938-1947: Policy Formulation and Implementation from Munich Through the Early Years of the Cold War." Doctoral dissertation, Ohio State University, 1972.

232 COSÍO VILLEGAS, Daniel. *American Extremes.* Trans. Américo Paredes. Austin, Tex., 1964. U.S. relations with Mexico and Latin America.

233 COTNER, T. E., and C. E. CASTENADA, eds. *Essays in Mexican History.* Austin, Tex., 1958.

234 COX, Isaac J. *Nicaragua and the United States, 1909-1927.* Boston, 1927.

235 CRAIG, Richard B. *The Bracero Program: Interest Groups and Foreign Policy.* Austin, Tex., 1971.

236 DOZER, Donald Marquand. *Are We Good Neighbors? Three Decades of Inter-American Relations, 1930-1960.* Gainesville, Fla., 1959. Reprinted 1961.

237 DOZER, Donald Marquand, ed. *The Monroe Doctrine, Its Modern Significance.* New York, 1965.†

238 DUFFY, Edward Gerald. "Politics of Expediency: Diplomatic Relations Between the United States and Venezuela During the Juan Vicente Gómez Era." Doctoral dissertation, Pennsylvania State University, 1970. Covers 1908-1935.

239 DUGGAN, Laurence. *The Americas: The Search for Hemispheric Security.* New York, 1949.

240 EALY, Lawrence O. *Yanqui Politics and the Isthmian Canal.* University Park, Pa., 1971. Covers the years 1840-1970.

241 EASUM, Donald Boyd. "The British-Argentine-United States Triangle: A Case Study in International Relations." Doctoral dissertation, Princeton University, 1953. Covers 1918-1946.

242 EVANS, H. C., Jr. *Chile and Its Relations with the United States.* Durham, N.C., 1927.

243   FITZGIBBON, Russell H. *Cuba and the United States, 1900-1935.* Menasha, Wis., 1935.

244   FONER, P. S. *A History of Cuba and Its Relations with the United States.* 2 vols. New York, 1962-1963. Vol. 2 covers 1845-1895.

245   GANTENBEIN, J. W., ed. *The Evolution of Our Latin-American Policy: A Documentary Record.* New York, 1950.

246   GIVENS, Larry Dale. "Official United States' Attitudes Toward Latin American Military Regimes, 1933-1960." Doctoral dissertation, University of California, Davis, 1970.

247   GODFREY, Erwina Edwards. "The Influence of Economic Factors on United States-Brazilian Relations: 1940-1960." Doctoral dissertation, University of Kentucky, 1960.

248   GREGORY, Gladys. *The Chamizal Settlement: A View from El Paso.* El Paso, Tex., 1963.† The U.S.-Mexican boundary problem.

249   HACKETT, Charles W. *The Mexican Revolution and the United States, 1910-1926.* Boston, 1926.

250   HART, A. B. *Monroe Doctrine: An Interpretation.* Boston, 1916.

251   HILL, L. F. *Diplomatic Relations Between the United States and Brazil.* Durham, N.C., 1932.

252   HUNDLEY, Norris, Jr. *Dividing the Waters: A Century of Controversy Between the United States and Mexico.* Berkeley, Cal., 1966.

253   INMAN, Samuel Guy. *Inter-American Conferences 1826-1954: History and Problems.* Washington, 1965.

254   JENKS, Leland Hamilton. *Our Cuban Colony: A Study in Sugar.* New York, 1928.

255   JONES, Chester Lloyd. *The Caribbean Since 1900.* New York, 1936.

256   KANE, William Everett. *Civil Strife in Latin America: A Legal History of U.S. Involvement.* Baltimore, 1972.

257   KARNES, Thomas L., ed. *Readings in the Latin American Policy of the United States.* Tucson, Ariz., 1972.

258   KNIGHT, Melvin M. *The Americans in Santo Domingo.* New York, 1928.

259   LANGLEY, Lester D. *The Cuban Policy of the United States: A Brief History.* New York, 1968.†

260   LIEUWEN, Edwin. *U.S. Policy in Latin America: A Short History.* New York, 1965.

261   LISS, Sheldon B. *The Canal: Aspects of United States-Panamanian Relations.* Notre Dame, Ind., 1967.

262   LISS, Sheldon B. *A Century of Disagreement: The Chamizal Conflict, 1864-1964.* Washington, 1965.

263   LIVERMORE, Seward W. "Battleship Diplomacy in South America, 1905-1925." *J Mod Hist,* XVI (1944), 31-48.

264   LOGAN, John A. *No Transfer: An American Security Principle.* New Haven, Conn., 1961.

265   McCAIN, William D. *The United States and the Republic of Panama.* Durham, N.C., 1937.

266   MACHADO, Manuel A., Jr. *An Industry in Crisis: Mexican-United States Cooperation in the Control of Foot-and-Mouth Disease.* Berkeley, Cal., 1968.

267   MACK, Gerstle. *The Land Divided: A History of the Panama Canal and Other Isthmian Canal Projects.* New York, 1944.

268   MARSH, Margaret C. *The Bankers in Bolivia: A Study in American Foreign Investment.* New York, 1928.

269   MECHAM, J. Lloyd. *A Survey of United States-Latin American Relations.* Boston, 1965.

270   MECHAM, J. Lloyd. *The United States and Inter-American Security, 1889-1960.* Austin, Tex., 1961.

271   MILLETT, Allan R. "The United States and Cuba: The Uncomfortable 'Abrazo,' 1898-1968." *Twentieth-Century American Foreign Policy.* See 64.

272   MONTAGUE, Ludwell L. *Haiti and the United States, 1714-1938.* Durham, N.C., 1940.

273   MOUNT, Graeme Stewart. "American Imperialism in Panama." Doctoral dissertation, University of Toronto, 1969. Covers the period 1846-1968.

274   MUNRO, Dana G. *Intervention and Dollar Diplomacy in the Caribbean, 1900-1921.* Princeton, N.J., 1964.

275   PADELFORD, Norman J. *The Panama Canal in Peace and War.* New York, 1942.

276   PARKS, E. Taylor. *Colombia and the United States, 1765-1934.* Durham, N.C., 1935.

277   PERKINS, Dexter. *A History of the Monroe Doctrine.* Boston, 1955.†

278   PERKINS, Dexter. *The United States and the Caribbean.* 2d ed. Cambridge, Mass., 1966.

279   PETERSON, Dale William. "The Diplomatic and Commercial Relations Between the United States and Peru from 1883 to 1918." Doctoral dissertation, University of Minnesota, 1969.

279-A PETERSON, Harold F. *Argentina and the United States, 1810-1960.* Albany, N.Y., 1964.

280   PIERSON, William Whatley, Jr. "The Political Influences of an Inter-Oceanic Canal, 1826-1926." *His Am Hist Rev,* VI (1926), 205-231.

281   PIKE, Fredrick B. *Chile and the United States, 1880-1962: The Emergence of Chile's Social Crisis and the Challenge to United States Diplomacy.* Notre Dame, Ind., 1963.

282   RICHARD, Alfred Charles, Jr. "The Panama Canal in American National Consciousness 1870-1922." Doctoral dissertation, Boston University, 1969.

283 RIPPY, J. Fred. *The Capitalists and Colombia*. New York, 1931.

284 RONNING, C. Neal. *Law and Politics in Inter-American Diplomacy*. New York, 1963.

285 SMITH, Robert F. *The United States and Cuba: Business and Diplomacy, 1917-1960.* New York, 1960.

286 TANNENBAUM, Frank. *Ten Keys to Latin America*. New York, 1962.

287 THOMAS, Hugh. *Cuba: The Pursuit of Freedom*. New York, 1971. Includes sections on Cuba's relations with the U.S.

288 TURCHEN, Lesta Van Der Wert. "The Oil Expropriation Controversy, 1917-1942, in United States-Mexican Relations." Doctoral dissertation, Purdue University, 1972.

289 WELLES, Sumner. *Naboth's Vineyard: The Dominican Republic, 1844-1924*. 2 vols. New York, 1928.

290 WHITAKER, Arthur P. *The United States and Argentina*. Cambridge, Mass., 1954.

291 WHITAKER, Arthur P. *The United States and South America: The Northern Republics*. Cambridge, Mass., 1948.

292 WHITAKER, Arthur P. *The Western Hemisphere Idea: Its Rise and Decline*. Ithaca, N.Y., 1954.

293 ZORRILLA, Luis G. *Historia de las Relaciones entre México y los Estados Unidos de América 1800-1958*. 2 vols. Mexico City, 1965-1966.

5. Selected Studies Related to American Diplomatic History

Public Opinion and Other Influences on Policy

294 BAILEY, Thomas A. *The Man in the Street: The Impact of American Public Opinion on Foreign Policy*. New York, 1948.

295 CRAIG, Richard B. *The Bracero Program: Interest Groups and Foreign Policy*. See 235.

296 DECONDE, Alexander. "The South and Isolationism." *J S Hist*, XXIV (1958), 332-346.

297 FEIG, Konnilyn Gay. "The Northwest and America's International Relations, 1919-1941: A Regional Study of the Domestic Formulation of Foreign Policy." Doctoral dissertation, University of Washington, 1970.

298 GALLUP, George H., ed. *The Gallup Poll; Public Opinion, 1935-1971*. 3 vols. New York, 1972.

299   GERSON, Louis L. *The Hyphenate in Recent American Politics and Diplomacy.* Lawrence, Kans., 1964.

300   GERSON, Louis L. "Immigrant Groups and American Foreign Policy." *Issues and Conflicts.* See 50.

301   GRASSMUCK, George L. *Sectional Biases in Congress on Foreign Policy.* Baltimore, 1951.

302   GRECO, John F. "A Foundation for Internationalism: The Carnegie Endowment for International Peace, 1933-1941." Doctoral dissertation, Syracuse University, 1971.

303   HERO, Alfred O., Jr. "American Negroes and U.S. Foreign Policy: 1937-1967." *J Confl Res,* XIII (1969), 220-251.

304   HERO, Alfred O., Jr. "Liberalism-Conservatism Revisited: Foreign vs. Domestic Federal Policies, 1937-1967." *Pub Opin Q,* XXXIII (1969), 399-408. Linkage of foreign and domestic policies.

305   HERO, Alfred O., Jr., and Emil STARR. *The Reuther-Meany Foreign Policy Dispute: Union Leaders and Members View World Affairs.* Dobbs Ferry, N.Y., 1970. From the 1930's through the 1960's.

306   HERO, Alfred O., Jr. *The Southerner and World Affairs.* Baton Rouge, La., 1965.

307   HILL, Thomas Michael. "The Senate Leadership and International Policy: From Lodge to Vandenberg." Doctoral dissertation, Washington University (St. Louis), 1970.

308   LANDECKER, Manfred. *The President and Public Opinion: Leadership in Foreign Affairs.* Washington, 1968. F.D.R. and Truman.

309   LOEWENHEIM, Francis L., ed. *The Historian and the Diplomat: The Role of History and Historians in American Foreign Policy.* New York, 1966.

310   MAY, Ernest R. "An American Tradition in Foreign Policy: The Role of Public Opinion." *Theory and Practice in American Politics.* Ed. William H. Nelson. Chicago, 1964.

311   RADOSH, Ronald. *American Labor and United States Foreign Policy.* New York, 1969.

312   RAPPAPORT, Armin. *The Navy League of the United States.* Detroit, 1962.

313   RIESELBACH, Leroy N. *The Roots of Isolationism: Congressional Voting and Presidential Leadership in Foreign Policy.* Indianapolis, 1966. Covers the period 1939-1958.

314   ROGERS, William C., Barbara STUHLER, and Donald KOENIG. "A Comparison of Informed and General Public Opinion on U.S. Foreign Policy." *Pub Opin Q,* XXXI (1967), 242-252.

315   ROSENAU, James N., ed. *Domestic Sources of Foreign Policy.* New York, 1967.

316   ZIEGLER, John Alan. "The *Progressive's* Views on Foreign Affairs, 1909-1941: A Case Study of Liberal Economic Isolationism." Doctoral dissertation, Syracuse University, 1970. About the magazine founded by Robert M. LaFollette.

Institutions and Practices of Diplomacy

317   BAILEY, Thomas A. *The Art of Diplomacy: The American Experience.* New York, 1968.

318   BARNES, William, and John H. MORGAN. *The Foreign Service of the United States: Origins, Development, and Functions.* Washington, 1961.

319   BYRD, Elbert M., Jr. *Treaties and Executive Agreements in the United States: Their Separate Roles and Limitations.* The Hague, 1960.

320   CARROLL, Holbert N. *The House of Representatives and Foreign Affairs.* Pittsburgh, 1958.

321   CORBETT, Percy E. *Law in Diplomacy.* Princeton, N.J., 1959.

322   DAHL, Robert A. *Congress and Foreign Policy.* New York, 1950.†

323   DANGERFIELD, Royden J. *In Defense of the Senate.* Norman, Okla., 1933.

324   DECONDE, Alexander. *The American Secretary of State: An Interpretation.* New York, 1962.†

325   DENNISON, Eleanor E. *The Senate Foreign Relations Committee.* Stanford, Cal., 1942.

326   DESTLER, I. M. *Presidents, Bureaucrats, and Foreign Policy.* Princeton, N.J., 1972.

327   DULLES, Eleanor Lansing. *American Foreign Policy in the Making.* New York, 1968.

328   EUBANK, Keith. *The Summit Conferences, 1919-1960.* Norman, Okla., 1966.

329   FLEMING, Denna F. *The United States and the World Court.* Garden City, N.Y., 1945.

330   HALL, H. Duncan. *Mandates, Dependencies, and Trusteeships.* Washington, 1948.

331   HARMON, Robert B. *The Art and Practice of Diplomacy: A Selected and Annotated Guide.* Metuchen, N.J., 1971.

332   HARRIS, Joseph P. *The Advice and Consent of the Senate.* Berkeley, Cal., 1953.

333   HARTMANN, Frederick H. *The Relations of Nations.* New York, 1973.

334   HEINRICHS, Waldo H., Jr. "Bureaucracy and Professionalism in the Development of American Career Diplomacy." *Twentieth-Century American Foreign Policy.* See 64.

335   HILL, Norman L. *Mr. Secretary of State.* New York, 1963.

336   HOLT, W. Stull. *Treaties Defeated by the Senate: A Study of the Struggle Between President and Senate over the Conduct of Foreign Relations.* Baltimore, 1933.

337   ILCHMAN, W. F. *Professional Diplomacy in the United States: A Study in Administrative History.* Chicago, 1961.

338   JANIS, Irving L. *Victims of Groupthink: A Psychological Study of Foreign-Policy Decisions and Fiascoes.* Boston, 1972.† Discusses Pearl Harbor, the Korean War, the Bay of Pigs, and Vietnam.

339   JEWELL, Malcolm E. *Senatorial Politics and Foreign Policy.* Lexington, Ky., 1962.

340   JOHNSON, Richard A. *The Administration of United States Foreign Policy.* Austin, Tex., 1971.

341   KUEHL, Warren F. *Seeking World Order: The United States and International Organization to 1920.* Nashville, Tenn., 1969.

342   LANGER, Robert. *Seizure of Territory: The Stimson Doctrine and Related Principles in Legal Theory and Diplomatic Practice.* Princeton, N.J., 1947.

343   MCCLURE, Wallace. *International Executive Agreements.* New York, 1941.

344   MCDOUGAL, Myres S., and Asher LANS. "Treaties and Congressional-Executive or Presidential Agreements: Interchangeable Instruments of National Policy." *Studies in World Public Order.* Ed. Myres S. McDougal, *et al.* New Haven, Conn., 1960.

345   MCKENNA, Joseph C. *Diplomatic Protest in Foreign Policy: Analysis and Case Studies.* Chicago, 1962.

346   MILLETT, Stephen Malcolm. "The Constitutionality of Executive Agreements: An Analysis of *United States v. Belmont.*" Doctoral dissertation, Ohio State University, 1972. The 1937 Supreme Court decision.

347   MODELSKI, George. *Principles of World Politics.* New York, 1972.

348   PLISCHKE, Elmer. "International Conferencing and the Summit: Macro-Analysis of Presidential Participation." *Orbis,* XIV (1971), 673-713.

349   PLISCHKE, Elmer. "The President's Right to Go Abroad." *Orbis,* XV (1972), 755-783.

350   PLISCHKE, Elmer. *Summit Diplomacy: Personal Diplomacy of the President of the United States.* College Park, Md., 1958.

351   PRICE, Don K., ed. *The Secretary of State.* Englewood Cliffs, N.J., 1960.

352   ROBINSON, Edgar E., *et al. Powers of the President in Foreign Affairs, 1945-1965.* San Francisco, 1966.

353   SAPIN, Burton M. *The Making of United States Foreign Policy.* New York, 1966.†

354   SCHLESINGER, Arthur, Jr. "Congress and the Making of American Foreign Policy." *For Aff,* LI (1972-73), 78-113. Survey of twentieth-century practice.

355   SCHULZINGER, Robert D. "The Making of the Diplomatic Mind: The Training, Outlook, and Style of United States Foreign Service Officers, 1906-1928." Doctoral dissertation, Yale University, 1971.

356   SNYDER, Richard C., *et al.,* eds. *Foreign Policy Decision-Making.* New York, 1962.

357   SORENSEN, Thomas C. *The Word War: The Story of American Propaganda.* New York, 1968. From World War I to the present.

358 SPAULDING, E. W. *Ambassadors Ordinary and Extraordinary*. Washington, 1961.

359 STEBBINS, Phillip Eugene. "A History of the Role of the United States Supreme Court in Foreign Policy." Doctoral dissertation, Ohio State University, 1966.

360 STEPHENS, Oren. *Facts to a Candid World: America's Overseas Information Program*. Stanford, Cal., 1955. Begins with World War I.

361 STUART, Graham H. *American Diplomatic and Consular Practice*. 2d ed. New York, 1962.

362 STUART, Graham H. *The Department of State: A History of Its Organization, Procedure, and Personnel*. New York, 1949.

363 WESTPHAL, A. C. F. *The House Committee on Foreign Affairs*. New York, 1942.

364 WILCOX, Francis O. *Congress, the Executive and Foreign Policy*. New York, 1971. The separation of powers.

365 WOOD, John R., and Jean SERRES. *Diplomatic Ceremonial and Protocol*. New York, 1970.

366 WRISTON, Henry R. *Executive Agents in American Foreign Relations*. Baltimore, 1929.

Economic Aspects of Foreign Policy

367 CHALK, Frank Robert. "The United States and the International Struggle for Rubber, 1914-1941." Doctoral dissertation, University of Wisconsin, 1970.

368 COHEN, Benjamin J., ed. *American Foreign Economic Policy*. New York, 1968. Readings.

369 CURTI, Merle E. *American Philanthrophy Abroad*. New Brunswick, N.J., 1963.

370 CURTI, Merle E., and Kendall BIRR. *Prelude to Point Four: American Technical Missions Overseas, 1838-1938*. Madison, Wis., 1954.

371 DANIEL, Robert L. *American Philanthropy in the Near East, 1820-1960*. Athens, Ohio, 1970.

372 DEUTSCH, Karl W., and Alexander ECKSTEIN. "National Industrialization and the Declining Share of the International Economic Sector, 1890-1959." *Wor Pol*, XIII (1961), 267-299. Statistics on U.S. foreign trade.

373 ELLIOTT, William Y. *The Political Economy of American Foreign Policy: Report of a Study Group*. New York, 1955.

374 HESS, Gary R. *Sam Higginbotham of Allahabad, Pioneer of Point Four to India*. Charlottesville, Va., 1967. The contribution of an American agriculturalist and missionary.

375 HUDSON, Michael. *Super Imperialism: The Economic Strategy of American Empire*. New York, 1972. Foreign economic policy since World War I.

376 KINDLEBERGER, Charles P. *American Business Abroad.* New Haven, Conn., 1969.

377 LEWIS, Cleona. *America's Stake in International Investments.* Washington, 1938. Valuable statistics.

378 MADDEN, John T., *et al. America's Experience as a Creditor Nation.* New York, 1937.

379 MIKESELL, Raymond F., *et al. Foreign Investment in the Petroleum and Mineral Industries: Case Studies of Investor-Host Country Relations.* Baltimore, 1971. Includes case studies of American companies in the Middle East and Latin America.

380 PHELPS, Clyde William. *The Foreign Extension of American Banks.* New York, 1927.

381 SNYDER, Richard C. *The Most-Favored-Nation Clause.* New York, 1946.

382 TAUSSIG, F. W. *Tariff History of the United States.* 8th ed. New York, 1931.

383 WILLIAMS, Benjamin H. *The Economic Foreign Policy of the United States.* New York, 1929.

Strategy and Military Force

384 ALBION, R. G., and J. B. POPE. *Sea Lanes in Wartime.* New York, 1942.

385 CONN, Stetson. "Changing Concepts of National Defense in the United States, 1937-1947." *Mil Aff,* XXVIII (Spring 1964), 1-7.

386 FRIEDMAN, Leon, ed. *The Law of War; A Documentary History.* Foreword by Telford Taylor. 2 vols. New York, 1972.

387 GRABER, Doris A. *Crisis Diplomacy: A History of U.S. Intervention Policies and Practices.* Washington, 1959.

388 GREENE, Fred. "The Military View of American National Policy, 1904-1940." *Am Hist Rev,* LXVI (1961), 354-377.

389 GRENVILLE, John A. S. "Diplomacy and War Plans in the United States, 1890-1917." *Transactions, Royal Historical Society,* ser. 5, XI (1961), 1-21.

390 GRENVILLE, John A. S., and George Berkeley YOUNG. *Politics, Strategy, and American Diplomacy: Studies in Foreign Policy, 1873-1917.* New Haven, Conn., 1966.

391 HAMMOND, Paul Y. *Organizing for Defense: The American Military Establishment in the Twentieth Century.* Princeton, N.J., 1961.

392 HASSLER, Warren W., Jr. *The President as Commander in Chief.* Menlo Park, Cal., 1971.†

393 HUNTINGTON, Samuel P. *The Soldier and the State: The Theory and Politics of Civil-Military Relations.* Cambridge, Mass. 1957.†

394 HUZAR, Elias. *The Purse and the Sword.* Ithaca, N.Y., 1950. Congress and the armed forces, 1933-1950.

395   IKLÉ, Fred Charles. *Every War Must End.* New York, 1971.† Processes by which twentieth-century wars have been brought to a close.

396   KARSTEN, Peter. *The Naval Aristocracy: The Golden Age of Annapolis and the Emergence of Modern American Navalism.* New York, 1972.

397   KYRE, Martin, and Joan KYRE. *Military Occupation and National Security.* Washington, 1968.

398   LIVEZEY, William E. *Mahan on Sea Power.* Norman, Okla., 1947.

399   MAHAN, Alfred Thayer. *From Sail to Steam: Recollections of a Naval Life.* New York, 1907.

400   MAHAN, Alfred Thayer. *The Interest of America in Sea Power, Present and Future.* Boston, 1897.

401   MAY, Ernest R. "The Development of Political-Military Consultation in the United States." *Pol Sci Q,* LXX (1955), 161-180.

402   MAY, Ernest R., ed. *The Ultimate Decision: The President as Commander in Chief.* New York, 1960. Contains essays on McKinley, Wilson, F.D.R., Truman, and "Eisenhower and After."

403   MILLIS, Walter. *Arms and Men.* New York, 1956.†

404   MILLIS, Walter, *et al. Arms and the State: Civil-Military Elements in National Policy.* New York, 1958.

405   MITCHELL, D. W. *History of the Modern American Navy from 1883 Through Pearl Harbor.* New York, 1946.

406   NELSON, Keith L., ed. *The Impact of War on American Life: The Twentieth-Century Experience.* New York, 1971.† Readings.

407   O'CONNOR, Raymond G., ed. *American Defense Policy in Perspective: From Colonial Times to the Present.* New York, 1965.†

408   OGLEY, Roderick. *The Theory and Practice of Neutrality in the Twentieth Century.* New York, 1970.

409   PULESTON, William D. *Mahan: The Life and Work of Alfred Thayer Mahan.* New Haven, Conn., 1939.

410   PURSELL, Carroll W., Jr., ed. *The Military-Industrial Complex.* New York, 1973.† World War I to the present. Statistics and contemporary commentaries.

411   RANDLE, Robert F. *The Origins of Peace: A Study of Peacemaking and the Structure of Peace Settlements.* New York, 1973. Describes how wars are ended.

412   ROSSITER, Clinton. *The Supreme Court and the Commander-in-Chief.* Ithaca, N.Y., 1951.

413   SMITH, William Young. "The Search for National Security Planning Machinery, 1906-1947." Doctoral dissertation, Harvard University, 1961.

414   SPROUT, Harold, and Margaret SPROUT. *The Rise of American Naval Power, 1776-1918.* Princeton, N.J., 1939.†

415   STROMBERG, Roland N., *Collective Security and American Foreign Policy from the League of Nations to NATO*. New York, 1963.

416   STROMBERG, Roland N. "The Idea of Collective Security." *J Hist Ideas*, XVII (1956), 250-263.

417   STROMBERG, Roland N. "The Riddle of Collective Security." *Issues and Conflicts*. See 50.

418   WHITEMAN, Harold Bartlett, Jr. "Norman H. Davis and the Search for International Peace and Security, 1917-1944." Doctoral dissertation, Yale University, 1958.

Peace Movements

419   BROCK, Peter. *Pacifism in the United States from the Colonial Era to the First World War*. Princeton, N.J., 1968.

420   CHATFIELD, Charles. *For Peace and Justice: Pacifism in America, 1914-1941*. Knoxville, Tenn., 1971.†

421   CHATFIELD, Charles, ed. *Peace Movements in America*. New York, 1973.† Eleven articles which first appeared in *American Studies*, XIII (Spring 1972).

422   CURTI, Merle E. *Peace or War: The American Struggle, 1636-1936*. New York, 1936.

423   FERRELL, Robert H. "The Peace Movement." *Isolation and Security*. See 72.

424   HERMAN, Sondra R. *Eleven Against War: Studies in American Internationalist Thought, 1898-1921*. Stanford, Cal., 1969.†

425   MARCHAND, C. Roland. *The American Peace Movement and Social Reform, 1898-1918*. Princeton, N.J., 1973.

426   NELSON, John K. *The Peace Prophets: American Pacifist Thought, 1919-1941*. Chapel Hill, N.C., 1967.

427   WITTNER, Lawrence S. *Rebels Against War: The American Peace Movement, 1941-1960*. New York, 1969.

Individual Topics

428   BENNETT, Marion T. *American Immigration Policies: A History*. Washington, 1963.

429   DIVINE, Robert A. *American Immigration Policy, 1924-1952*. New Haven, Conn., 1957.

430   GARIS, Roy L. *Immigration Restrictions*. New York, 1927.

431   GAY, James Thomas. "American Fur Seal Diplomacy." Doctoral dissertation, University of Georgia, 1971. Before and after the 1911 North Pacific Sealing Convention.

432   KAHN, David. *The Codebreakers*. New York, 1966.

433　SHEPHERD, George W., Jr., ed. *Racial Influences on American Foreign Policy.* New York, 1970. Contemporary and rudimentary.

434　TAYLOR, Arnold H. *American Diplomacy and the Narcotics Traffic, 1900-1939: A Study in International Humanitarian Reform.* Durham, N.C., 1969.

II. Years of Expanding Interests, 1890-1913

1. General

435　ANDERSON, Donald F. *William Howard Taft: A Conservative's Conception of the Presidency.* Ithaca, N.Y., 1973.

436　ARMSTRONG, W. M. *E. L. Godkin and American Foreign Policy, 1865-1900.* New York, 1957.

437　BEALE, Howard K. *Theodore Roosevelt and the Rise of America to World Power.* Baltimore, 1956.†

438　BLAKE, Nelson M. "Ambassadors at the Court of Theodore Roosevelt." *Miss Val Hist Rev,* XLII (1955), 179-206.

439　BLUM, John Morton. *The Republican Roosevelt.* Cambridge, Mass., 1954.†

440　BRAEMAN, John. *Albert J. Beveridge, American Nationalist.* Chicago, 1971. About a leading imperialist.

441　CARSON, Donald Keith. "Richard Olney: Secretary of State, 1895-1897." Doctoral dissertation, University of Kentucky, 1969.

442　CASTLE, W. R., Jr. "John Watson Foster." *Secretaries of State.* Vol. 8. See 60.

443　CHESSMAN, G. Wallace. *Theodore Roosevelt and the Politics of Power.* Boston, 1968.†

444　CLEMENTS, Kendrick Alling. "William Jennings Bryan and Democratic Foreign Policy, 1896-1915." Doctoral dissertation, University of California, Berkeley, 1970.

445　CLYMER, Kenton James. "The Gentleman as Diplomat: The Social Thought and International Outlook of John Hay." Doctoral dissertation, University of Michigan, 1971.

446　COLETTA, Paolo E. *The Presidency of William Howard Taft.* Lawrence, Kans., 1973.

447 COLETTA, Paolo E., ed. *Threshold to American Internationalism: Essays on the Foreign Policies of William McKinley*. New York, 1970.

448 COLETTA, Paolo E. "William McKinley and the Conduct of United States Foreign Relations." *Threshold to American Internationalism*. See 447.

449 COY, Dwight Richard. "Cushman K. Davis and American Foreign Policy, 1887-1900." Doctoral dissertation, University of Minnesota, 1965. Davis was chairman of Senate Foreign Relations Committee.

450 DENNETT, Tyler. *John Hay: From Poetry to Politics*. New York, 1933.

451 DENNIS, Alfred L. P. *Adventures in American Diplomacy, 1896-1906*. New York, 1928.

452 DENNIS, Alfred L. P. "John Hay." *Secretaries of State*. Vol. 9. See 60.

453 DULEBOHN, G. R. *Principles of Foreign Policy Under the Cleveland Administrations*. Philadelphia, 1941.

454 DULLES, Foster Rhea. *Prelude to World Power: American Diplomatic History, 1860-1900*. New York, 1965.

455 EINSTEIN, Lewis. *A Diplomat Looks Back*. Ed. Lawrence E. Gelfand. New Haven, Conn., 1968. A wide-ranging memoir.

456 EINSTEIN, Lewis D. *Roosevelt: His Mind in Action*. Boston, 1930.

457 EPPINGA, Richard Jay. "Aristocrat, Nationalist, Diplomat: The Life and Career of Huntington Wilson." Doctoral dissertation, Michigan State University, 1972. Wilson was active in the Theodore Roosevelt and Taft administrations.

458 ESTHUS, Raymond A. *Theodore Roosevelt and the International Rivalries*. Waltham, Mass., 1970.†

459 FAULKNER, Harold U. *Politics, Reform, and Expansion, 1890-1900*. New York, 1959.

460 FOSTER, John W. *Diplomatic Memoirs*. 2 vols. Boston, 1909.

461 FOWLER, Wilton B. "American Foreign Policy in the Progressive Era: The Dictates of Defense and Strategy." *The Progressive Era*. Ed. Lewis L. Gould. Syracuse, N.Y., 1974.

462 FREYTAG, Dierk. *Die Vereinigten Staaten auf dem Weg zur Intervention: Studien zur amerikanischen Aussenpolitik 1910-1914*. Heidelberg, 1971.

463 GARDNER, Lloyd C. "American Foreign Policy 1900-1921: A Second Look at the Realist Critique of American Diplomacy." *Towards a New Past: Dissenting Essays in American History*. Ed. Barton J. Bernstein. New York, 1968.†

464 GARRATY, John A. *Lodge*. See 902.

465 GRESHAM, Matilda. *Life of Walter Quintin Gresham, 1832-1895*. 2 vols. Chicago, 1919.

466 GREW, Joseph C. *Turbulent Era: A Diplomatic Record of Forty Years, 1904-1945*. Ed. Walter Johnson. Boston, 1952.

467 HARBAUGH, William H. *Power and Responsibility: The Life and Times of Theodore Roosevelt*. New York, 1961.

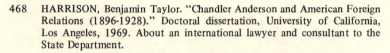

468 HARRISON, Benjamin Taylor. "Chandler Anderson and American Foreign Relations (1896-1928)." Doctoral dissertation, University of California, Los Angeles, 1969. About an international lawyer and consultant to the State Department.

469 HAY, John. *Letters of John Hay and Extracts from Diary*. 3 vols. Washington, 1908.

470 HEINRICHS, Waldo, Jr. *American Ambassador: Joseph C. Grew and the Development of the United States Diplomatic Tradition*. Boston, 1967.

471 HOAR, George Frisbie. *Autobiography of Seventy Years*. 2 vols. New York, 1903.

472 HOLBO, Paul S. "Economics, Emotion, and Expansion: An Emerging Foreign Policy." *The Gilded Age*. Ed. H. Wayne Morgan. Rev. ed. Syracuse, N.Y., 1970.†

473 HOLBO, Paul S. "Perspectives on American Foreign Policy, 1890-1916: Expansion and World Power." *Soc Stud*, LVIII (1967), 246-256. A bibliographical essay.

474 JAMES, Henry. *Richard Olney and His Public Service*. Boston, 1923.

475 JESSUP, Philip C. *Elihu Root*. 2 vols. New York, 1938.

476 KENNAN, George. *E. H. Harriman*. 2 vols. Boston, 1922.

477 LEOPOLD, Richard W. *Elihu Root and the Conservative Tradition*. Boston, 1954.†

478 LIVEZEY. *Mahan*. See 398.

479 LOCKEY, J. B. "James Gillespie Blaine." *Secretaries of State*. Vol. 8. See 60.

480 LODGE, Henry Cabot, ed. *Selections from the Correspondence of Theodore Roosevelt and Henry Cabot Lodge*. 2 vols. New York, 1925.

481 MAY, Ernest R. "Emergence to World Power." *The Reconstruction of American History*. Ed. John Higham. New York, 1962.†

482 MAY, Ernest R. *Imperial Democracy: The Emergence of America as a Great Power*. New York, 1961.†

483 MEGARGEE, Richard. "The Diplomacy of John Bassett Moore: Realism in American Foreign Policy." Doctoral dissertation, Northwestern University, 1963.

484 MORGAN, H. Wayne. *William McKinley and His America*. Syracuse, N.Y., 1963.

485 MORISON, Elting E., *et al.*, eds. *The Letters of Theodore Roosevelt*. 8 vols. Cambridge, Mass., 1951-1954.

486 MULHOLLAN, Paige Elliott. "Philander C. Knox and Dollar Diplomacy, 1909-1913." Doctoral dissertation, University of Texas, 1966.

487 NEVINS, Allan. *Grover Cleveland: A Study in Courage*. New York, 1932.

488 NEVINS, Allan. *Henry White: Thirty Years of American Diplomacy*. New York, 1930.

489 PHILLIPS, Frances Marie. "John Watson Foster, 1836-1917." Doctoral dissertation, University of New Mexico, 1956.

490 PHILLIPS, William. *Ventures in Diplomacy*. Portland, Me., 1952. Phillips was active in the administrations of T.R., Wilson, and F.D.R.

491 PLESUR, Milton. *America's Outward Thrust: Approaches to Foreign Affairs, 1865-1890*. DeKalb, Ill., 1971.

492 PRATT, Julius W. *America and World Leadership, 1900-1921*. New York, 1967.† Originally published as *Challenge and Rejection*.

493 PRINGLE, Henry F. *The Life and Times of William Howard Taft*. 2 vols. New York, 1939.

494 PRINGLE, Henry F. *Theodore Roosevelt: A Biography*. New York, 1931.†

495 RADKE, August Carl. "John Tyler Morgan, an Expansionist Senator, 1877-1907." Doctoral dissertation, University of Washington, 1953. Morgan was a Democrat on the Senate Foreign Relations Committee.

496 ROOSEVELT, Theodore. *Theodore Roosevelt: An Autobiography*. New York, 1916.

497 SCHOLES, Walter V., and Marie V. SCHOLES. *The Foreign Policies of the Taft Administration*. Columbia, Mo., 1970.

498 SCHUYLER, M. "Walter Quintin Gresham" and "Richard Olney." *Secretaries of State*. Vol. 8. See 60.

499 SCOTT, J. B. "Elihu Root" and "Robert Bacon." *Secretaries of State*. Vol. 9. See 60.

500 SEARS, L. M. "John Sherman." *Secretaries of State*. Vol. 9. See 60.

501 SHIPPEE, L. B., and R. B. WAY. "William Rufus Day." *Secretaries of State*. Vol. 9. See 60.

502 SPETTER, Allan. "Harrison and Blaine: Foreign Policy, 1889-1893." *Indiana Magazine of History*, LXV (1969), 215-227.

503 TANSILL, Charles C. *The Foreign Policy of Thomas F. Bayard, 1885-1897*. New York, 1940.

504 THAYER, William R. *The Life and Letters of John Hay*. 2 vols. Boston, 1915.

505 TYLER, Alice Felt. *The Foreign Policy of James G. Blaine*. Minneapolis, 1927.

506 VARG, Paul A. "The United States a World Power, 1900-1917: Myth or Reality?" *Twentieth-Century American Foreign Policy*. See 64.

507 VOLWILER, A. T. *The Correspondence Between Benjamin Harrison and James G. Blaine, 1882-1893*. Philadelphia, 1940.

508 VOLWILER, A. T. "Harrison, Blaine, and Foreign Policy, 1889-1893." *Proc Am Philos Soc*, LXXIX (1938), 637-648.

509 WELLS, Samuel F., Jr. "The Challenge of Power: American Diplomacy, 1900-1921." *The Unfinished Century*. See 96.

510 WHITE, Andrew Dickson. *Autobiography of Andrew Dickson White.* 2 vols. New York, 1905. The 1899 Hague Conference and other diplomatic assignments.

511 WILSON, Francis M. Huntington. *Memoirs of an Ex-Diplomat.* Boston, 1945. Huntington served under T.R. and Taft.

512 WILSON, Henry Lane. *Diplomatic Episodes in Mexico, Belgium, and Chile.* New York, 1927.

513 WRIGHT, H. F. "Philander C. Knox." *Secretaries of State.* Vol. 9. See 60.

514 YOUNGER, Edward. *John A. Kasson: Politics and Diplomacy from Lincoln to McKinley.* Iowa City, Iowa, 1955.

2. Imperialism

The Phenomenon Analyzed

515 AMBROSIUS, Lloyd E. "Turner's Frontier Thesis and the Modern American Empire: A Review Essay." *Civil War History,* XVII (1971), 332-339.

516 BAILEY, Thomas A. "Was the Presidential Election of 1900 a Mandate on Imperialism?" *Miss Val Hist Rev,* XXIV (1937), 43-52.

517 BURTON, David H. *Theodore Roosevelt, Confident Imperialist.* Philadelphia, 1968.†

518 GATEWOOD, Willard B., Jr. "A Negro Editor on Imperialism: John Mitchell, 1898-1901." *Jour Q,* XLIX (1972), 43-50, 60.

519 HEALY, David. *US Expansionism: The Imperialist Urge in the 1890s.* Madison, Wis., 1970.

520 HOFSTADTER, Richard. "Manifest Destiny and the Philippines." *America in Crisis.* Ed. Daniel Aaron. New York, 1952.

521 KENNEDY, Padraic Colum. "La Follette's Imperialist Flirtation." *Pac Hist Rev,* XXIX (1960), 131-144.

522 KENNEDY, Philip W. "The Racial Overtones of Imperialism as a Campaign Issue, 1900." *Mid-Am,* XLVIII (1966), 196-205.

523 KNUDSON, David L. T. "A Note on Walter LaFeber, Captain Mahan, and the Use of Historical Sources." *Pac Hist Rev,* XL (1971), 519-522.

524 LAFEBER Walter. *The New Empire: An Interpretation of American Expansion, 1860-1898.* Ithaca, N.Y., 1964.†

525 LAFEBER, Walter. "A Note on the 'Mercantilistic Imperialism' of Alfred Thayer Mahan." *Miss Val Hist Rev,* XLVIII (1962), 674-685.

526 LANGER, William L. *The Diplomacy of Imperialism.* 2 vols. New York, 1935. Mostly European.

527 LEUCHTENBURG, William E. "Progressivism and Imperialism: The Progressive Movement and American Foreign Policy, 1898-1916." *Miss Val Hist Rev*, XXXIX (1952), 483-504.

528 MCKEE, Delber L. "Samuel Gompers, the A.F. of L., and Imperialism, 1895-1900." *Historian*, XXI (1959), 187-199.

529 MARKOWITZ, Gerald Edward. "Progressive Imperialism: Consensus and Conflict in the Progressive Movement on Foreign Policy, 1898-1917." Doctoral dissertation, University of Wisconsin, 1971.

530 MAY, Ernest R. *American Imperialism: A Speculative Essay*. New York, 1968. Previously published in different form in *Perspectives in American History*, I (1967), 123-283.

531 MEYERHUBER, Carl Irving, Jr., "Henry Cabot Lodge, Massachusetts, and the New Manifest Destiny." Doctoral dissertation, University of California, San Diego, 1972.

532 MILLER, Richard H. *American Imperialism in 1898: The Quest for National Fulfillment*. New York, 1970.

533 NICHOLS, Jeannette P. "The United States Congress and Imperialism, 1861-1897." *J Econ Hist*, XXI (1961), 526-538.

534 PERKINS, Whitney T. *Denial of Empire: The United States and Its Dependencies*. Leyden, 1962.

535 PRATT, Julius W. *America's Colonial Experiment: How the United States Gained, Governed, and in Part Gave Away a Colonial Empire*. Englewood Cliffs, N.J., 1950.

536 PRATT, Julius W. *Expansionists of 1898: The Acquisition of Hawaii and the Spanish Islands*. Baltimore, 1936.†

537 PRATT, Julius W. "The 'Large Policy' of 1898." *Miss Val Hist Rev*, XIX (1932), 219-242.

538 THOMPSON, J. A. "William Appleman Williams and the 'American Empire.' " *J Am Stud*, VII (1973), 91-104. Review article.

539 VEVIER, Charles. "Brooks Adams and the Ambivalence of American Foreign Policy." *World Affairs Quarterly*, XXX (1959), 3-18.

540 WILLIAMS, William A. "Brooks Adams and American Expansion." *N Eng Q*, XXV (1952), 217-232.

541 WILLIAMS, William A. *The Roots of the Modern American Empire: A Study of the Growth and Shaping of Social Consciousness in a Marketplace Society*. New York, 1969.

Hawaii, Samoa

542 APPEL, J. C. "American Labor and the Annexation of Hawaii: A Study in Logic and Economic Interest." *Pac Hist Rev*, XXIII (1954), 1-18.

543 BAILEY, Thomas A. "The United States and Hawaii During the Spanish-American War." *Am Hist Rev*, XXXVI (1931), 552-560.

544 BAKER, George W., Jr. "Benjamin Harrison and Hawaiian Annexation: A Reinterpretation." *Pac Hist Rev*, XXXIII (1964), 295-309.

545 ELLISON, Joseph W. "The Partition of Samoa: A Study in Imperialism and Diplomacy." *Pac Hist Rev*, VIII (1939), 259-288.

546 OSBORNE, Thomas J. "The Main Reason for Hawaiian Annexation in July, 1898." *Oregon Historical Quarterly*, LXXI (1970), 161-178.

547 PRATT, Julius W. *Expansionists of 1898*. See 536.

548 PRATT, Julius W. "The Hawaiian Revolution: Re-Interpretation." *Pac Hist Rev*, I (1932), 273-294.

549 QUINN, Pearle E. "The Diplomatic Struggle for the Carolines, 1898." *Pac Hist Rev*, XIV (1945), 290-302.

550 ROWLAND, Donald. "The Establishment of the Republic of Hawaii, 1893-1894." *Pac Hist Rev*, IV (1935), 201-220.

551 RUSS, William A., Jr. "Hawaiian Labor and Immigration Problems Before Annexation." *J Mod Hist*, XV (1943), 207-222.

552 RUSS, William A., Jr. *The Hawaiian Republic (1894-1898) and Its Struggle to Win Annexation*. Selinsgrove, Pa., 1961.

553 RUSS, William A., Jr. *The Hawaiian Revolution, 1893-1894*. Selinsgrove Pa., 1959.

554 RUSS, William A., Jr. "The Role of Sugar in Hawaiian Annexation." *Pac Hist Rev*, XII (1943), 339-350.

555 RYDEN, George H. *The Foreign Policy of the United States in Relation to Samoa*. New Haven, Conn., 1933.

556 STEVENS, Sylvester K. *American Expansion in Hawaii, 1842-1898*. Harrisburg, Pa., 1945.

557 TATE, Merze. "Great Britain and the Sovereignty of Hawaii." *Pac Hist Rev*, XXXI (1962), 327-348.

558 TATE, Merze. *Hawaii: Reciprocity or Annexation*. East Lansing, Mich., 1968.

559 TATE, Merze. "Hawaii: A Symbol of Anglo-American Rapprochement." *Pol Sci Q*, LXXIX (1964), 555-575.

560 TATE, Merze. "The Myth of Hawaii's Swing Toward Australasia and Canada." *Pac Hist Rev*, XXXIII (1964), 273-293.

561 WEIGLE, Richard D. "Sugar and the Hawaiian Revolution." *Pac Hist Rev*, XVI (1947), 41-58.

Cuba, War with Spain, the Philippines

562 APPEL, John C. "The Unionization of Florida Cigarmakers and the Coming of the War with Spain." *His Am Hist Rev*, XXXVI (1956), 38-49.

563 AUXIER, George W. "Middle Western Newspapers and the Spanish-American War, 1895-1898." *Miss Val Hist Rev*, XXVI (1940), 523-534.

564 AUXIER, George W. "The Propaganda Activities of the Cuban *Junta* in Precipitating the Spanish-American War, 1895-1898." *His Am Hist Rev*, XIX (1939), 286-305.

565 BAILEY, Thomas A. "Dewey and the Germans at Manila Bay." *Am Hist Rev*, XLV (1939), 59-81.

566 BENTON, E. J. *International Law and Diplomacy of the Spanish-American War*. Baltimore, 1908.

567 BROWN, Charles H. *The Correspondents' War: Journalists in the Spanish-American War*. New York, 1967.†

568 CHADWICK, French Ensor. *The Relations of the United States and Spain: Diplomacy*. New York, 1909.

569 COLETTA, Paolo E. "Bryan, McKinley, and the Treaty of Paris." *Pac Hist Rev*, XXVI (1957), 131-146.

570 COLETTA, Paolo E. "McKinley, the Peace Negotiations, and the Acquisition of the Philippines." *Pac Hist Rev*, XXX (1961), 341-350.

571 COLETTA, Paolo E. "The Peace Negotiations and the Treaty of Paris." *Threshold to American Internationalism*. See 447.

572 COSMAS, Graham A. *An Army for Empire: The United States Army in the Spanish-American War*. Columbia, Mo., 1972.

573 DEWEY, George. *Autobiography of George Dewey, Admiral of the Navy*. New York, 1913.

574 EGGERT, Gerald G. "Our Man in Havana: Fitzhugh Lee." *His Am Hist Rev*, XLVII (1967), 463-485.

575 FERRARA, Orestes. *The Last Spanish War: Revelations in Diplomacy*. New York, 1937.

576 FONER, Philip S. "Why the United States Went to War with Spain in 1898." *Sci Soc*, XXXII (1968), 39-65.

577 FREIDEL, Frank. *The Splendid Little War*. Boston, 1958. Many pictures.

578 GILMORE, N. Ray. "Mexico and the Spanish-American War." *His Am Hist Rev*, XLIII (1963), 511-525.

579 GRENVILLE, John A. S. "American Naval Preparations for War with Spain, 1896-1898." *J Am Stud*, II (1968), 33-47.

580 HINES, Thomas S. "The Imperial Facade: Daniel H. Burnham and American Architectural Planning in the Philippines." *Pac Hist Rev*, XLI (1972), 33-53.

581 HITCHMAN, James H. *Leonard Wood and Cuban Independence, 1898-1902*. The Hague, 1971.

582 HOLBO, Paul S. "The Convergence of Moods and the Cuban-Bond 'Conspiracy' of 1898." *J Am Hist*, LV (1968), 54-72.

583 HOLBO, Paul S. "Presidential Leadership in Foreign Affairs: William McKinley and the Turpie-Foraker Amendment." *Am Hist Rev*, LXXII (1967), 1321-1335. Concerns Cuba, 1898.

584 MAHAN, Alfred Thayer. *Lessons of the War with Spain.* Boston, 1899.

585 MILLIS, Walter. *The Martial Spirit: A Study of Our War with Spain.* Boston, 1931.†

586 MORGAN, H. Wayne. *America's Road to Empire: The War with Spain and Overseas Expansion.* New York, 1965.†

587 MORGAN, H. Wayne. "The DeLome Letter: A New Appraisal." *Historian,* XXVI (1963), 36-49.

588 NICHOLSON, Philip Y. "George Dewey and the Transformation of American Foreign Policy." Doctoral dissertation, University of New Mexico, 1971.

589 O'CONNOR, Nancy L. "The Spanish-American War: A Re-Evaluation of Its Causes." *Sci Soc,* XXII (1958), 129-143.

590 PERKINS, Whitney T. "The New Dependencies Under McKinley." *Threshold to American Internationalism.* See 447.

591 PRATT, Julius W. "American Business and the Spanish-American War." *His Am Hist Rev,* XIV (1934), 163-201.

592 PRATT, Julius W. "The Coming of War with Spain." *Threshold to American Internationalism.* See 447.

593 QUINT, Howard H. "American Socialists and the Spanish-American War." *Am Q,* X (1958), 131-141.

594 READNOUR, Harry Warren. "General Fitzhugh Lee, 1835-1905: A Biographical Study." Doctoral dissertation, University of Virginia, 1971. Lee was U.S. consul-general, Havana, 1898.

595 RIPPY, J. Fred. "The European Powers and the Spanish American War." *James Sprunt Historical Studies,* XIX (1927), 22-52.

596 SEARS, Louis Martin. "French Opinion of the Spanish-American War." *His Am Hist Rev,* VII (1927), 25-44.

597 SHELBY, C. C. "Mexico and the Spanish-American War: Some Contemporary Expressions of Opinion." *Essays in Mexican History.* See 233.

598 SHIPPEE, Lester B. "Germany and the Spanish-American War." *Am Hist Rev,* XXX (1925), 754-777.

599 SKLAR, Martin J. "The N.A.M. and Foreign Markets on the Eve of the Spanish-American War." *Sci Soc,* XXIII (1959), 133-162.

600 SNYDER, Phil Lyman. "Mission, Empire, or Force of Circumstances? A Study of the American Decision to Annex the Philippine Islands." Doctoral dissertation, Stanford University, 1972.

601 SPECTOR, Ronald. "Who Planned the Attack on Manila Bay?" *Mid-Am,* LII (1971), 94-102.

602 STANLEY, Peter William. "A Nation in the Making: The Philippines and the United States, 1899-1921." Doctoral dissertation, Harvard University, 1970.

603 WALKER, L. W. "Guam's Seizure by the United States in 1898." *Pac Hist Rev,* XIV (1945), 1-12.

604   WERKING, Richard H. "Senator Henry Cabot Lodge and the Philippines: A Note on American Territorial Expansion." *Pac Hist Rev*, XLII (1973), 234-240.

605   WILKERSON, Marcus M. *Public Opinion and the Spanish-American War.* Baton Rouge, La., 1932. Reprinted, New York, 1967.

606   WISAN, Joseph E. *The Cuban Crisis as Reflected in the New York Press.* New York, 1934.

607   WOLFF, Leon. *Little Brown Brother: How the United States Purchased and Pacified the Philippine Islands at the Century's Turn.* Garden City, N.Y., 1961.

Anti-Imperialism

608   BARON, Harold. "Anti-Imperialism and the Democrats." *Sci Soc*, XXI (1957), 222-239.

609   BEISNER, Robert L. "1898 and 1968: The Anti-Imperialists and the Doves." *Pol Sci Q*, LXXXV (1970), 187-216.

610   BEISNER, Robert L. *Twelve Against Empire: The Anti-Imperialists 1898-1900.* New York, 1968.

611   COLETTA, Paolo E. "Bryan, Anti-Imperialism, and Missionary Diplomacy." *Nebraska History*, XLIV (1963), 167-187.

612   FREIDEL, Frank. "Dissent in the Spanish-American War and the Philippine Insurrection." *Dissent in Three American Wars.* By Samuel Eliot MORISON, Frederick MERK, and Frank FREIDEL. Cambridge, Mass., 1970.

613   HARRINGTON, Fred Harvey. "The Anti-Imperialist Movement in the United States, 1898-1900." *Miss Val Hist Rev*, XXII (1935), 211-230.

614   LASCH, Christopher. "The Anti-Imperialists, the Philippines, and the Inequality of Man." *J S Hist*, XXIV (1958), 319-331.

615   PRATT, Julius W. "Collapse of Anti-Imperialism." *American Mercury*, XXXI (1934), 269-278.

616   SCHIRMER, Daniel B. *Republic or Empire: American Resistance to the Philippine War.* Cambridge, Mass., 1972.

617   TOMPKINS, E. Berkeley. *Anti-Imperialism in the United States: The Great Debate, 1890-1920.* Philadelphia, 1970.

618   TOMPKINS, E. Berkeley. "The Old Guard: A Study of the Anti-Imperialist Leadership." *Historian*, XXX (1968), 366-388.

619   TOMPKINS, E. Berkeley. "Scylla and Charybdis: The Anti-Imperialist Dilemma in the Election of 1900." *Pac Hist Rev*, XXXVI (1967), 143-161.

620   WELCH, Richard E., Jr. *George Frisbie Hoar and the Half-Breed Republicans.* Cambridge, Mass., 1972. About a leading anti-imperialist.

621   WELCH, Richard E., Jr. "Motives and Policy Objectives of Anti-Imperialists, 1898." *Mid-Am*, LI (1969), 119-129.

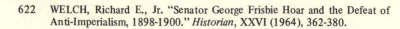

622 WELCH, Richard E., Jr. "Senator George Frisbie Hoar and the Defeat of Anti-Imperialism, 1898-1900." *Historian*, XXVI (1964), 362-380.

3. Relations with Canada and Great Britain

623 BAILEY, Thomas A. "Theodore Roosevelt and the Alaska Boundary Settlement." *Can Hist Rev*, XVIII (1937), 123-130.

624 BAYARD, Ross Hawthorne. "Anti-Americanism in Canada and the Abortive Reciprocity Agreement of 1911." Doctoral dissertation, University of South Carolina, 1971.

625 BLAKE, Nelson M. "England and the United States, 1897-1899." *Essays ... Blakeslee*. See 90.

626 BLAKE, Nelson M. "The Olney-Pauncefote Treaty of 1897." *Am Hist Rev*, L (1945), 228-243.

627 BORCHARD, Edwin M. "The North Atlantic Coast Fisheries Arbitration." *Columbia Law Review*, XI (1911), 1-23.

628 BOURNE, Kenneth. *Britain and the Balance of Power in North America, 1815-1908*. Berkeley, Cal., 1967.

629 BROWN, R. Craig. *Canada's National Policy, 1883-1900: A Study in Canadian-American Relations*. Princeton, N.J., 1964.

630 BROWN, R. Craig. "Goldwin Smith and Anti-Imperialism." *Can Hist Rev*, XLIII (1962), 93-105. Compares British and American imperialism.

631 CAMPBELL, Alexander E. *Great Britain and the United States, 1895-1903*. London, 1960.

632 CAMPBELL, Charles S., Jr. "The Anglo-American Crisis in the Bering Sea, 1890-1891." *Miss Val Hist Rev*, XLVIII (1961), 393-414.

633 CAMPBELL, Charles S., Jr. "Anglo-American Relations, 1897-1901." *Threshold to American Internationalism*. See 447.

634 CAMPBELL, Charles S., Jr. *Anglo-American Understanding, 1898-1903*. Baltimore, 1957.

635 CAMPBELL, John P. "Taft, Roosevelt, and the Arbitration Treaties of 1911." *J Am Hist*, LIII (1966), 279-298.

636 CLEMENTS, Kendrick A. "Manifest Destiny and Canadian Reciprocity in 1911." *Pac Hist Rev*, XLII (1973), 32-52.

637 COLE, Donald. "Allen Aylesworth on the Alaska Boundary Award." *Can Hist Rev*, LII (1971), 472-477. Considers the effects of T. R.'s threats.

638 ELLIS, L. Ethan. *Reciprocity, 1911: A Study in Canadian-American Relations*. New Haven, Conn., 1939.

639 FERGUSON, John H. *American Diplomacy and the Boer War*. Philadelphia, 1939.

640 GARRATY, John A. "Henry Cabot Lodge and the Alaska Boundary Tribunal." *N Eng Q*, XXIV (1951), 469-494.

641 GELBER, Lionel M. *The Rise of Anglo-American Friendship: A Study in World Politics, 1898-1906.* New York, 1938.

642 GLUEK, Alvin C., Jr. "The Passamaquoddy Bay Treaty, 1910: A Diplomatic Sideshow in Canadian-American Relations." *Can Hist Rev*, XLVII (1966), 1-21.

643 GRENVILLE, John A. S. "Great Britain and the Isthmian Canal, 1898-1901." *Am Hist Rev*, LXI (1955), 48-69.

644 GWYNN, Stephen. *Spring Rice.* See 1123.

645 HEINDEL, Richard H. *The American Impact on Great Britain, 1898-1914.* Philadelphia, 1940.

646 HUSSEY, Lyman Andrew, Jr. "Anglo-Canadian Relations During the Roosevelt Era, 1901-1908." Doctoral dissertation, University of Georgia, 1969.

647 KITCHENS, Allen Hampton. "Ambassador Extraordinary: The Diplomatic Career of Joseph Hodges Choate." Doctoral dissertation, George Washington University, 1971. Choate was U.S. Ambassador to Britain, 1899-1905.

648 LANSING, Robert. "The North Atlantic Coast Fisheries Arbitration." *Am J Int Law*, V (1911), 1-31.

649 NEALE, R. G. *Great Britain and United States Expansion: 1898-1900.* East Lansing, Mich., 1966.

650 NEARY, Peter. "Grey, Bryce, and the Settlement of Canadian-American Differences." *Can Hist Rev*, XLIX (1968), 357-380.

651 PERKINS, Bradford. *The Great Rapprochement: England and the United States, 1895-1914.* New York, 1968.

652 ROTHSTEIN, Morton. "America in the International Rivalry for the British Wheat Market, 1860-1914." *Miss Val Hist Rev*, XLVII (1960), 401-418.

653 TANSILL, C. C. *Canadian-American Relations, 1875-1911.* New Haven, Conn., 1943.

654 TOMPKINS, S. R. "Drawing the Alaskan Boundary." *Can Hist Rev*, XXVI (1945), 1-24.

655 WARD, Alan J. *Ireland and Anglo-American Relations, 1899-1921.* Toronto, 1969.

656 WARNER, D. F. *The Idea of Continental Union: Agitation for the Annexation of Canada to the United States, 1849-1893.* Lexington, Ky., 1960.

657 WELLS, Samuel F., Jr. "Anglo-American Friendship, 1904-1914: The Strategic Aspect." Doctoral dissertation, Harvard University, 1967.

4. Relations with Europe and Russia

658 ASKEW, William C., and J. Fred RIPPY. "The United States and Europe's Strife, 1908-1913." *J Pol*, IV (1942), 68-79.

659 CASSEDY, James H. "Applied Microscopy and American Pork Diplomacy: Charles Wardell Stiles in Germany 1898-1899." *Isis*, LXII (1971), 5-20.

660 COHEN, Naomi W. "The Abrogation of the Russo-American Treaty of 1832." *Jewish Social Studies*, XXV (1963), 3-41.

661 DUNCAN, Bingham. "Protectionism and Pork: Whitelaw Reid as Diplomat, 1889-1891." *Ag Hist*, XXXIII (1959), 190-195.

662 EGAN, Clifford L. "Pressure Groups, the Department of State, and the Abrogation of the Russian-American Treaty of 1832." *Proc Am Phil Soc*, CXV (1971), 328-334. Pressure on President Taft.

663 JACKSON, Shirley Fulton. "The United States and Spain 1898-1918." Doctoral dissertation, Florida State University, 1967.

664 KREIDER, John K. "Diplomatic Relations Between Germany and the United States 1906-1913." Doctoral dissertation, Pennsylvania State University, 1969.

665 LEWIS, Tom Tandy. "Franco-American Diplomatic Relations, 1898-1907." Doctoral dissertation, University of Oklahoma, 1971.

666 MEYER, Luciana R.-W. "German-American Migration and the Bancroft Naturalization Treaties, 1868-1910." Doctoral dissertation, C.U.N.Y., 1970.

667 MOTT, T. Bentley. *Myron T. Herrick: Friend of France.* New York, 1930. Herrick was Ambassador to France under Taft.

668 PARSONS, Edward B. "The German-American Crisis of 1902-1903." *Historian*, XXXIII (1971), 436-452.

669 SCHIEBER, Clara E. *The Transformation of American Sentiment Toward Germany, 1870-1914.* Boston, 1923.

670 SIMON, Matthew, and David E. NOVACK. "Some Dimensions of the American Commercial Invasion of Europe, 1871-1914: An Introductory Essay." *J Econ Hist*, XXIV (1964), 591-605.

671 SNYDER, L. L. "The American-German Pork Dispute, 1879-1891." *J Mod Hist*, XVII (1945), 16-28.

672 TRANI, Eugene P. "Russia in 1905: The View from the American Embassy." *Rev Pol*, XXXI (1969), 48-65.

673 VAGTS, Alfred. *Deutschland und die Vereinigten Staaten in der Weltpolitik, 1890-1906.* 2 vols. New York, 1935.

5. Relations with the Middle East and Africa

674 COHEN, Naomi W. "Ambassador Straus in Turkey, 1909-1910: A Note on Dollar Diplomacy." *Miss Val Hist Rev*, XLV (1959), 632-642.

675 DAVIS, Harold E. "The Citizenship of Jon Perdicaris." *J Mod Hist*, XIII (1941), 517-526. Subject of dispute with Morocco.

676 DENOVO, John A. "A Railroad for Turkey: The Chester Project, 1908-1913." *Bus Hist Rev*, XXXIII (1959), 300-329.

677 FENDALL, Lonny Ward. "Theodore Roosevelt and Africa: Deliberate Non-Involvement in the Scramble for Territory and Influence." Doctoral dissertation, University of Oregon, 1972.

678 FERGUSON, John A. *Boer War*. See 639.

679 McSTALLSWORTH, Paul. "The United States and the Congo Question, 1884-1914." Doctoral dissertation, Ohio State University, 1954.

680 NOER, Thomas John. "The United States and South Africa, 1870-1914." Doctoral dissertation, University of Minnesota, 1972.

681 PHILLIPS, Dennis Heath. "The American Presence in Morocco, 1880-1904." Doctoral dissertation, University of Wisconsin, 1972.

6. Relations with Asia and the Pacific

682 BAILEY, Thomas A. "Japan's Protest Against the Annexation of Hawaii." *J Mod Hist*, III (1931), 46-51.

683 BAILEY, Thomas A. "The Lodge Corollary to the Monroe Doctrine." *Pol Sci Q*, XLVIII (1933), 220-239.

684 BAILEY, Thomas A. "The North Pacific Sealing Convention of 1911." *Pac Hist Rev*, IV (1935), 1-14.

685 BAILEY, Thomas A. "The Root-Takahira Agreement of 1908." *Pac Hist Rev*, IX (1940), 19-35.

686 BAILEY, Thomas A. *Theodore Roosevelt and the Japanese-American Crises*. Stanford, Cal., 1934.

687 BLAZSIK, Gloria Eva. "Theodore Roosevelt's Far Eastern Policy and the T'ang Shao-Yi Mission." Doctoral dissertation, Georgetown University, 1969. Mission from China, 1908.

688 BOSE, Nemai Sadhan. *American Attitude and Policy to the Nationalist Movement in China (1911-1921)*. Bombay, 1970.

689 BRAISTED, William R. "China, the United States Navy, and the Bethlehem Steel Company, 1909-1920." *Bus Hist Rev*, XLII (1968), 50-66.

690 BRAISTED, William R. "The Open Door and the Boxer Uprising." *Threshold to American Internationalism*. See 447.

691 BRAISTED, William R. "The United States and the American China Development Company." *Far Eastern Quarterly*, XI (1952), 147-166.

692 BUELL, Raymond L. "The Development of the Anti-Japanese Agitation in the United States." *Pol Sci Q*, XXXVII (1922), 605-638.

693 CAMERON, Meribeth E. "American Recognition Policy Toward the Republic of China, 1912-1913." *Pac Hist Rev*, II (1933), 214-230.

694 CARUTHERS, Sandra. "Charles Legendre: American Diplomacy and Expansionism in Meiji Japan, 1868-1893." Doctoral dissertation, University of Colorado, 1966.

695 CASSEY, John William. "The Mission of Charles Denby and International Rivalries in the Far East, 1885-1898." Doctoral dissertation, University of Southern California, 1959.

696 CHAMBERLIN, Eugene K. "The Japanese Scare at Magdalena Bay." *Pac Hist Rev*, XXIV (1955), 345-359.

697 CHAY, Jongsuk. "The Taft-Katsura Memorandum Reconsidered." *Pac Hist Rev*, XXXVII (1968), 321-326.

698 CHONG, Key Ray. "The Abortive American-Chinese Project for Chinese Revolution, 1908-1911." *Pac Hist Rev*, XLI (1972), 54-70.

699 CLINARD, Outten J. *Japan's Influence on American Naval Power, 1897-1917*. Berkeley, Cal., 1947.

700 CROLY, Herbert. *Willard Straight*. New York, 1924. Straight was an advocate of American involvement in China.

701 DANIELS, Roger. *The Politics of Prejudice: The Anti-Japanese Movement in California and the Struggle for Japanese Exclusion.* Berkeley, Cal., 1962.

702 DENNETT, Tyler. "The Open Door." *Empire in the East.* Ed. Joseph Barnes. New York, 1934.

703 DENNETT, Tyler. *Roosevelt and the Russo-Japanese War.* Garden City, N.Y., 1925.

704 DORWART, Jeffery Michael. "The Pigtail War: The American Response to the Sino-Japanese War of 1894-1895." Doctoral dissertation, University of Massachusetts, 1971.

705 ESTHUS, Raymond A. "The Changing Concept of the Open Door, 1899-1910." *Miss Val Hist Rev*, XLVI (1959), 435-454.

706 ESTHUS, Raymond A. "The Taft-Katsura Agreement—Reality or Myth?" *J Mod Hist*, XXXI (1959), 46-51.

707 ESTHUS, Raymond A. *Theodore Roosevelt and Japan.* Seattle, 1966.

708 EYRE, James K., Jr. "Japan and the American Annexation of the Philippines." *Pac Hist Rev*, XI (1942), 55-71.

709 EYRE, James K., Jr. "Russia and the American Acquisition of the Philippines." *Miss Val Hist Rev*, XXVIII (1942), 539-562.

710 FAIRBANK, John K. " 'American China Policy' to 1898: A Misconception." *Pac Hist Rev*, XXXIX (1970), 409-420.

711 FIELD, Frederick V. *American Participation in the China Consortiums.* Chicago, 1931.

712 FORD, Andrew Thomas. "The Diplomacy of the Boxer Uprising with Special Reference to American Foreign Policy." Doctoral dissertation, University of Wisconsin, 1971.

713   FOSTER, John W. *American Diplomacy in the Orient*. Boston, 1903.

714   GORDON, Donald C. "Roosevelt's 'Smart Yankee Trick.' " *Pac Hist Rev*, XXX (1961), 351-358. U.S., Japan, and the British Empire.

715   HALL, Luella J. "The Abortive German-American-Chinese Entente of 1907-1908." *J Mod Hist*, I (1929), 219-235.

716   HARRINGTON, Fred H. *God, Mammon, and the Japanese: Dr. Horace N. Allen and Korean-American Relations, 1884-1905*. Madison, Wis., 1944.

717   HUNT, Michael H. "The American Remission of the Boxer Indemnity: A Reappraisal." *J Asian Stud*, XXXI (1972), 539-559.

718   HUNT, Michael H. *Frontier Defense and the Open Door: Manchuria in Chinese-American Relations, 1895-1911*. New Haven, Conn., 1973.

719   IRICK, Robert L. "The Chinchow-Aigun Railroad and the Knox Neutralization Plan in Ch'ing Diplomacy." *Papers on China*, XIII (1959), 80-112.

720   IRIYE, Akira. *Pacific Estrangement: Japanese and American Expansion, 1897-1911*. Cambridge, Mass., 1972.

721   ISRAEL, Jerry. *Progressivism and the Open Door: America and China, 1905-1921*. Pittsburgh, 1971.

722   KAHN, Helen Dodson. "The Great Game of Empire: Willard D. Straight and American Far Eastern Policy." Doctoral dissertation, Cornell University, 1968.

723   KELLY, John S. *A Forgotten Conference: The Negotiations at Peking, 1900-1901*. Geneva, 1962. Boxer troubles.

724   KNIGHT, Barry Lee. "American Trade and Investment in China, 1890-1910." Doctoral dissertation, Michigan State University, 1968.

725   LIVERMORE, Seward W. "American Strategy Diplomacy in the South Pacific, 1890-1914." *Pac Hist Rev*, XII (1943), 33-51.

726   LORENCE, James J. "Business and Reform: The American Asiatic Association and the Exclusion Laws, 1905-1907." *Pac Hist Rev*, XXXIX (1970), 421-438.

727   MCCLELLAN, Robert. *The Heathen Chinese: A Study of American Attitudes Toward China, 1890-1905*. Columbus, Ohio, 1971.

728   MCCORMICK, Thomas J. "Insular Imperialism and the Open Door: The China Market and the Spanish-American War." *Pac Hist Rev*, XXXII (1963), 155-169.

729   MCCORMICK, Thomas J. *China Market: America's Quest for Informal Empire, 1893-1901*. Chicago, 1967.†

730   MILLER, Jesse A. "The United States and Chinese Territorial Integrity, 1908." *Essays . . . Blakeslee*. See 90.

731   MINGER, Ralph E. "Taft's Mission to Japan: A Study in Personal Diplomacy." *Pac Hist Rev*, XXX (1961), 279-294.

732 NEU, Charles E. "Theodore Roosevelt and the American Involvement in the Far East, 1901-1909." *Pac Hist Rev*, XXXV (1966), 433-449.

733 NEU, Charles E. *An Uncertain Friendship: Theodore Roosevelt and Japan, 1906-1909.* Cambridge, Mass., 1967.

734 OSBORN, Clarence G. "American Extraterritorial Jurisdiction in China to 1906: A Study of American Policy." Doctoral dissertation, Stanford University, 1935.

735 PALMER, Spencer, ed. *Korean-American Relations: Documents Pertaining to the Far Eastern Diplomacy of the United States.* Vol. 2: *Period of Growing Influence, 1887-1895.* Berkeley, Cal., 1963.

736 PARSONS, Edward B. "Roosevelt's Containment of the Russo-Japanese War." *Pac Hist Rev*, XXXVIII (1969), 21-43.

737 PAULSEN, George E. "The Abrogation of the Gresham-Yang Treaty." *Pac Hist Rev*, XL (1971), 457-477. The treaty that prohibited immigration of Chinese laborers was abrogated in 1904.

738 PRESSMAN, Harvey. "Hay, Rockhill, and China's Integrity: A Reappraisal." *Papers on China*, XIII (1959), 61-79.

739 PRICE, Allen T. "American Missions and American Diplomacy in China, 1830-1900." Doctoral dissertation, Harvard University, 1932.

740 PURCELL, Victor. *The Boxer Uprising: A Background Study.* Cambridge, England, 1963.

741 REID, John G. *The Manchu Abdication and the Powers, 1908-1912.* Berkeley, Cal., 1935.

742 SAXTON, Alexander. *The Indispensable Enemy: Labor and the Anti-Chinese Movement in California.* Berkeley and Los Angeles, 1971.

743 TAN, C. C. *The Boxer Catastrophe.* New York, 1955.

744 TATE, E. Mowbray. "U.S. Gunboats on the Yangtze: History and Political Aspects, 1842-1922." *Studies on Asia*, VII (1966), 121-132.

745 TRANI, Eugene P. *The Treaty of Portsmouth; An Adventure in American Diplomacy.* Lexington, Ky., 1969. Conclusion of the Russo-Japanese War.

746 TREAT, Payson J. *Diplomatic Relations Between the United States and Japan, 1853-1905.* 3 vols. Stanford, Cal., 1932-1938.

747 VARG, Paul A. *The Making of a Myth: The United States and China, 1897-1912.* East Lansing, Mich., 1968.

748 VARG, Paul A. "The Myth of the China Market, 1890-1914." *Am Hist Rev*, LXXIII (1968), 742-758.

749 VARG, Paul A. *Open Door Diplomat: The Life of W. W. Rockhill.* Urbana, Ill., 1952.

750 VARG, Paul A. "William Woodville Rockhill's Influence on the Boxer Negotiations." *Pac Hist Rev*, XVIII (1949), 369-380.

751   VEVIER, Charles. "The Open Door: An Idea in Action, 1906-1913." *Pac Hist Rev*, XXIV (1955), 49-62.

752   VEVIER, Charles. *The United States and China, 1906-1913: A Study of Finance and Diplomacy.* New Brunswick, N.J., 1955.

753   WHITE, John Albert. *The Diplomacy of the Russo-Japanese War.* Princeton, N.J., 1964.

754   YOUNG, Marilyn Blatt. "American Expansion, 1870-1900: The Far East." *Towards a New Past: Dissenting Essays in American History.* Ed. Barton J. Bernstein. New York, 1968.†

755   YOUNG, Marilyn B. *The Rhetoric of Empire: American China Policy, 1895-1901.* Cambridge, Mass., 1968.

756   ZABRISKIE, Edward H. *American-Russian Rivalry in the Far East: A Study in Diplomacy and Power Politics, 1895-1914.* Philadelphia, 1946.

7. Relations with Latin America

757   AMERINGER, Charles D. "The Panama Canal Lobby of Philippe Bunau-Varilla and William Nelson Cromwell." *Am Hist Rev*, LXVIII (1963), 346-363.

758   AMERINGER, Charles D. "Philippe Bunau-Varilla: New Light on the Panama Canal Treaty." *His Am Hist Rev*, XLVI (1966), 28-52.

759   ATKINS, George Pope. "McKinley and Latin America." *Threshold to American Internationalism.* See 447.

760   BAILEY, Thomas A. "Interest in a Nicaragua Canal, 1903-1931." *His Am Hist Rev*, XVI (1936), 2-28.

761   BASTERT, Russell H. "A New Approach to the Origins of Blaine's Pan American Policy." *His Am Hist Rev*, XXXIX (1959), 375-412.

762   BERBUSSE, Edward J. "Neutrality-Diplomacy of the United States and Mexico, 1910-1911." *The Americas*, XII (1956), 265-283.

763   BERBUSSE, Edward J. *The United States in Puerto Rico 1898-1900.* Chapel Hill, N.C., 1966.

764   BLAISDELL, Lowell L. "Henry Lane Wilson and the Overthrow of Madero." *Southwest Social Science Quarterly*, XLIII (1962), 126-135.

765   BLAKE, Nelson M. "Background of Cleveland's Venezuelan Policy." *Am Hist Rev*, XLVII (1942), 259-277.

766   BLASIER, Cole. "The United States and Madero." *J Latin Am Stud*, IV (1972), 207-231.

767   BUNAU-VARILLA, Philippe. *Panama: The Creation, Destruction, and Resurrection.* New York, 1914.

768   BURNS, E. Bradford. *The Unwritten Alliance: Rio-Branco and Brazilian-American Relations.* New York, 1966. Spans the decade 1902-1912.

769 CALLCOTT, Wilfred H. *The Caribbean Policy of the United States, 1890-1920.* Baltimore, 1942.

770 CALVERT, Peter. *The Mexican Revolution 1910-1914: The Diplomacy of Anglo-American Conflict.* Cambridge, Eng., 1968.

771 CALVERT, Peter. "The Murray Contract: An Episode in International Finance and Diplomacy." *Pac Hist Rev*, XXXV (1966), 203-224. Anglo-American loan competition in Colombia.

772 CARRERAS, Charles Edward. "United States Economic Penetration of Venezuela and Its Effects on Diplomacy: 1895-1906." Doctoral dissertation, University of North Carolina, 1971.

773 CHILD, Clifton J. "The Venezuela-British Guiana Boundary Arbitration of 1899." *Am J Int Law*, XLIV (1950), 682-693.

774 CLEVELAND, Grover. *Presidential Problems.* New York, 1904. Includes a long chapter on Venezuela.

775 CLIFFORD, John Garry. "Admiral Dewey and the Germans, 1903: A New Perspective." *Mid-Am*, XLIX (1967), 214-220. Venezuela.

776 COKER, William S. "The Panama Canal Tolls Controversy: A Different Perspective." *J Am Hist*, LV (1968), 555-564.

777 COSÍO VILLEGAS, Daniel. *The United States Versus Porfirio Diaz.* Lincoln, Neb., 1964.

778 CUMMINS, Lejeune. "The Formulation of the 'Platt' Amendment." *The Americas*, XXIII (1967), 370-389.

779 DAHL, Victor C. "Uruguay Under Juan Idiarte Borda: An American Diplomat's Observations." *His Am Hist Rev*, XLVI (1966), 66-77. Covers the years 1894-1897.

780 DENNIS, William Cullen. "The Venezuela-British Guiana Boundary Arbitration of 1899." *Am J Int Law*, XLIV (1950), 720-727.

781 FENTON, P. F. "Diplomatic Relations of the United States and Venezuela, 1880-1915." *His Am Hist Rev*, VIII (1928), 330-356.

782 FINDLING, John Ellis. "The United States and Zelaya: A Study in the Diplomacy of Expediency." Doctoral dissertation, University of Texas, 1971. Nicaragua, 1893-1909.

783 FOSSUM, Paul R. "The Anglo-Venezuelan Boundary Controversy." *His Am Hist Rev*, VIII (1928), 299-329.

784 FRIEDLANDER, Robert A. "A Reassessment of Roosevelt's Role in the Panamanian Revolution of 1903." *W Pol Q*, XIV (1961), 535-543.

785 GREGG, Robert D. *The Influence of Border Troubles on Relations Between the United States and Mexico 1876-1910.* Baltimore, 1937.

786 GRIEB, Kenneth J. "Standard Oil and the Financing of the Mexican Revolution." *California Historical Society Quarterly*, L (1971), 159-171. Covers 1911-1914.

787 GRIEB, Kenneth J. *The United States and Huerta.* Lincoln, Nebr., 1969. U.S. relations with Mexico, 1913-1914.

788 HALEY, P. Edward. *Revolution and Intervention: The Diplomacy of Taft and Wilson with Mexico, 1910-1917.* Cambridge, Mass., 1970.

789 HARDY, Osgood. "The Itata Incident." *His Am Hist Rev,* V (1922), 195-226. The 1891 U.S. government seizure of a Chilean ship.

790 HARDY, Osgood. "Was Patrick Egan a 'Blundering Minister'?" *His Am Hist Rev,* VIII (1928), 65-81. Egan was minister to Chile.

791 HEALY, David F. *The United States in Cuba, 1898-1902: Generals, Politicians, and the Search for Policy.* Madison, Wis., 1963.

792 HENDRICKSON, Embert J. "Roosevelt's Second Venezuela Controversy." *His Am Hist Rev,* L (1970), 482-498.

793 HILL, Howard C. *Roosevelt and the Caribbean.* Chicago, 1927.

794 HIMELHOCH, Myra. "Frederick Douglass and Haiti's Mole St. Nicolas." *J Neg Hist,* LVI (1971), 161-180. Port au Prince discussion, 1889-1891.

795 HITCHMAN, James H. "The Platt Amendment Revisited: A Bibliographical Survey." *The Americas,* XXIII (1967), 343-369.

796 HOLBO, Paul S. "Perilous Obscurity: Public Diplomacy and the Press in the Venezuelan Crisis, 1902-1903." *Historian,* XXXII (1970), 428-448.

797 KARLIN, J. Alexander. "The Italo-American Incident of 1891 and the Road to Reunion." *J S Hist,* VIII (1942), 242-258.

798 KIST, Glenn Joseph. "The Role of Thomas C. Dawson in United States-Latin American Diplomatic Relations 1897-1912." Doctoral dissertation, Loyola University, Chicago, 1971.

799 LAFEBER, Walter. "The Background of Cleveland's Venezuelan Policy: A Reinterpretation." *Am Hist Rev,* LXVI (1961), 947-967.

800 LAFEBER, Walter. "United States Depression Diplomacy and the Brazilian Revolution, 1893-1894." *His Am Hist Rev,* XL (1960), 107-118.

801 LANE, Jack C. "Instrument for Empire: The American Military Government in Cuba, 1899-1902." *Sci Soc,* XXXVI (1972), 314-330.

802 LINDSELL, Harold. *The Chilean-American Controversy of 1891-1892.* New York, 1943.

803 LIVERMORE, Seward W. "Theodore Roosevelt, the American Navy, and the Venezuela Crisis of 1902-1903." *Am Hist Rev,* LI (1946), 452-471.

804 LOCKMILLER, D. A. *Magoon in Cuba.* Chapel Hill, N.C., 1938. Magoon was a U.S. agent, 1906-1909.

805 McGANN, Thomas F. *Argentina, the United States, and the Inter-American System, 1880-1914.* Cambridge, Mass., 1957.

806 MASINGILL, Eugene Frank. "The Diplomatic Career of Henry Lane Wilson in Latin America." Doctoral dissertation, Louisiana State University, 1957.

807 MATHEWS, Joseph J. "Informal Diplomacy in the Venezuela Crisis of 1896." *Miss Val Hist Rev,* L (1963), 195-212.

808 MELLANDER, G. A. *The United States in Panamanian Politics: The Intriguing Formative Years.* Danville, Ill., 1971. Covers 1903-1908.

809 MILLETT, Allan R. "The General Staff and the Cuban Intervention of 1906." *Mil Aff*, XXXI (1967), 113-119.

810 MILLETT, Allan Reed. *The Politics of Intervention: The Military Occupation of Cuba, 1906-1909.* Columbus, Ohio, 1968.

811 MINER, Dwight C. *The Fight for the Panama Route: The Story of the Spooner Act and the Hay-Herran Treaty.* New York, 1940.

812 MINGER, Ralph. "William H. Taft and the United States Intervention in Cuba in 1906." *His Am Hist Rev*, XLI (1961), 75-89.

813 MUNRO, Dana G. "Dollar Diplomacy in Nicaragua, 1909-1913." *His Am Hist Rev*, XXXVIII (1958), 209-234.

814 MURPHY, Donald Joseph. "Professors, Publicists, and Pan Americanism, 1905-1917: A Study in the Origins of the Use of 'Experts' in Shaping American Foreign Policy." Doctoral dissertation, University of Wisconsin, 1970.

815 NETTLES, H. Edward. "The Drago Doctrine in International Law and Politics." *His Am Hist Rev*, VIII (1928), 204-223.

816 PATTERSON, John. "Latin-American Reactions to the Panama Revolution of 1903." *His Am Hist Rev*, XXIV (1944), 342-351.

817 PÉREZ, Louis A., Jr. "Supervision of a Protectorate: The United States and the Cuban Army, 1898-1908." *His Am Hist Rev*, LII (1972), 250-271.

818 PLATT, D. C. M. "The Allied Coercion of Venezuela, 1902-1903: A Reassessment." *Int-Am Econ Aff*, XV (1962), 3-28.

819 POWELL, Anna R. "Relations Between the United States and Nicaragua, 1898-1916." *His Am Hist Rev*, VIII (1928), 43-64.

820 RELYEA, P. S. *Relations Between the United States and Mexico Under Porfirio Diaz, 1876-1910.* Northampton, Mass., 1924.

821 RIPPY, J. Fred. "Antecedents of the Roosevelt Corollary of the Monroe Doctrine." *Pac Hist Rev*, IX (1940), 267-279.

822 RIPPY, J. Fred. "The British Bondholders and the Roosevelt Corollary of the Monroe Doctrine." *Pol Sci Q*, XLIX (1934), 195-206.

823 RIPPY, J. Fred. "The Initiation of the Customs Receivership in the Dominican Republic." *His Am Hist Rev*, XVII (1937), 419-457.

824 RIPPY, J. Fred. "Some Contemporary Mexican Reactions to Cleveland's Venezuelan Message." *Pol Sci Q*, XXXIX (1924), 280-292.

825 ROMNEY, Joseph Barnard. "American Interests in Mexico: Development and Impact During the Rule of Porfirio Diaz, 1876-1911." Doctoral dissertation, University of Utah, 1969.

826 SCHIFF, Warren. "German Military Penetration into Mexico During the Late Diaz Period." *His Am Hist Rev*, XXXIX (1959), 568-579.

827   SCHOENRICH, Otto. "The Venezuela-British Guiana Boundary Dispute."
       Am J Int Law, XLIII (1949), 523-530.

828   SEARS, Louis Martin. "Frederick Douglass and the Mission to Haiti, 1889-
       1891." *His Am Hist Rev*, XXI (1941), 222-238.

829   SENSABAUGH, Leon F. "The Coffee-Trust Question in United States-
       Brazilian Relations: 1912-1913." *His Am Hist Rev*, XXVI (1946), 480-496.

830   SHERMAN, W. B. *The Diplomatic and Commercial Relations of the United
       States and Chile, 1820-1914.* Boston, 1926.

831   SMITH, Robert F. "Cuba: Laboratory for Dollar Diplomacy, 1898-1917."
       Historian, XXVIII (1966), 586-609.

832   SMITH, Theodore Clark. "Secretary Olney's Real Credit in the Venezuela
       Affair." *Proc Mass Hist Soc*, LXV (1933), 112-147.

833   THOMAS, Ann Van Wynen, and A. J. THOMAS, Jr. *Non-Intervention: The
       Law and Its Import in the Americas.* Dallas, Tex., 1956.

834   TURNER, Frederick C. "Anti-Americanism in Mexico, 1910-1913." *His
       Am Hist Rev*, XLVII (1967), 502-518.

835   WEBER, Francis J. "The Pious Fund of the Californias." *His Am Hist Rev*,
       XLIII (1963), 78-94. First American case before the Hague Court.

836   WILLIAMS, Mary W. *Anglo-American Isthmian Diplomacy, 1815-1915.*
       Baltimore, 1916. Reprinted, New York, 1965.

837   YOUNG, George B. "Intervention Under the Monroe Doctrine: The Olney
       Corollary." *Pol Sci Q*, LVII (1942), 247-280.

8. *Economic Matters*

838   ABRAHAMS, Paul Philip. "The Foreign Expansion of American Finance
       and Its Relationship to the Foreign Economic Policies of the United States,
       1907-1921." Doctoral dissertation, University of Wisconsin, 1967.

839   BEST, Gary Dean. "Financing a Foreign War: Jacob H. Schiff and Japan,
       1904-05." *American Jewish Historical Quarterly*, LXI (1972), 313-324.

840   CAMPBELL, Charles S., Jr. *Special Business Interests and the Open Door
       Policy.* New Haven, Conn., 1951.

841   DOZER, Donald Marquand. "Secretary of State Elihu Root and Consular
       Reorganization." *Miss Val Hist Rev*, XXIX (1942), 339-350.

842   ERSHKOWITZ, Herbert. *The Attitude of American Business Toward
       American Foreign Policy, 1900-1916.* University Park, Pa., 1967.

843   GARDNER, Lloyd C., ed. *A Different Frontier: Selected Readings in the
       Foundations of American Economic Expansion.* Chicago, 1966.†

844   HINCKLEY, Frank H. *American Consular Jurisdiction in the Orient.* Wash-
       ington, 1906. Extraterritoriality in Turkey and East Asia.

845   HOFFMAN, Charles. "The Depression of the Nineties." *J Econ Hist*, XVI (1956), 137-164. Some statistics on exports, balance-of-payments.

846   KAUFMAN, Burton I. "Organization for Foreign Trade Expansion." See 1301.

847   KAUFMAN, Burton I. "The Organizational Dimension of United States Economic Foreign Policy, 1900-1920." *Bus Hist Rev*, XLVI (1972), 17-44.

848   LAFEBER, Walter. "The American Business Community and Cleveland's Venezuelan Message." *Bus Hist Rev*, XXXIV (1960), 393-402.

849   LORENCE, James John. "The American Asiatic Association, 1898-1925: Organized Business and the Myth of the China Market." Doctoral dissertation, University of Wisconsin, 1970.

850   PATERSON, Thomas G. "American Businessmen and Consular Service Reform, 1890's to 1906." *Bus Hist Rev*, XL (1966), 77-97.

851   PRISCO, Salvatore, III. *John Barrett, Progressive Era Diplomat; A Study of a Commercial Expansionist, 1887-1920.* University, Ala., 1973.

852   SCHONBERGER, Howard B. *Transportation to the Seaboard; "Communication Revolution" and American Foreign Policy, 1860-1900.* Westport, Conn., 1971.

853   SKLAR, Martin J. "The N.A.M. and Foreign Markets." See 599.

854   TERRILL, Tom E. *The Tariff, Politics, and American Foreign Policy, 1874-1901.* Westport, Conn., 1973.

855   WILKINS, Mira. *The Emergence of Multinational Enterprise: American Business Abroad from the Colonial Era to 1914.* Cambridge, Mass., 1970.

9. The Navy, Strategy, and the Hope for Disarmament

856   BAILEY, Thomas A. "The World Cruise of the American Battleship Fleet, 1907-1909." *Pac Hist Rev*, I (1932), 389-423.

857   BRAISTED, William R. "The Philippine Naval Base Problem, 1898-1909." *Miss Val Hist Rev*, XLI (1954), 21-40.

858   BRAISTED, William R. *The United States Navy in the Pacific, 1897-1909.* Austin, Tex., 1958.

859   BRAISTED, William Reynolds. *The United States Navy in the Pacific, 1909-1922.* Austin, Tex., 1971.

860   BRAISTED, William R. "The United States Navy's Dilemma in the Pacific, 1906-1909." *Pac Hist Rev*, XXVI (1957), 235-244.

861   CHALLENER, Richard D. *Admirals, Generals, and American Foreign Policy, 1898-1914.* Princeton, N.J., 1973.

862   CHOATE, Joseph H. *The Two Hague Conferences.* Princeton, N.J., 1913.

863   CLIFFORD, John Garry. "Admiral Dewey and the Germans." See 775.

864   CLINARD, Outten J. *Japan's Influence on American Naval Power.* See 699.

865   DAVIS, Calvin D. *The United States and the First Hague Peace Conference.* Ithaca, N.Y., 1962.

866   HART, Robert A. *The Great White Fleet: Its Voyage Around the World, 1907-1909.* Boston, 1965.

867   HEALY, David. "McKinley as Commander-in-Chief." *Threshold to American Internationalism.* See 447.

868   KARSTEN, Peter. "The Nature of 'Influence': Roosevelt, Mahan and the Concept of Sea Power." *Am Q,* XXIII (1971), 585-600.

869   LIVERMORE, Seward W. "American Naval-Base Policy in the Far East, 1850-1914." *Pac Hist Rev,* XIII (1944), 113-135.

870   LIVERMORE, Seward W. "The American Navy as a Factor in World Politics, 1903-1913." *Am Hist Rev,* LXIII (1958), 863-879.

871   LONG, John D. *The New American Navy.* 2 vols. New York, 1903.

872   MAHAN, Alfred Thayer. *Interest of America in Sea Power.* See 400 and 398.

873   MORTON, Louis. "Military and Naval Preparations for the Defense of the Philippines During the War Scare of 1907." *Mil Aff,* XIII (1949), 95-104.

874   POHL, James W. "The General Staff and American Military Policy: The Formative Period, 1898-1917." Doctoral dissertation, University of Texas, 1967.

875   PRATT, Julius W. "Alfred Thayer Mahan." *The Marcus W. Jernegan Essays in American Historiography.* Chicago, 1937.

876   SCOTT, James Brown. *The Hague Peace Conferences of 1899 and 1907.* 2 vols. Baltimore, 1909.

877   SNOWBARGER, Willis E. "Pearl Harbor in Pacific Strategy, 1898-1908." *Historian,* XIX (1957), 361-384.

878   STILLSON, Albert C. "Military Policy Without Political Guidance: Theodore Roosevelt's Navy." *Mil Aff,* XXV (1961), 18-31.

879   TATE, Merze. *The Disarmament Illusion: The Movement for a Limitation of Armaments to 1907.* New York, 1942.

880   WELLS, Samuel F., Jr. "British Strategic Withdrawal from the Western Hemisphere, 1904-1906." *Can Hist Rev,* XLIX (1968), 335-356.

III. Wilson, World War I, and the Versailles Settlement, 1913-1921

1. General

881 ALLEN, Howard W. "Republican Reformers and Foreign Policy, 1913-1917." *Mid-Am*, XLIV (1962), 222-229.

882 Anonymous (FULLER, Joseph V.). "William Jennings Bryan." *Secretaries of State*. Vol. 10. See 60.

883 BAKER, Ray Stannard, and William E. DODD, eds. *The Public Papers of Woodrow Wilson*. 6 vols. New York, 1925-1927.

884 BARUCH, Bernard M. *The Public Years*. New York, 1960.

885 BELL, Herbert C. F. *Woodrow Wilson and the People*. New York, 1945.

886 BELL, Sidney. *Righteous Conquest: Woodrow Wilson and the Evolution of the New Diplomacy*. Port Washington, N.Y., 1972.

887 BLOCK, Robert Hoyt. "Southern Opinion of Woodrow Wilson's Foreign Policies, 1913-1917." Doctoral dissertation, Duke University, 1968.

888 BLUM, John M. *Woodrow Wilson and the Politics of Morality*. Boston, 1956.†

889 BRAEMAN, John, Ed. *Wilson*. Englewood Cliffs, N.J., 1972.† Excerpts from writings by and about Woodrow Wilson.

890 BRYAN, William Jennings, and Mary Baird BRYAN. *The Memoirs of William Jennings Bryan*. Philadelphia, 1925.

891 BUEHRIG, Edward H., ed. *Wilson's Foreign Policy in Perspective*. Bloomington, Ind., 1957. Essays by several scholars.

892 BUEHRIG, Edward H. *Woodrow Wilson and the Balance of Power*. Bloomington, Ind., 1955.

893 CLEMENTS, Kendrick Alling. "Bryan." See 444.

894 COLETTA, Paolo E. "Secretary of State William Jennings Bryan and 'Deserving Democrats.' " *Mid-Am*, XLVIII (1966), 75-98.

895 COLETTA, Paolo E. *William Jennings Bryan*. 3 vols. Lincoln, Nebr., 1964-1969.

896   COOK, Blanche Wiesen. "Woodrow Wilson and the Antimilitarists, 1914-1917." Doctoral dissertation, Johns Hopkins University, 1970.

897   CRONON, E. David, ed. *The Cabinet Diaries of Josephus Daniels, 1913-1921*. Lincoln, Nebr., 1963.

898   CURTI, Merle E. *Bryan and World Peace*. Northampton, Mass., 1931.

899   DEWITT, Howard Arthur. "Hiram W. Johnson and American Foreign Policy, 1917-1941." Doctoral dissertation, University of Arizona, 1972.

900   FOWLER, Wilton B. "American Foreign Policy in the Progressive Era." See 461.

901   GARDNER, Lloyd C. "American Foreign Policy 1900-1921." See 463.

902   GARRATY, John A. *Henry Cabot Lodge*. New York, 1953.

903   GARRATY, John A. *Woodrow Wilson*. New York, 1956.

903-A GEORGE, Alexander L., and Juliette L. GEORGE. *Woodrow Wilson and Colonel House: A Personality Study*. New York, 1956.

904   GRAHAM, Otis L., Jr. *The Great Campaigns: Reform and War in America 1900-1928*. Englewood Cliffs, N.J., 1971.†

905   GRAYSON, Cary T. *Woodrow Wilson: An Intimate Memoir*. New York, 1960.

906   GREW, Joseph C. *Turbulent Era*. See 466.

907   HARRISON, Benjamin Taylor. "Chandler Anderson." See 468.

908   HEINRICHS, Waldo, Jr. *Grew*. See 470.

909   HOLBO, Paul S. "Perspectives on American Foreign Policy." See 473.

910   HOOVER, Herbert. *Memoirs*. See 1353.

911   JESSUP, Philip C. *Root*. See 475.

912   JOHNSON, Claudius O. *Borah of Idaho*. New York, 1936. Reissued, Seattle, 1967.†

913   KOENIG, Louis W. *Bryan: A Political Biography of William Jennings Bryan*. New York, 1971.

914   LEOPOLD, Richard W. *Root*. See 477.

915   LEVIN, N. Gordon, Jr. *Woodrow Wilson and World Politics: America's Response to War and Revolution*. New York, 1968.†

916   LEVINE, Lawrence W. *Defender of the Faith, William Jennings Bryan: The Last Decade, 1915-1925*. New York, 1965.

917   LINK, Arthur S. *The Higher Realism of Woodrow Wilson and Other Essays*. Nashville, Tenn., 1971.

918   LINK, Arthur S. *Wilson*. 5 vols. to date. Princeton, N.J., 1947-1965.

919   LINK, Arthur S. *Woodrow Wilson: A Brief Biography*. Cleveland, 1963.†

920   LINK, Arthur S., ed. *Woodrow Wilson: A Profile*. New York, 1968.

921   LINK, Arthur S. *Woodrow Wilson and the Progressive Era, 1910-1917*. New York, 1954.

922   LIVERMORE, Seward W. " 'Deserving Democrats': The Foreign Service Under Woodrow Wilson." *S Atl Q*, LXIX (1970), 144-160.

923   McKENNA, Marian C. *Borah*. Ann Arbor, 1961.

923-A NOTTER, Harley. *The Origins of the Foreign Policy of Woodrow Wilson*. Baltimore, 1937.

924   PHILLIPS, William. *Ventures in Diplomacy*. See 490.

925   PRATT, Julius W. *America and World Leadership*. See 492.

926   PRATT, Julius W. "Robert Lansing." *Secretaries of State*. Vol. 10. See 60.

927   SCHILLING, Warner Roller. "Admirals and Foreign Policy, 1913-1919." Doctoral dissertation, Yale University, 1953.

928   SEYMOUR, Charles, ed. *The Intimate Papers of Colonel House*. 4 vols. Boston, 1926-1928.

929   SMITH, Daniel M. *Aftermath of War: Bainbridge Colby and Wilsonian Diplomacy, 1920-1921*. Philadelphia, 1970.

930   SPARGO, John. "Bainbridge Colby." *Secretaries of State*. Vol. 10. See 60.

931   TOMPKINS, E. Berkeley. *Anti-Imperialism*. See 617.

932   VARG, Paul A. "The United States a World Power." See 506.

933   VIERECK, George S. *The Strangest Friendship in History: Woodrow Wilson and Colonel House*. New York, 1932.

934   WEINSTEIN, Edwin A. "Woodrow Wilson's Neurological Illness." *J Am Hist*, LVII (1970), 324-351.

935   WELLS, Samuel F., Jr. "The Challenge of Power." See 509.

936   WELLS, Samuel F., Jr. "New Perspectives on Wilsonian Diplomacy: The Secular Evangelism of American Political Economy; A Review Essay." *Perspectives in American History*, VI (1972), 389-419.

937   WEST, Sister Rachel. "The Department of State, at Home and Abroad, on the Eve of World War I, 1913-1914." Doctoral dissertation, Indiana University, 1972. An administrative study.

2. America and the First World War

General

938   CLIFFORD, John Garry. *The Citizen Soldiers: The Plattsburg Training Camp Movement, 1913-1920.* Lexington, Ky., 1972.

939   GIDDENS, Jackson A. "American Foreign Propaganda in World War I." Doctoral dissertation, Fletcher School, 1967.

940   HOOVER, Herbert. *An American Epic; Famine in Forty-Five Nations: The Battle on the Front Line, 1914-1923.* Chicago, 1961.

941   JUSSERAND, Jean Jules. *Le sentiment américain pendant la guerre.* Paris, 1931.

942   MAYER, Arno J. "World War I." *The Comparative Approach to American History.* Ed. C. Vann Woodward. New York, 1968.†

943   PALMER, Frederick. *Bliss, Peacemaker: The Life and Letters of General Tasker Howard Bliss.* New York, 1934.

944   PAXSON, Frederic L. *American Democracy and the World War.* 3 vols. Boston, 1936-1948.

945   READ, J. M. *Atrocity Propaganda, 1914-1919.* New Haven, Conn., 1941.

946   REINERTSON, John. "Colonel House, Woodrow Wilson and European Socialism, 1917-1919." Doctoral dissertation, University of Wisconsin, 1971.

947   SMITH, Daniel M. *The Great Departure: The United States and World War I, 1914-1920.* New York, 1965.†

948   STEPHENSON, George M. "The Attitude of Swedish Americans Toward the World War." *Proceedings, Mississippi Valley Historical Association*, X, Part I (1918-1919), 79-84.

949   SURFACE, Frank M., and Raymond L. BLAND. *American Food in the World War and Reconstruction Period.* Stanford, Cal., 1931.

950   THOMPSON, J. A. "An Imperialist and the First World War: The Case of Albert J. Beveridge." *J Am Stud*, V (1971), 133-150.

951   TRATTNER, Walter I. "Progressivism and World War I: A Re-appraisal." *Mid-Am*, XLIV (1962), 131-145.

952   WITTKE, Carl. *German-Americans and the World War.* Columbus, Ohio, 1936.

953   ZEMAN, Z. A. B. *The Gentlemen Negotiators: A Diplomatic History of the First World War.* New York, 1971.

Neutrality and the Decision for War

954 ALBION, R. G., and J. B. POPE. *Sea Lanes in Wartime.* See 384.

955 BAILEY, Thomas A. "German Documents Relating to the *Lusitania*." *J Mod Hist*, VIII (1936), 320-337.

956 BAILEY, Thomas A. "The Sinking of the *Lusitania*." *Am Hist Rev*, XLI (1935-1936), 54-73.

957 BAILEY, Thomas A. "The United States and the Blacklist During the Great War." *J Mod Hist*, VI (1934), 14-36.

958 BERNSTORFF, J. H. von. *My Three Years in America.* London, 1920. Bernstorff was the German ambassador to the U.S.

959 BILLINGTON, Monroe. "The Gore Resolution of 1916." *Mid-Am*, XLVII (1965), 89-98.

960 BIRDSALL, Paul. "Neutrality and Economic Pressures, 1914-1917." *Sci Soc*, III (1939), 217-228.

960-A BIRNBAUM, Karl E. *Peace Moves and U-Boat Warfare: A Study of Imperial Germany's Policy Towards the United States, April 18, 1916-January 9, 1917.* Stockholm, 1958.

961 BRUNAUER, Esther C. "The Peace Proposals of December 1916-January 1917." *J Mod Hist*, IV (1932), 544-571.

962 BUCHANAN, A. Russell. "Theodore Roosevelt and American Neutrality, 1914-1917." *Am Hist Rev*, XLIII (1938), 775-790.

963 BUEHRIG, Edward H. "Wilson's Neutrality Re-examined." *Wor Pol*, III (1952), 1-19.

964 CHILD, Clifton J. *The German-Americans in Politics, 1914-1917.* Madison, Wis., 1939.

965 COLETTA, Paolo E., ed. "Bryan Briefs Lansing." *Pac Hist Rev*, XXVII (1958), 383-396.

966 COOPER, John Milton, Jr. "The British Response to the House-Grey Memorandum: New Evidence and New Questions." *J Am Hist*, LIX (1973), 958-971.

967 COOPER, John Milton, Jr. *The Vanity of Power; American Isolation and the First World War, 1914-1917.* Westport, Conn., 1969.

968 CRIGHTON, J. C. "The *Wilhelmina*: An Adventure in the Assertion and Exercise of American Trading Rights During the World War." *Am J Int Law*, XXXIV (1940), 74-88.

969 CUDDY, Edward. "Irish-American Propagandists and American Neutrality, 1914-1917." *Mid-Am*, XLIX (1967), 252-275.

970 DAVIS, Gerald H. "The 'Ancona' Affair: A Case of Preventive Diplomacy." *J Mod Hist*, XXXVIII (1966), 267-277.

971 ESSLINGER, Dean R. "American, German and Irish Attitudes Toward Neutrality, 1914-1917: A Study of Catholic Minorities." *Cath Hist Rev*, LIII (1967), 194-216.

972 FULLER, Joseph V. "The Genesis of the Munitions Traffic." *J Mod Hist*, VI (1934), 280-293.

973 GREGORY, Ross. *The Origins of American Intervention in the First World War*. New York, 1971.†

974 HARBAUGH, William H. "Wilson, Roosevelt, and Interventionism, 1914-1917: A Study of Domestic Influence on the Formulation of American Foreign Policy." Doctoral dissertation, Northwestern University, 1954.

975 HERSHEY, Burnett. *The Odyssey of Henry Ford and the Great Peace Ship*. New York, 1967.

976 HIRST, David Wayne. "German Propaganda in the United States, 1914-1917." Doctoral dissertation, Northwestern University, 1962.

977 HOWE, Frederic C. *Why War*. New York, 1916. New ed. Intro. by Wilton B. Fowler, Seattle, 1970.

978 KERR, Thomas J. "German-Americans and Neutrality in the 1916 Election." *Mid-Am*, XLIII (1961), 95-105.

979 LEARY, William M., Jr. "Woodrow Wilson, Irish-Americans, and the Election of 1916." *J Am Hist*, LIV (1967), 57-72.

980 LEOPOLD, Richard W. "The Problem of American Intervention, 1917: An Historical Retrospect." *Wor Pol*, II (1950), 405-425.

981 LINK, Arthur S. "The Middle West and the Coming of World War I." *Ohio State Archeological and Historical Quarterly*, LXII (1953), 109-121.

982 LINK, Arthur S. *Wilson*. Vol. III: *The Struggle for Neutrality 1914-1915*. Vol. IV: *Confusions and Crises 1915-1916*. Vol. V: *Campaigns for Progressivism and Peace 1916-1917*. See 918.

983 LOCHNER, Louis P. *America's Don Quixote: Henry Ford's Attempt to Save Europe*. London, 1924.

984 LOWITT, Richard. "The Armed-Ship Bill Controversy: A Legislative View." *Mid-Am*, XLVI (1964), 38-47.

985 MAY, Ernest R. *American Intervention: 1917 and 1941*. Pamphlet. Washington, 1960. Historiography.

986 MORRISSEY, Alice M. *The American Defense of Neutral Rights, 1914-1917*. Cambridge, Mass., 1939.

987 OGLEY, Roderick. *Theory and Practice of Neutrality*. See 408.

988 O'KEEFE, Kevin J. "A Thousand Deadlines: The New York City Press and American Neutrality, 1914-1917." Doctoral dissertation, New York University, 1971.

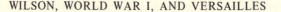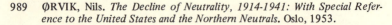

989 ØRVIK, Nils. *The Decline of Neutrality, 1914-1941: With Special Reference to the United States and the Northern Neutrals.* Oslo, 1953.

990 PATTERSON, David S. "Woodrow Wilson and the Mediation Movement, 1914-17." *Historian*, XXXIII (1971), 535-556.

991 PETERSON, Horace C. *Propaganda for War: The Campaign Against American Neutrality, 1914-1917.* Norman, Okla., 1939.

992 PHILLIPS, E. C. "American Participation in Belligerent Commercial Controls, 1914-1917." *Am J Int Law*, XXVII (1933), 675-693.

993 RAPPAPORT, Armin. *The British Press and Wilsonian Neutrality.* Stanford, Cal., 1951.

994 SAVAGE, Carlton. *Policy of the United States Toward Maritime Commerce in War.* 2 vols. Washington, 1934-1936.

995 SEYMOUR, Charles. *American Neutrality, 1914-1917.* New Haven, Conn., 1935.

996 SIMPSON, Colin. *The Lusitania.* Boston, 1973. A pointed study of the 1915 sinking.

997 SINEY, Marion C. "British Negotiations with American Meat Packers, 1915-1917: A Study of Belligerent Trade Controls." *J Mod Hist*, XXIII (1951), 343-453.

998 SMITH, Daniel M. *Robert Lansing and American Neutrality, 1914-1917.* Berkeley, Cal., 1958.

999 SMITH, Daniel M. "Robert Lansing and the Formulation of American Neutrality Policies, 1914-1915." *Miss Val Hist Rev*, XLIII (1956), 59-81.

1000 SMITH, Daniel M. "National Interest and American Intervention, 1917: An Historiographical Appraisal." *J Am Hist*, LII (1965), 5-24.

1001 SMITH, Gaddis. *Britain's Clandestine Submarines, 1914-1915.* New Haven, Conn., 1964. Involves American neutrality.

1002 SPENCER, Samuel R., Jr. *Decision for War, 1917: The Laconia Sinking and the Zimmermann Telegram as Key Factors in the Public Reaction Against Germany.* Rindge, N.H., 1953.

1003 SQUIRES, James D. *British Propaganda at Home and in the United States from 1914 to 1917.* Cambridge, Mass., 1935.

1004 SUTTON, Walter A. "Progressive Republican Senators and the Submarine Crisis, 1915-1916." *Mid-Am*, XLVII (1965), 75-88.

1005 SYRETT, Harold C. "The Business Press and American Neutrality, 1914-1917." *Miss Val Hist Rev*, XXXII (1945), 215-230.

1006 TASSIER, Suzanne. *La Belgique et l'entrée en guerre des Etats-Unis, 1914-1917.* Brussels, 1951.

1007 TUCHMAN, Barbara W. *The Zimmermann Telegram.* New York, 1958.†

1008 TURLINGTON, E. C. *Neutrality: Its History, Economics, and Law–The World War Period.* Ed. Philip C. Jessup and F. Deak. New York, 1936.

1009   TUTTLE, Peter Guertin. "The Ford Peace Ship: Volunteer Diplomacy in the Twentieth Century." Doctoral dissertation, Yale University, 1958. About the 1915 voyage.

1010   VAN ALSTYNE, Richard W. "The Policy of the United States Regarding the Declaration of London, at the Outbreak of the Great War." *J Mod Hist*, VII (1935), 434-447.

1011   VAN ALSTYNE, Richard W. "Private American Loans to the Allies, 1914-1916." *Pac Hist Rev*, II (1933), 180-193.

1012   WARD, Robert D. "The Origins and Activities of the National Security League, 1914-1919." *Miss Val Hist Rev*, XLVII (1960), 51-65.

American Belligerency

1013   BAILEY, Thomas A. *The Policy of the United States Towards the Neutrals, 1917-1918*. Baltimore, 1942.

1014   BEAVER, Daniel R. *Newton D. Baker and the American War Effort, 1917-1919*. Lincoln, Nebr., 1966.

1015   BLAKEY, George T. *Historians on the Homefront: American Propagandists for the Great War*. Lexington, Ky., 1970.

1016   BLISS, Tasker H. "The Evolution of the Unified Command." *For Aff*, I (1922), No. 2, 1-30.

1017   BRUNTZ, George G. *Allied Propaganda and the Collapse of the German Empire in 1918*. Stanford, Cal., 1938.

1018   BUCHANAN, A. Russell. "American Editors Examine American War Aims and Plans in April, 1917." *Pac Hist Rev*, IX (1940), 253-265.

1019   COFFMAN, Edward M. *The Hilt of the Sword: The Career of Peyton C. March*. Madison, Wis., 1966.

1020   COFFMAN, Edward M. *The War to End All Wars*. New York, 1968. Military emphasis.

1021   CREEL, George. *How We Advertised America*. New York, 1920.

1022   DEWEERD, Harvey A. *President Wilson Fights His War: World War I and the American Intervention*. New York, 1968.

1023   EPSTEIN, Klaus. "The Development of German-Austrian War Aims in the Spring of 1917." *Journal of Central European Affairs*, XVII (1957), 24-47.

1024   FOWLER, Wilton B. *British-American Relations, 1917-1918: The Role of Sir William Wiseman*. Princeton, N.J., 1969. Wiseman acted as a wartime liaison with President Wilson and Colonel House.

1025   HALPERIN, S. William. "Anatomy of an Armistice." *J Mod Hist*, XLIII (1971), 107-112. A review of the 1918 armistice.

1026   HERWIG, Holger H., and David F. TRASK. "The Failure of Imperial Germany's Undersea Offensive Against World Shipping, February 1917-October 1918." *Historian*, XXXIII (1971), 611-636.

1027 INGRAM, Alton Earl. "The Root Mission to Russia, 1917." Doctoral dissertation, Louisiana State University, 1970.

1028 LANSING, Robert. *War Memoirs of Robert Lansing.* New York, 1935.

1029 LIVERMORE, Seward W. *Politics Is Adjourned: Woodrow Wilson and the War Congress, 1916-1918.* Middletown, Conn., 1966.†

1030 MAYER, Arno J. *Political Origins of the New Diplomacy, 1917-1918.* New Haven Conn., 1959. Issued as *Wilson vs. Lenin,* Cleveland, 1964.†

1031 MOCK, James R., and Cedric LARSON. *Words That Won the War: The Story of the Committee on Public Information, 1917-1919.* Princeton, N.J., 1939.

1032 MORISON, Elting E. *Admiral Sims and the Modern American Navy.* Boston, 1942.

1033 NELSON, Keith L. "What Colonel House Overlooked in the Armistice." *Mid-Am,* LI (1969), 75-91.

1033-A NORING, Nina J. "American Coalition Diplomacy and the Armistice, 1918-1919." Doctoral dissertation, University of Iowa, 1972.

1034 PALMER, Frederick. *Newton D. Baker: America at War.* 2 vols. New York, 1931. Baker was Secretary of War.

1035 PARSONS, Edward Budd. "Admiral Sims' Mission in Europe in 1917-1919 and Some Aspects of United States Naval and Foreign Wartime Policy." Doctoral dissertation, S.U.N.Y., Buffalo, 1971.

1036 PERSHING, John J. *My Experiences in the World War.* 2 vols. New York, 1931.

1037 PETERSON, Horace C., and Gilbert C. FITE. *Opponents of War, 1917-1918.* Madison, Wis., 1957.

1038 RUDIN, Harry R. *Armistice 1918.* New Haven, Conn., 1944.

1039 SIMS, William S., and Burton J. HENDRICK. *The Victory at Sea.* New York, 1920.

1040 SNELL, John L. "Wilsonian Rhetoric Goes to War." *Historian,* XIV (1952), 191-208.

1041 SPECTOR, Ronald. " 'You're Not Going to Send Soldiers Over There Are You!' The American Search for an Alternative to the Western Front 1916-1917." *Mil Aff,* XXXVI (1972), 1-4.

1042 TRASK, David F. *Captains and Cabinets: Anglo-American Naval Relations, 1917-1918.* Columbia, Mo., 1972.

1043 TRASK, David F. "Political-Military Consultation Among Allies." *Military Review,* XXXIX (1959), 20-28. Compares the two World Wars.

1044 TRASK, David F. *The United States in the Supreme War Council: American War Aims and Inter-Allied Strategy, 1917-1918.* Middletown, Conn., 1961.

1045 United States Department of the Army. *United States Army in the World War.* 17 vols. Washington, 1948.

1046 WEINSTEIN, James. "Anti-War Sentiment and the Socialist Party, 1917-1918." *Pol Sci Q*, LXXIV (1959), 215-239.

The Peace Conference at Paris

1047 ALBRECHT-CARRIÉ René. *Italy at the Paris Peace Conference*. New York, 1938.

1048 BAILEY, Thomas A. *Woodrow Wilson and the Lost Peace*. New York, 1944.†

1049 BANE, Suda Lorena, and Ralph H. LUTZ, eds. *Organization of American Relief in Europe, 1918-1919*. Stanford, Cal., 1943.

1050 BARUCH, Bernard M. *The Making of the Reparation and Economic Sections of the Treaty*. New York, 1920.

1051 BEER, George Louis. *African Questions*. See 1198.

1052 BERLE, Beatrice Bishop, and Beal Jacobs TRAVIS, eds. *From the Papers of Adolf A. Berle: Navigating the Rapids 1918-1971*. New York, 1973. On the Paris Peace Conference and many other topics.

1053 BONSAL, Stephen. *Suitors and Suppliants: The Little Nations at Versailles*. New York, 1946.

1054 BONSAL, Stephen. *Unfinished Business*. Garden City, N.Y., 1944.

1055 BRYSON, Thomas A. "Walter George Smith and the Armenian Question at the Paris Peace Conference, 1919." *Records of the American Catholic Historical Society of Philadelphia*, LXXXI (1970), 3-26.

1056 BURNETT, Philip M. *Reparation at the Paris Peace Conference from the Standpoint of the American Delegation*. 2 vols. New York, 1940.

1057 CURRY, George W. "Woodrow Wilson, Jan Smuts, and the Versailles Settlement." *Am Hist Rev*, LXVI (1961), 968-986.

1058 DEAK, Francis. *Hungary at the Paris Peace Conference*. New York, 1942.

1059 GELFAND, Lawrence E. *The Inquiry: American Preparations for Peace, 1917-1919*. New Haven, Conn., 1963.

1060 HASKINS, C. H., and R. H. LORD. *Some Problems of the Peace Conference*. Cambridge, Mass., 1920.

1061 HOUSE, Edward M., and Charles SEYMOUR, eds. *What Really Happened at Paris*. New York, 1921.

1061-A KLATCHKO, Mary. "Anglo-American Naval Competition, 1918-1922." Doctoral dissertation, Columbia University, 1962.

1062 LANSING, Robert. *The Big Four and Others of the Peace Conference*. Boston, 1921.

1063 LANSING, Robert. *The Peace Negotiations: A Personal Narrative*. Boston, 1921.

1064   LEDERER, Ivo J. *Yugoslavia at the Paris Peace Conference: A Study in Frontier-Making*. New Haven, Conn., 1963.

1065   LLOYD GEORGE, David. *Memoirs of the Peace Conference*. 2 vols. New Haven, Conn., 1939.

1065-A MANTOUX, Paul. *Les Délibérations du Conseil des Quatre (24 Mars-28 Juin 1919)*. 2 vols. Paris, 1955. English translation by J. B. Whitton: *Paris Peace Conference, 1919; Proceedings of the Council of Four, March 24-April 18*. Geneva, 1964.

1066   MARTIN, Laurence W. "Woodrow Wilson's Appeals to the People of Europe: British Radical Influence on the President's Strategy." *Pol Sci Q*, LXXIV (1959), 498-516.

1067   MAYER, Arno J. *Politics and Diplomacy of Peacemaking: Containment and Counterrevolution at Versailles, 1918-1919*. New York, 1967.

1067-A MILLER, David Hunter. *The Drafting of the Covenant*. 2 vols. New York, 1928.

1068   MILLER, David Hunter. *My Diary at the Conference at Paris*. 21 vols. Washington, 1928. Only a small number of copies were printed.

1068-A MITCHELL, Kell Freeman, Jr. "Frank L. Polk and the Paris Peace Conference, 1919." Doctoral dissertation, University of Georgia, 1966.

1069   NICOLSON, Harold. *Peacemaking 1919*. New York, 1939.†

1069-A O'GRADY, Joseph P., ed. *The Immigrants' Influence on Wilson's Peace Proposals*. Lexington, Ky., 1967. Contains articles on the British, Czechs, Germans, Irish, Italians, Jews, Magyars, Poles, Ruthenians, Slovaks, and South Slavs.

1070   RIZOPOULOS, Nicholas X. "Greece at the Paris Peace Conference, 1919." Doctoral dissertation, Yale University, 1963.

1071   SCHULZ, Gerhard. *Revolutions and Peace Treaties 1917-1920*. Trans. Marian Jackson. New York, 1972.

1072   SEYMOUR, Charles. *Letters from the Paris Peace Conference*. Ed. Harold B. Whiteman, Jr. New Haven, Conn., 1965.

1073   SEYMOUR, Charles. "The Paris Education of Woodrow Wilson." *Va Q Rev*, XXXII (1956), 578-593.

1074   SEYMOUR, Charles. "Woodrow Wilson and Self-Determination in the Tyrol." *Va Q Rev*, XXXVIII (1962), 567-587.

1075   SHOTWELL, James T. *At the Paris Peace Conference*. New York, 1937.

1076   STARTT, James D. "The Uneasy Partnership: Wilson and the Press at Paris," *Mid-Am*, LII (1970), 55-69.

1077   STARTT, James D. "Wilson's Mission to Paris: The Making of a Decision." *Historian*, XXX (1969), 599-616.

1077-A STRICKLAND, Roscoe Lee, Jr. "Czechoslovakia at the Paris Peace Conference, 1919." Doctoral dissertation, University of North Carolina, 1958.

1078   TEMPERLEY, H. W. V., ed. *A History of the Peace Conference of Paris, 1920-24.* 6 vols. New York, 1920-1924.

1079   TILLMAN, Seth P. *Anglo-American Relations at the Paris Peace Conference of 1919.* Princeton, N.J., 1961.

1080   TRASK, David F. *General Tasker Howard Bliss and the "Sessions of the World," 1919.* Philadelphia, 1966.

The Treaty/League Controversy at Home

1081   ADLER, Selig. "The Congressional Election of 1918." *S Atl Q*, XXXVI (1937), 447-465.

1082   AMBROSIUS, Lloyd E. "Wilson, the Republicans, and French Security After World War I." *J Am Hist*, LIX (1972), 341-352.

1083   BAGBY, Wesley M. "Woodrow Wilson, a Third Term, and the Solemn Referendum." *Am Hist Rev*, LX (1955), 567-575.

1084   BAILEY, Thomas A. *Woodrow Wilson and the Great Betrayal.* New York, 1945.†

1085   BARTLETT, Ruhl J. *The League to Enforce Peace.* Chapel Hill, N.C., 1944.

1086   BOOTHE, Leon E. "Anglo-American Pro-League Groups Lead Wilson 1915-18." *Mid-Am*, LI (1969), 92-107.

1087   DUFF, John B. "The Versailles Treaty and the Irish-Americans." *J Am Hist*, LV (1968), 582-598.

1088   FISCHER, Robert James. "Henry Cabot Lodge's Concept of Foreign Policy and the League of Nations." Doctoral dissertation, University of Georgia, 1971.

1089   FLANNAGAN, John H., Jr. "The Disillusionment of a Progressive: U.S. Senator David I. Walsh and the League of Nations Issue, 1918-1920." *N Eng Q*, XLI (1968), 483-504.

1090   FLEMING, Denna F. *The United States and the League of Nations, 1918-1920.* New York, 1938.

1091   FOSDICK, Raymond B. *Letters on the League of Nations from the Files of Raymond B. Fosdick.* Princeton, N.J., 1966.

1092   GRANTHAM, Dewey W., Jr. "The Southern Senators and the League of Nations, 1918-1920." *North Carolina Historical Review*, XXVI (1949), 187-205.

1093   HELBICH, Wolfgang J. "American Liberals in the League of Nations Controversy." *Pub Opin Q*, XXXI (1968), 568-596.

1094   HEWES, James E., Jr. "Henry Cabot Lodge and the League of Nations." *Proc Am Phil Soc*, CXIV (1970), 245-255.

1095   KEYNES, John Maynard. *The Economic Consequences of the Peace.* New York, 1920.

1096   LANCASTER, James L. "The Protestant Churches and the Fight for Ratification of the Versailles Treaty." *Pub Opin Q*, XXXI (1968), 597-619.

1097   LODGE, Henry Cabot. *The Senate and the League of Nations.* New York, 1925.

1098   LOGAN, Rayford W. *The Senate and the Versailles Mandate System.* Washington, 1945.

1099   LOWER, Richard C. "Hiram Johnson: The Making of an Irreconcilable." *Pac Hist Rev*, XLI (1972), 505-526.

1099-A MANTOUX, Etienne. *The Carthaginian Peace, or the Economic Consequences of Mr. Keynes.* New York, 1952. See 1095.

1100   MAXWELL, Kenneth R. "Irish-Americans and the Fight for Treaty Ratification." *Pub Opin Q*, XXXI (1968), 620-641.

1101   MERRITT, Richard L. "Woodrow Wilson and the 'Great and Solemn Referendum,' 1920." *Rev Pol*, XXVII (1965), 78-104.

1102   MERVIN, David. "Henry Cabot Lodge and the League of Nations." *J Am Stud*, IV (1971), 201-214.

1103   PERKINS, Dexter. "Woodrow Wilson's Tour." *America in Crisis.* Ed. Daniel Aaron. New York, 1952.

1104   PHIFER, Gregg. "Woodrow Wilson's Swing Around the Circle in Defense of His League." *Florida State University Studies*, XXIII (1956), 65-102.

1105   POMEROY, Earl S. "Sentiment for a Strong Peace, 1917-1919." *S Atl Q*, XLIII (1944), 325-337.

1106   STONE, Ralph A. "The Irreconcilables' Alternatives to the League of Nations." *Mid-Am*, XLIX (1967), 163-173.

1107   STONE, Ralph. *The Irreconcilables; The Fight Against the League of Nations.* Lexington, Ky., 1970.

1108   STONE, Ralph A. "Two Illinois Senators Among the Irreconcilables." *Miss Val Hist Rev*, L (1963), 443-465.

1109   STROMBERG, Roland N. "Uncertainties and Obscurities About the League of Nations." *J Hist Ideas*, XXXIII (1972), 139-154.

1110   VINSON, John Chalmers. *Referendum for Isolation: Defeat of Article X of the League of Nations Covenant.* Athens, Ga., 1961.

1111   WIMER, Kurt. "Woodrow Wilson and a Third Nomination." *Pennsylvania History*, XXIX (1962), 193-211.

1112   WIMER, Kurt. "Woodrow Wilson Tries Conciliation: An Effort That Failed." *Historian*, XXV (1963), 419-438.

1113   WIMER, Kurt. "Woodrow Wilson's Plan for a Vote of Confidence." *Pennsylvania History*, XXVIII (1961), 279-293.

1114   WIMER, Kurt. "Woodrow Wilson's Plans to Enter the League of Nations Through an Executive Agreement." *W Pol Q*, XI (1958), 800-812.

3. *Relations with Canada and Great Britain*

1115 BOOTHE, Leon. "A Fettered Envoy: Lord Grey's Special Mission to the United States, 1919-1920." *Rev Pol*, XXXIII (1971), 78-94.

1116 BOTHWELL, Robert. "Canadian Representation at Washington: A Study in Colonial Responsibility." *Can Hist Rev*, LIII (1972), 125-148. Covers 1912-1920.

1117 CHRISTY, Florence Jean. "Anglo-American Diplomacy and the Decline of the British Empire, 1919-1930: The British View." Doctoral dissertation, University of Georgia, 1970.

1118 DIGNAN, Don K. "The Hindu Conspiracy in Anglo-American Relations During World War I." *Pac Hist Rev*, XL (1971), 57-76.

1119 FOWLER, Wilton B. *British-American Relations.* See 1024.

1120 FRY, Michael G. *Illusions of Security: North Atlantic Diplomacy, 1918-22.* Toronto, 1972. Relations among Canada, Britain, and the United States.

1121 GREGORY, Ross. "The Superfluous Ambassador: Walter Hines Page's Return to Washington, 1916." *Historian*, XXVIII (1966), 389-404.

1122 GREGORY, Ross. *Walter Hines Page, Ambassador to the Court of St. James's.* Lexington, Ky., 1970.

1123 GWYNN, Stephen, ed. *The Letters and Friendships of Sir Cecil Spring Rice.* 2 vols. Boston, 1929.

1124 HENDRICK, Burton J. *The Life and Letters of Walter Hines Page.* 3 vols. New York, 1923-1925.

1125 KERNEK, Sterling. "The British Government's Reaction to President Wilson's 'Peace' Note of December, 1916." *Historical Journal*, XIII (1970), 721-766.

1126 KIHL, Mary R. "A Failure of Ambassadorial Diplomacy." *J Am Hist*, LVII (1970), 636-653. Discusses Ambassador Page in London and British Ambassador Spring Rice in Washington.

1127 KLEIN, Ira. "Whitehall, Washington, and the Anglo-Japanese Alliance, 1919-1921." *Pac Hist Rev*, XLI (1972), 460-483.

1128 LINK, Arthur S. "The Cotton Crisis, the South, and Anglo-American Diplomacy, 1914-1915." *Studies in Southern History in Memory of Albert Ray Newsome, 1894-1951.* Ed. J. C. Sitterson. Chapel Hill, N.C., 1957.

1129 LLOYD GEORGE, David. *War Memoirs of David Lloyd George.* 6 vols. Boston, 1933-1936.

1130 MCDONALD, J. Kenneth. "Lloyd George and the Search for a Postwar Naval Policy, 1919." *Lloyd George: Twelve Essays.* Ed. A. J. P. Taylor. New York, 1971.

1130-A MARTIN, Laurence W. *Peace Without Victory: Woodrow Wilson and the British Liberals.* New Haven, Conn., 1958.

1131 WARD, Alan J. *Ireland and Anglo-American Relations.* See 655.

1131-A WILLIAMS, Joyce Ellen. "Colonel House and Sir Edward Grey: A Study in Anglo-American Diplomacy." Doctoral dissertation, Indiana University, 1971.

1132 WOODWARD, David R. "Great Britain and President Wilson's Efforts to End World War I in 1916." *Maryland Historian*, I (1970), 45-58.

4. Relations with Europe and Russia

1133 AMBROSIUS, Lloyd Eugene. "The United States and the Weimar Republic, 1918-1923: From the Armistice to the Ruhr Occupation." Doctoral dissertation, University of Illinois, 1967.

1134 BARANY, George. "Wilsonian Central Europe: Lansing's Contribution." *Historian*, XXVIII (1966), 224-251.

1135 BONADIO, Felice A. "The Failure of German Propaganda in the United States, 1914-1917." *Mid-Am*, XLI (1959), 40-57.

1136 CUDDY, Edward. "Pro-Germanism and American Catholicism, 1914-1917." *Cath Hist Rev*, LIV (1968), 427-454.

1137 CUMMING, C. K., and Walter W. PETTIT, eds. *Russian-American Relations, March 1917-March 1920: Documents and Papers.* New York, 1920.

1138 DAVIS, Gerald H. "The Diplomatic Relations Between the United States and Austria-Hungary, 1913-1917." Doctoral dissertation, Vanderbilt University, 1958.

1139 DEVASIA, Arackal Thomas. "The United States and the Formation of Greater Romania, 1914-1918: A Study in Diplomacy and Propaganda." Doctoral dissertation, Boston College, 1970.

1140 DUMBA, Constantin. *Memoirs of a Diplomat.* Boston, 1932. Dumba was Austrian ambassador to the U.S.

1141 EGAN, Maurice F. *Ten Years near the German Frontier.* New York, 1919. Memoir of American minister to Denmark.

1142 FARNSWORTH, Beatrice. *William C. Bullitt and the Soviet Union.* Bloomington, Ind., 1967.

1143 FIKE, Claude E. "The Influence of the Creel Committee and the American Red Cross on Russian-American Relations, 1917-1919." *J Mod Hist*, XXXI (1959), 93-109.

1144 FIKE, Claude E. "The United States and Russian Territorial Problems, 1917-1920." *Historian*, XXIV (1962), 331-346.

1145 FRANCIS, David R. *Russia from the American Embassy: April, 1916-November, 1918.* New York, 1921.

1146 FUSCO, Jeremiah Nicholas. "Diplomatic Relations Between Italy and the United States 1913-1917." Doctoral dissertation, George Washington University, 1969.

1147 GAWOREK, Norbert Horst. "Allied Economic Warfare Against Soviet Russia from November 1917 to March 1921." Doctoral dissertation, University of Wisconsin, 1970.

1148 GERARD, James W. *My Four Years in Germany*. New York, 1917. Gerard was American ambassador to Germany.

1149 GERSON, Louis L. *Woodrow Wilson and the Rebirth of Poland, 1914-1920: A Study in the Influence on American Policy of Minority Groups of Foreign Origin*. New Haven, Conn., 1953.

1150 GIBSON, Hugh. *A Journal from Our Legation in Belgium*. New York, 1917. Gibson was American minister to Belgium.

1151 GOULD, John Wells. "Italy and the United States, 1914-1918: Background to Confrontation." Doctoral dissertation, Yale University, 1969.

1152 GRAVES, William S. *America's Siberian Adventure, 1918-1920*. New York, 1931. Graves was commander of the expedition.

1153 JACKSON, Shirley Fulton. "United States and Spain." See 664.

1154 JOHNSON, Niel M. *George Sylvester Viereck, German-American Propagandist*. Urbana, Ill., 1972.

1155 JORDAN, Laylon Wayne. "America's Mussolini: The United States and Italy, 1919-1936." Doctoral dissertation, University of Virginia, 1972.

1156 KENNAN, George F. *Soviet-American Relations, 1917-1920*. 2 vols. to date. Princeton, N.J., 1956-1958.†

1157 KENNAN, George F. "Soviet Historiography and America's Role in the Intervention." *Am Hist Rev*, LXV (1960), 302-322.

1158 KOHLENBERG, Gilbert C. "David Rowland Francis: American Business Man in Russia." *Mid-Am*, XL (1958), 195-217.

1159 LASCH, Christopher. "American Intervention in Siberia: A Reinterpretation." *Pol Sci Q*, LXXVII (1962), 205-223.

1160 LIVERMORE, Seward W. "The Azores in American Strategy-Diplomacy, 1917-1919." *J Mod Hist*, XX (1948), 197-211.

1161 MADDOX, Robert James. "Woodrow Wilson, the Russian Embassy and Siberian Intervention." *Pac Hist Rev*, XXXVI (1967), 435-448.

1162 MAMATEY, Victor S. "The United States and Bulgaria in World War I." *American Slavic and East European Review*, XII (1953), 233-257.

1163 MAMATEY, Victor S. "The United States and the Dissolution of Austria-Hungary." *Journal of Central European Affairs*, X (1950), 256-270.

1164 MAMATEY, Victor S. *The United States and East Central Europe, 1914-1918: A Study of Wilsonian Diplomacy and Propaganda*. Princeton, N.J., 1957.

1165 MARYE, George T. *Nearing the End in Imperial Russia*. Philadelphia, 1929. Marye was American ambassador to Russia, 1914-1916.

1166   MEIBURGER, Sister Anne Vincent. *Efforts of Raymond Robins Toward the Recognition of Soviet Russia and the Outlawry of War, 1917-1933.* Washington, 1958.

1167   MORRIS, Ira Nelson. *From an American Legation.* New York, 1923. Morris was minister to Sweden.

1168   NELSON, Harold L. *Land and Power: British and Allied Policy on Germany's Frontiers, 1916-1919.* Toronto, 1963. "Allied" includes the U.S.

1169   NELSON, Keith L. "The First American Military Occupation in Germany, 1918-1923." Doctoral dissertation, University of California, Berkeley, 1965.

1170   NEVINS, Allan, ed. *The Letters and Journals of Brand Whitlock.* 2 vols. New York, 1936.

1171   PAGE, Thomas Nelson. *Italy and the World War.* New York, 1920.

1172   RADOSH, Ronald. "John Spargo and Wilson's Russian Policy." *J Am Hist,* LII (1965), 548-565.

1173   RICHARDSON, Norval. *My Diplomatic Education.* New York, 1923. About Italy from 1913 to 1920.

1174   ST. JOHN, Jacqueline D. "John F. Stevens: American Assistance to Russian and Siberian Railroads, 1917-1922." Doctoral dissertation, University of Oklahoma, 1969.

1175   SAVAGE, Harry Howard. "Official Policies and Relations of the United States with the Provisional Government of Russia, March-November 1917." Doctoral dissertation, University of Minnesota, 1971.

1176   SCHUMAN, Frederick L. *American Policy Toward Russia Since 1917.* New York, 1928.

1177   SHARP, William Graves. *The War Memoirs of William Graves Sharp, American Minister to France, 1914-1919.* London, 1931.

1178   SILVERLIGHT, John. *The Victors' Dilemma: Allied Intervention in the Russian Civil War.* New York, 1970.

1179   SISSON, Edgar. *One Hundred Red Days: A Personal Chronicle of the Bolshevik Revolution.* New Haven, Conn., 1931.

1180   SNELL, John L. "German Socialist Reaction to Wilsonian Diplomacy: From Neutrality to Belligerency." *Journal of Central European Affairs,* IX (1949), 61-79.

1181   SNELL, John L. "Wilson on Germany and the Fourteen Points." *J Mod Hist,* XXVI (1954), 364-369.

1182   SNELL, John L. "Wilson's Peace Program and German Socialism, January-March, 1918." *Miss Val Hist Rev,* XXXVIII (1951), 187-214.

1183   STRAKHOVSKY, Leonid I. *Intervention at Archangel: The Story of Allied Intervention and Russian Counter-Revolution in North Russia, 1918-1920.* Princeton, N.J., 1944.

1184   STRAKHOVSKY, Leonid I. *The Origins of American Intervention in North Russia.* Princeton, N.J., 1937.

1185   TARULIS, Albert N. *American-Baltic Relations 1918-1922: The Struggle over Recognition.* Washington, 1965.

1186   THOMPSON, John M. *Russia, Bolshevism, and the Versailles Peace.* Princeton, N.J., 1966.

1187   ULLMAN, Richard H. *Anglo-Soviet Relations, 1917-1921.* 3 vols. Princeton, N.J., 1961-1972.

1188   UNTERBERGER, Betty M. *America's Siberian Expedition, 1918-1920.* Durham, N.C., 1956.

1189   UNTERBERGER, Betty M. "The Russian Revolution and Wilson's Far Eastern Policy." *Russian Review,* XVI (1957), No. 2, 35-46.

1190   VENTRY, Lance T. "The Impact of the United States Committee on Public Information on Italian Participation in the First World War." Doctoral dissertation, Catholic University of America, 1968.

1191   VOPICKA, Charles J. *Secrets of the Balkans: Seven Years of a Diplomat's Life in the Storm Centre of Europe.* Chicago, 1921. Vopicka was American wartime minister to Rumania, Serbia, and Bulgaria.

1192   WARTH, Robert D. *The Allies and the Russian Revolution.* Durham, N.C., 1954.

1193   WHITE, John Albert. *The Siberian Intervention.* Princeton, N.J., 1950.

1194   WHITLOCK, Brand. *Belgium: A Personal Narrative.* 2 vols. New York, 1919. Whitlock was American minister to Belgium.

1195   WILLIAMS, William A. "American Intervention in Russia, 1917-1920." *Studies on the Left,* III (1963), No. 4, 24-48; IV (1964), No. 1, 39-56.

1196   YATES, Louis A. R. *The United States and French Security, 1917-1921.* New York, 1957.

1197   ŽIVOJINOVIĆ Dragoljub Radovan. "The United States and Italy, April 1917-April 1919, with Special Reference to the Creation of the Yugoslav State." Doctoral dissertation, University of Pennsylvania, 1966.

5. Relations with the Middle East and Africa

1198   BEER, George Louis. *African Questions at the Paris Peace Conference.* New York, 1923. Reprinted, London, 1968.

1199   BRYSON, Thomas A. "The Armenia-America Society: A Factor in American-Turkish Relations, 1919-1924." *Records of the American Catholic Historical Society of Philadelphia,* LXXXII (1971), 83-105.

1200   CONTEE, Clarence G. "Du Bois, the NAACP, and the Pan-African Congress of 1919." *J Neg Hist,* LVII (1972), 13-28.

1201 DANIEL, Robert L. "The Armenian Question and American-Turkish Relations, 1914-1927." *Miss Val Hist Rev*, XLVI (1959), 252-275.

1202 EVANS, Laurence. *United States Policy and the Partition of Turkey, 1914-1924*. Baltimore, 1965.

1203 GIDNEY, James P. *A Mandate for Armenia*. Kent, Ohio, 1967.

1204 HOWARD, Harry N. *The King-Crane Commission: An American Inquiry in the Middle East*. Beirut, 1963.

1205 LEBOW, Richard Ned. "Woodrow Wilson and the Balfour Declaration." *J Mod Hist*, XL (1968), 501-523.

1206 LOUIS, Wm. Roger. "The United States and the African Peace Settlement of 1919: The Pilgrimage of George Louis Beer." *Journal of African History*, IV (1963), 413-433.

1207 MCKINLEY, Edward Harvey. "American Relations with Tropical Africa, 1919-1939." Doctoral dissertation, University of Wisconsin, 1971.

1208 MORGENTHAU, Henry. *Ambassador Morgenthau's Story*. New York, 1918. Morgenthau was American ambassador to Turkey.

1209 TRASK, Roger R. *United States Response to Turkish Nationalism*. See 181.

6. *Relations with Asia and the Pacific*

1210 ASADA, Sadao. "Japan and the United States, 1915-25." Doctoral dissertation, Yale University, 1963.

1211 BAILEY, Thomas A. "California, Japan and the Alien Land Legislation of 1913." *Pac Hist Rev*, I (1932), 36-59.

1212 BEERS, Burton F. "Robert Lansing's Proposed Bargain with Japan." *Pac Hist Rev*, XXVI (1957), 391-400.

1213 BEERS, Burton F. *Vain Endeavor: Robert Lansing's Attempts to End the American-Japanese Rivalry*. Durham, N.C., 1962.

1214 BOSE, Nemai Sadhan. *American Attitude . . . to the Nationalist Movement in China*. See 688.

1215 BRAISTED, William R. "China, the United States Navy, and the Bethlehem Steel Company." See 689.

1216 BRAISTED, William R. "The United States and the American China Development Company." *Far Eastern Quarterly*, XI (1952), 147-165.

1217 COHEN, Warren I. "America and the May Fourth Movement, the Response to Chinese Nationalism, 1917-1921." *Pac Hist Rev*, XXXV (1966), 88-94.

1218 CURRY, Roy W. *Woodrow Wilson and Far Eastern Policy, 1913-1921*. New York, 1957.

1219 DANIELS, Roger. "William Jennings Bryan and the Japanese." *Southern California Quarterly*, XLVIII (1966), 227-240.

1220   DAVIS, Clarence Baldwin. "The Defensive Diplomacy of British Imperialism in the Far East, 1915-1922: Japan and the United States as Partners and Rivals." Doctoral dissertation, University of Wisconsin, 1972.

1221   FIELD, Frederick V. *Consortiums*. See 711.

1222   FIFIELD, Russell H. "Disposal of the Carolines, Marshalls, and Marianas at the Paris Peace Conference." *Am Hist Rev*, LI (1946), 472-479.

1223   FIFIELD, Russell H. *Woodrow Wilson and the Far East: The Diplomacy of the Shantung Question*. New York, 1952.

1224   HOSACK, Robert E. "The Shantung Question and the Senate." *S Atl Q*, XLIII (1944), 181-193.

1225   ISRAEL, Jerry. *Progressivism and the Open Door*. See 721.

1226   KAMIKAWA, Hikomatsu. *Japan-American Diplomatic Relations*. See 203.

1227   LEVI, Werner. "American Attitudes Toward Pacific Islands, 1914-1919." *Pac Hist Rev*, XVII (1948), 55-64.

1228   LI, Tien-yi. *Woodrow Wilson's China Policy, 1913-1917*. New York, 1952.

1229   MANNING, Clarence A. *The Siberian Fiasco*. New York, 1952.

1230   MAY, Ernest R. "American Policy and Japan's Entrance into World War I." *Miss Val Hist Rev*, XL (1953), 279-290.

1231   MITCHELL, Kell F., Jr. "Diplomacy and Prejudice: The Morris-Shidehara Negotiations, 1920-1921." *Pac Hist Rev*, XXXIX (1970), 85-104.

1232   MORLEY, James W. *The Japanese Thrust into Siberia*. New York, 1957.

1233   MUNSON, Vivian Lorraine. "American Merchants of Capital in China: The Second Chinese Banking Consortium." Doctoral dissertation, University of Wisconsin, 1968. The consortium was formed in 1917.

1234   PUGACH, Noel. "Making the Open Door Work: Paul S. Reinsch in China, 1913-1919." *Pac Hist Rev*, XXXVIII (1969), 157-175.

1235   PUGACH, Noel H. "Standard Oil and Petroleum Development in Early Republican China." *Bus Hist Rev*, XLV (1971), 452-473.

1236   REINSCH, Paul S. *An American Diplomat in China*. Garden City, N.Y., 1922.

1237   SAFFORD, Jeffrey J. "Experiment in Containment: The United States Steel Embargo and Japan, 1917-1918." *Pac Hist Rev*, XXXIX (1970), 439-451.

1238   TATE, E. Mowbray. "U.S. Gunboats on the Yangtze." See 744.

1239   TRANI, Eugene P. "Woodrow Wilson, China, and the Missionaries, 1913-1921." *Journal of Presbyterian History*, XLIX (1971), 328-351.

1239-A UNTERBERGER, Betty M. *America's Siberian Expedition*. See 1188.

1240   VINSON, John Chalmers. "The Annulment of the Lansing-Ishii Agreement." *Pac Hist Rev*, XXVII (1958), 57-69.

1241   WEST, Philip. "Yenching University and American-Chinese Relations, 1917-1937." Doctoral dissertation, Harvard University, 1971.

7. Relations with Latin America

1242 ADLER, Selig. "Bryan and Wilsonian Caribbean Penetration." *His Am Hist Rev*, XX (1940), 198-226.

1243 BAKER, George W., Jr. "Ideals and Realities in the Wilson Administration's Relations with Honduras." *The Americas*, XXI (1964), 3-19.

1244 BAKER, George W., Jr. "Robert Lansing and the Purchase of the Danish West Indies." *Soc Stud*, LVII (1966), 64-71.

1245 BAKER, George W., Jr. "The Wilson Administration and Cuba, 1913-1921." *Mid-Am*, XLVI (1964), 48-63.

1246 BAKER, George W., Jr. "The Woodrow Wilson Administration and El Salvadoran Relations 1913-1921." *Soc Stud*, LVI (1965), 97-103.

1247 BAKER, George W., Jr. "The Woodrow Wilson Administration and Guatemalan Relations." *Historian*, XXVII (1965), 155-169.

1248 BAKER, George W., Jr. "Woodrow Wilson's Use of the Non-Recognition Policy in Costa Rica." *The Americas*, XXII (1965), 3-21.

1249 BALDRIDGE, Donald Carl. "Mexican Petroleum and the United States-Mexican Relations, 1919-1923." Doctoral dissertation, University of Arizona, 1971.

1250 BRADDY, Haldeen. *Pershing's Mission in Mexico*. El Paso, Tex., 1966.

1251 CALLCOTT, Wilfred Hardy. *Caribbean Policy*. See 769.

1252 CARTER, Purvis M. "Congressional and Public Reaction to Wilson's Caribbean Policy, 1913-1917." Doctoral dissertation, University of Colorado, 1970.

1253 CHAPMAN, Charles E. "The Development of the Intervention in Haiti." *His Am Hist Rev*, VII (1927), 299-319.

1254 CHAPMAN, Charles E. "The United States and the Dominican Republic." *His Am Hist Rev*, VII (1927), 84-91. About the 1916 intervention.

1255 CLENDENEN, Clarence C. *The United States and Pancho Villa*. Ithaca, N.Y., 1961.

1256 COLETTA, Paolo E. "William Jennings Bryan and the United States-Colombia Impasse, 1903-1921." *His Am Hist Rev*, XLVII (1967), 486-501.

1257 CUMBERLAND, Charles C. "The Jenkins Case and Mexican-American Relations." *His Am Hist Rev*, XXXI (1951), 586-607. A crisis in 1919.

1258 DARNELL, Michael Russell. "Henry P. Fletcher and American Diplomacy, 1902-1929." Doctoral dissertation, University of Colorado, 1972. Fletcher was envoy to Chile (1910-1916) and Mexico (1916-1920), and Under Secretary of State (1921-1925).

1259 EDWARDS, Warrick Ridgely, III. "United States-Mexican Relations, 1913-1916: Revolution, Oil, and Intervention." Doctoral dissertation, Louisiana State University, 1971.

1260 GOODELL, Stephen. "Woodrow Wilson in Latin America: Interpretations." *Historian*, XXVIII (1965), 96-127.

1261   HALEY, P. Edward. *Revolution and Intervention: The Diplomacy of Taft and Wilson with Mexico.* See 788.

1262   HILL, Larry D. "Woodrow Wilson's Executive Agents in Mexico: From the Beginning of His Administration to the Recognition of Venustiano Carranza." Doctoral dissertation, Louisiana State University, 1971.

1263   HINCKLEY, Ted C. "Wilson, Huerta, and the Twenty-One Gun Salute." *Historian*, XXII (1960), 197-206.

1264   JOHNSON, Robert Bruce. "The Punitive Expedition: A Military, Diplomatic, and Political History of Pershing's Chase After Pancho Villa, 1916-1917." Doctoral dissertation, University of Southern California, 1964.

1265   KAHLE, Louis G. "Robert Lansing and the Recognition of Venustiano Carranza." *His Am Hist Rev*, XXXVIII (1958), 353-372.

1266   KAPLAN, Edward Stephen. "The Latin American Policy of William Jennings Bryan, 1913-1915." Doctoral dissertation, New York University, 1970.

1267   KELSEY, Carl. "The American Intervention in Haiti and the Dominican Republic." *Ann Am Acad Pol Sci*, C (1922), 109-202.

1268   LINK, Arthur S. *La Politica de los Estados Unidos en América Latina, 1913-1916.* Mexico City and Buenos Aires, 1960.

1269   LINK, Arthur S. *Wilson.* See 918. Vols. 2-5 contain many chapters on Latin America, especially Mexico.

1270   LOWRY, Philip H. "The Mexican Policy of Woodrow Wilson." Doctoral dissertation, Yale University, 1949.

1271   MACCORKLE, S. A. *The American Policy of Recognition Towards Mexico.* Baltimore, 1933.

1272   MARTIN, Percy A. *Latin America and the War.* Baltimore, 1925.

1273   MAYER, Robert. "The Origins of the American Banking Empire in Latin America: Frank A. Vanderlip and the National City Bank." *J Interam Stud*, XV (1973), 60-72.

1274   MEYER, Leo J. "The United States and the Cuban Revolution of 1917." *His Am Hist Rev*, X (1930), 138-166.

1275   MEYER, Michael C. "The Arms of the Ypiranga." *His Am Hist Rev*, L (1970), 543-556. Backdrop to Wilson's intervention at Veracruz.

1276   MILLSPAUGH, Arthur C. *Haiti Under American Control, 1915-1930.* Boston, 1931.

1277   MOCK, James R. "The Creel Committee in Latin America." *His Am Hist Rev*, XXII (1942), 262-279.

1278   MOCK, James R., and Cedric LARSON. "Activities of the Mexico Section of the Creel Committee, 1917-1918." *Jour Q*, XVI (1939), 136-150.

1279   MURPHY, Donald Joseph. "Professors, Publicists, and Pan Americanism." See 814.

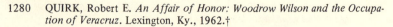

1280 QUIRK, Robert E. *An Affair of Honor: Woodrow Wilson and the Occupation of Veracruz.* Lexington, Ky., 1962.†

1281 ROSENBERG, Emily S. "Dollar Diplomacy Under Wilson: An Ecuadorean Case." *Int-Am Econ Aff,* XXV (1971), No. 2, 47-53.

1282 ROSENBERG, Emily S. "World War I and the Growth of United States Preponderance in Latin America." Doctoral dissertation, S.U.N.Y., Stony Brook, 1973.

1283 ROTBERG, Robert I., with Christopher K. CLAGUE. *Haiti: The Politics of Squalor.* Boston, 1971. Contains a chapter on the American occupation, 1915-34.

1284 SANDOS, James A. "German Involvement in Northern Mexico, 1915-1916: A New Look at the Columbus Raid." *His Am Hist Rev,* L (1970), 70-88.

1285 SANDOS, James A. "The Plan of San Diego: War & Diplomacy on the Texas Border, 1915-1916." *Arizona & the West,* XIV (1972), 5-24.

1286 SCHMIDT, Hans. *The United States Occupation of Haiti, 1915-1934.* New Brunswick, N.J., 1971.

1287 SCHOLES, Walter V., and Marie V. SCHOLES. "Wilson, Grey, and Huerta." *Pac Hist Rev,* XXXVII (1968), 151-158.

1288 SMITH, Daniel M. "Bainbridge Colby and the Good Neighbor Policy, 1920-1921." *Miss Val Hist Rev,* L (1963), 56-78.

1289 SMITH, Robert F. "The Formation and Development of the International Bankers' Committee on Mexico." *J Econ Hist,* XXIII (1963), 574-586.

1290 SMITH, Robert Freeman. *The United States and Revolutionary Nationalism in Mexico, 1916-1932.* Chicago, 1972.

1291 SWEET, Dana Royden. "A History of United States-Argentine Commercial Relations, 1918-1933: A Study of Competitive Farm Economies." Doctoral dissertation, Syracuse University, 1972.

1292 SWEETMAN, Jack. *The Landing at Veracruz: 1914. The First Complete Chronicle of a Strange Encounter in April, 1914, When the United States Navy Captured and Occupied the City of Veracruz, Mexico.* Annapolis, Md., 1968.

1293 TANSILL, Charles C. *The Purchase of the Danish West Indies.* Baltimore, 1932.

1294 TEITELBAUM, Louis M. *Woodrow Wilson and the Mexican Revolution (1913-1916): A History of United States-Mexican Relations from the Murder of Madero Until Villa's Provocation Across the Border.* New York, 1967.

1295 TROW, Clifford W. "Woodrow Wilson and the Mexican Interventionist Movement of 1919." *J Am Hist,* LVIII (1971), 46-72.

1296 TULCHIN, Joseph S. *The Aftermath of War: World War I and U.S. Policy Toward Latin America.* New York, 1971.

1297   WEITEKAMP, Raymond. "The Virgin Islands Purchase and the Coercion Myth." *Mid-Am*, LIV (1972), 75-93.

8. *Economic Matters*

1298   ABRAHAMS, Paul Philip. "Foreign Expansion of American Finance." See 838.

1299   DENOVO, John A. "The Movement for an Aggressive American Oil Policy Abroad, 1918-1920." *Am Hist Rev*, LXI (1956), 854-876.

1300   DIAMOND, William. *The Economic Thought of Woodrow Wilson*. Baltimore, 1943.

1301   KAUFMAN, Burton I. "Organization for Foreign Trade Expansion in the Mississippi Valley, 1900-1920." *Bus Hist Rev*, XLVI (1972), 444-465.

1302   KAUFMAN, Burton I. "The Organizational Dimension of United States Economic Foreign Policy." See 847.

1303   LORENCE, James John. "American Asiatic Association . . . Organized Business and the Myth of the China Market." See 849.

1304   PARRINI, Carl P. *Heir to Empire; United States Economic Diplomacy, 1916-1923*. Pittsburgh, 1969.

1305   PRISCO, Salvatore. *John Barrett*. See 851.

1306   SCHEIBER, Harry N. "World War I as Entrepreneurial Opportunity: Willard Straight and the American International Corporation." *Pol Sci Q*, LXXXIV (1969), 486-511.

1307   VAN METER, Robert Hardin, Jr. "The United States and European Recovery 1918-1923: A Study of Public Policy and Private Finance." Doctoral dissertation, University of Wisconsin, 1971.

IV. An Interlude of Peace: The 1920's and 1930's

1. General

1308 ABBOTT, Frank Winchester. "From Versailles to Munich: The Foreign Policy Association and American Foreign Policy." Doctoral dissertation, Texas Tech University, 1972.

1309 ADLER, Selig. *The Uncertain Giant, 1921-1941: American Foreign Policy Between the Wars*. New York, 1965.†

1310 ADLER, Selig. "The War-Guilt Question and American Disillusionment, 1918-1928." *J Mod Hist*, XXIII (1951), 1-28.

1311 ARMSTRONG, Hamilton Fish. *Peace and Counterpeace: From Wilson to Hitler*. New York, 1971.

1312 ASHBY, Leroy. *The Spearless Leader: Senator Borah and the Progressive Movement in the 1920's*. Urbana, Ill., 1972.

1313 BARNES, Harry Elmer. *Perpetual War*. See 1721.

1314 BEARD, Charles A. *The Open Door at Home*. New York, 1934.

1315 BERDAHL, Clarence A. *The Policy of the United States with Respect to the League of Nations*. New York, 1932.

1316 BILLINGTON, Ray Allen. "The Origins of Middle Western Isolationism." *Pol Sci Q*, LX (1945), 44-64.

1317 BLAKESLEE, George H. *The Recent Foreign Policy of the United States: Problems in American Cooperation with Other Powers*. New York, 1925.

1318 BLUM, John M. *From the Morgenthau Diaries: Years of Crisis, 1928-1938*. Boston, 1959. Morgenthau was F.D.R.'s Secretary of the Treasury.

1319 BOYLE, Peter G. "The Roots of Isolationism: A Case Study." *J Am Stud*, VI (1972), 41-54. The case of Hiram Johnson.

1320 BOYLE, Peter Gerard. "The Study of an Isolationist: Hiram Johnson." Doctoral dissertation, University of California, Los Angeles, 1971.

1321 BURNS, Richard Dean, and W. Addams DIXON. "Foreign Policy and the 'Democratic Myth': The Debate on the Ludlow Amendment." *Mid-Am*, XLVII (1965), 288-306.

1322 CANTRIL, Hadley, ed. *Public Opinion, 1935-1946*. Princeton, N.J., 1951. An important compilation of opinion polls.

1323 CARLETON, William G. "Isolationism and the Middle West." *Miss Val Hist Rev*, XXXIII (1946), 377-390.

1324   CARR, E. H. *The Twenty Years' Crisis, 1919-1939: An Introduction to the Study of International Relations*. New York, 1939.†

1325   COHEN, Warren I. *The American Revisionists: The Lessons of Intervention in World War I*. Chicago, 1967. Influential historians.

1326   COLE, Wayne S. *Senator Gerald P. Nye and American Foreign Relations*. Minneapolis, 1962.

1327   COLE, Wayne S. "Senator Key Pittman and American Neutrality Policies, 1933-1940." *Miss Val Hist Rev*, XLVI (1960), 644-662.

1328   CURRENT, Richard N. *Secretary Stimson: A Study in Statecraft*. New Brunswick, N.J., 1954.

1329   DANELSKI, David J., and Joseph S. TULCHIN, eds. *The Autobiographical Notes of Charles Evans Hughes*. Cambridge, Mass., 1973.

1330   DARNELL, Michael Russell. "Henry P. Fletcher." See 1258.

1331   DEWITT, Howard Arthur. "Hiram W. Johnson." See 899.

1332   DIVINE, Robert A. "Franklin D. Roosevelt and Collective Security, 1933." *Miss Val Hist Rev*, XLVIII (1961), 42-59.

1333   DIVINE, Robert A. *The Illusion of Neutrality*. Chicago, 1962.†

1334   DIVINE, Robert A. *Reluctant Belligerent*. See 1807.

1335   DONOVAN, John C. "Congressional Isolationists and the Roosevelt Foreign Policy." *Wor Pol*, III (1951), 299-316.

1336   DOWNING, Marvin Lee. "Hugh R. Wilson and American Relations with the League of Nations, 1927-1937." Doctoral dissertation, University of Oklahoma, 1970.

1337   DRUMMOND, Dwight F. *Passing of American Neutrality*. See 1808.

1338   EDWARDS, Jerome E. *The Foreign Policy of Col. McCormick's Tribune: 1929-1941*. Reno, Nev., 1971.

1339   ELLIS, L. Ethan. *Frank B. Kellogg and American Foreign Relations, 1925-1929*. New Brunswick, N.J., 1961.

1340   ELLIS, L. Ethan. *Republican Foreign Policy, 1921-1933*. New Brunswick, N.J., 1968.

1341   FERRELL, Robert H. *American Diplomacy in the Great Depression: Hoover-Stimson Foreign Policy, 1929-1933*. New Haven, Conn., 1957.

1342   FERRELL, Robert H. *Frank B. Kellogg* [and] *Henry L. Stimson. Secretaries of State*. Vol. 11. New York, 1963. See 79.

1343   FERRELL, Robert H. "The Price of Isolation; American Diplomacy, 1921-1945." *The Unfinished Century*. See 96.

1344   FLEMING, Denna F. *The United States and World Organization, 1920-1933*. New York, 1938.

1345   FREIDEL, Frank. *Franklin D. Roosevelt*. 3 vols. Boston, 1952-1956. In progress.

1346 GLAD, Betty. *Charles Evans Hughes and the Illusions of Innocence: A Study in American Diplomacy.* Urbana, Ill., 1966.

1347 GRAFF, Frank Warren. "The Strategy of Involvement: A Diplomatic Biography of Sumner Welles, 1933-1943." Doctoral dissertation, University of Michigan, 1971.

1348 HAIGHT, John McV., Jr. "Roosevelt and the Aftermath of the Quarantine Speech." *Rev Pol*, XXIV (1962), 233-259.

1349 HANKS, Richard Kay. "Hamilton Fish and American Isolationism, 1920-1944." Doctoral dissertation, University of California, Riverside, 1971. Fish was a Republican congressman from New York.

1350 HENDERSON, Gordon G. "Policy by Default: The Origin and Fate of the Prescott Letter." *Pol Sci Q*, LXXIX (1964), 76-95. Discusses policy toward Antarctica (1924).

1351 HICKS, John D. *Republican Ascendancy, 1921-1933.* New York, 1960.

1352 HOOKER, Nancy H., ed. *The Moffat Papers: Selections from the Diplomatic Journals of Jay Pierrepont Moffat, 1919-1943.* Cambridge, Mass., 1956.

1353 HOOVER, Herbert. *The Memoirs of Herbert Hoover.* 3 vols. New York, 1951-1952.

1354 HULL, Cordell. *The Memoirs of Cordell Hull.* 2 vols. New York, 1948.

1355 HYDE, C. C. "Charles Evans Hughes." *Secretaries of State.* Vol. 10. See 60.

1356 ISRAEL, Fred L. *Nevada's Key Pittman.* Lincoln, Neb., 1963. Pittman was the chairman of Senate Foreign Relations Committee.

1357 JABLON, Howard. "The State Department and Collective Security, 1933-34." *Historian*, XXXIII (1971), 248-263.

1358 JACOBS, Travis Beal. "Roosevelt's Quarantine Speech." *Historian*, XXIV (1962), 483-502.

1359 JOHNSON, Claudius O. *Borah of Idaho.* See 912.

1360 JONAS, Manfred. *Isolationism in America, 1935-1941.* New York, 1966.

1361 JONAS, Manfred. "The United States and the Failure of Collective Security in the 1930s." *Twentieth-Century American Foreign Policy.* See 64.

1362 KAUFMANN, William W. "Two American Ambassadors: Bullitt and Kennedy." *The Diplomats.* See 68.

1363 KENDALL, Richard H. "Edwin M. Borchard and the Defense of Traditional American Neutrality 1931-1941." Doctoral dissertation, Yale University, 1964.

1364 LANGER, William L., and S. Everett GLEASON. *The Challenge to Isolation, 1937-1940.* New York, 1952.

1365 LEUCHTENBURG, William E. *Franklin D. Roosevelt and the New Deal, 1932-1940.* New York, 1963.†

1366 LOWERRE, Nan Kathryn Jamieson. "Warren G. Harding and American Foreign Affairs, 1915-1923." Doctoral dissertation, Stanford University, 1968.

1367 MCCOY, Donald R. *Calvin Coolidge: The Quiet President.* New York, 1967.

1368 MCKENNA, Marian C. *Borah.* See 923.

1369 MADDOX, Robert J. "Another Look at the Legend of Isolationism in the 1920's." *Mid-Am*, LIII (1971), 35-43.

1370 MADDOX, Robert James. *William E. Borah and American Foreign Policy.* Baton Rouge, 1969.

1371 MOORE, Jamie Wallace. "The Logic of Isolation and Neutrality; American Foreign Policy 1933-1935." Doctoral dissertation, University of North Carolina, 1970.

1372 MORISON, Elting E. *Turmoil and Tradition: A Study of the Life and Times of Henry L. Stimson.* Boston, 1960.†

1373 MURRAY, Robert K. *The Harding Era: Warren G. Harding and His Administration.* Minneapolis, 1969.

1374 MYER, William S. *The Foreign Policies of Herbert Hoover, 1929-1933.* New York, 1940.

1375 NELSON, Keith L. "The 'Black Horror on the Rhine': Race as a Factor in Post-World War I Diplomacy." *J Mod Hist*, XLII (1970), 606-617. European and American reactions to the use of African troops in the war.

1376 NIXON, Edgar B., ed. *Franklin D. Roosevelt and Foreign Affairs.* 3 vols., Cambridge, Mass., 1969. Documents.

1377 OSTROWER, Gary B. "American Ambassador to the League of Nations— 1933: A Proposal Postponed." *Int Organ* XXV (1971), 46-58.

1378 OSTROWER, Gary Best. "The United States, the League of Nations, and Collective Security, 1931-1934." Doctoral dissertation, University of Rochester, 1970.

1379 PERKINS, Dexter. *Charles Evans Hughes and American Democratic Statesmanship.* Boston, 1956.

1380 PERKINS, Dexter. "The Department of State and American Public Opinion." *The Diplomats.* See 68.

1381 PETROV, Vladimir. *A Study in Diplomacy: The Story of Arthur Bliss Lane.* Chicago, 1971. Lane was a career diplomat in Latin America and Central Europe.

1382 PHILLIPS, William. *Ventures in Diplomacy.* See 490.

1383 PRATT, Julius W. *Cordell Hull.* 2 vols. New York, 1964. *Secretaries of State.* Vols. 12 and 13. See 79.

1384 PRATT, Julius W. "The Ordeal of Cordell Hull." *Rev Pol*, XXVIII (1966), 76-98. Cabinet competition for control of foreign policy under F.D.R.

1385 PUSEY, Merlo J. *Charles Evans Hughes.* 2 vols. New York, 1951.

1386 REDMOND, Kent G. "Henry L. Stimson and the Question of League Membership." *Historian*, XXV (1963), 200-212.

1387 ROOSEVELT, Elliott, ed. *F.D.R.: His Personal Letters, 1928-1945.* 2 vols. New York, 1950.

1388 RUSSELL, Francis. *The Shadow of Blooming Grove: Warren G. Harding in His Times.* New York, 1968.

1389 SCHLESINGER, Arthur M., Jr. *The Age of Roosevelt.* 3 vols to date. Boston, 1957-1960.†

1390 SHOWAN, Daniel P. "United States Policy Regarding League of Nations Social and Humanitarian Activities." Doctoral dissertation, Pennsylvania State University, 1969.

1391 SINCLAIR, Andrew. *The Available Man: The Life Behind the Masks of Warren Gamaliel Harding.* New York, 1965.

1392 SMITH, Robert Freeman. "American Foreign Relations 1920-1942." *Towards a New Past: Dissenting Essays in American History.* Ed Barton J. Bernstein. New York, 1968.†

1392-A SMUCKLER, Ralph H. "The Region of Isolationism." *Am Pol Sci Rev,* XLVII (1953), 386-401.

1393 STIMSON, Henry L., and McGeorge BUNDY. *On Active Service in Peace and War.* New York, 1948.

1394 WILLIAMS, William A. "The Legend of Isolationism in the 1920's." *Sci Soc,* XVIII (1954), 1-20.

1395 WILSON, Hugh R. *Diplomat Between Wars.* New York, 1941. A memoir.

1396 WILTZ, John E. *From Isolation to War, 1931-1941.* New York, 1968.†

1397 WILTZ, John E. *In Search of Peace: The Senate Munitions Inquiry, 1934.* Baton Rouge, 1963.

1398 WILTZ, John E. "The Nye Committee Revisited." *Historian,* XXIII (1961), 211-233.

1399 WIMER, Kurt, and Sarah WIMER. "The Harding Administration, the League of Nations, and the Separate Peace Treaty." *Rev Pol,* XXIX (1967), 13-24.

1400 WOODARD, Nelson Eugene. "Postwar Reconstruction and International Order: A Study of the Diplomacy of Charles Evans Hughes, 1921-1925." Doctoral dissertation, University of Wisconsin, 1970.

2. The Washington Conference, Strategy, and Arms Limitation

1401   ANDRADE, Ernest, Jr. "The United States Navy and the Washington Conference." *Historian*, XXXI (1969), 345-363.

1402   ASADA, Sadao. "Japan's 'Special Interests' and the Washington Conference, 1921-22." *Am Hist Rev*, LXVII (1961), 62-70.

1403   ATWATER, Elton. *American Regulations of Arms Exports*. New York, 1941.

1404   BERG, Meredith William. "Admiral William H. Standley and the Second London Naval Treaty, 1934-1936." *Historian*, XXXIII (1971), 215-236.

1405   BIRN, Donald S. "Britain and France at the Washington Conference, 1921-1922." Doctoral dissertation, Columbia University, 1964.

1406   BREBNER, J. Bartlet. "Canada, the Anglo-Japanese Alliance, and the Washington Conference." *Pol Sci Q*, L (1935), 45-58.

1407   BUCKLEY, Thomas H. *The United States and the Washington Conference, 1921-1922*. Knoxville, Tenn., 1970.

1408   BUELL, Raymond L. *The Washington Conference*. New York, 1922.

1409   BURNS, Richard Dean. "Origins of the United States' Arms Inspection Policies, 1926-46." *Disarmament and Arms Control*, II (1964), 157-169.

1410   BURNS, Richard Dean. "Regulating Submarine Warfare, 1921-41: A Case Study in Arms Control and Limited War." *Mil Aff*, XXXV (1971), 56-63.

1411   BURNS, Richard Dean, and Donald URQUIDI. *Disarmament in Historical Perspective: An Analysis of Selected Arms Control and Disarmament Agreements Between World Wars, 1919-1941*. 4 vols. Washington, 1968. This is U.S. Arms Control and Disarmament Agency Report No. RS-55.

1412   BYWATER, Hector D. *Seapower in the Pacific: A Study of American-Japanese Naval Problems*. New York, 1921.

1413   CARLTON, David. "Great Britain and the Coolidge Naval Disarmament Conference of 1927." *Pol Sci Q*, LXXXIII (1968), 573-598.

1414   CUSTER, Ben S. "The Geneva Conference for the Limitation of Naval Armament, 1927." Doctoral dissertation, Georgetown University, 1948.

1415   DEBOE, David Cornelius. "The United States and the Geneva Disarmament Conference, 1932-1934." Doctoral dissertation, Tulane University, 1969.

1416   DINGMAN, Roger. "Power in the Pacific: The Evolution of Japanese and American Naval Policies, 1918-1922." Doctoral dissertation, Harvard University, 1969.

1417   GALBRAITH, John S. "The Imperial Conference of 1921 and the Washington Conference." *Can Hist Rev* XXIX (1948), 143-152.

1418 GODFREY, James L. "Anglo-American Naval Conversations Preliminary to the London Naval Conference of 1930." *S Atl Q*, XLIX (1950), 303-316.

1419 GRANAT, Stanley J. "Chinese Participation at the Washington Conference: 1921-1922." Doctoral dissertation, Indiana University, 1969.

1420 HERZOG, James H. "The Role of the United States Navy in the Evolution and Execution of American Foreign Policy Relative to Japan, 1936-1941." Doctoral dissertation, Brown University, 1963.

1421 HOAG, C. Leonard. *Preface to Preparedness: The Washington Disarmament Conference and Public Opinion.* Washington, 1941.

1422 HOLBROOK, Francis Xavier. "United States National Defense and Trans-Pacific Commercial Air Routes, 1933-1941." Doctoral dissertation, Fordham University, 1969.

1423 ICHIHASHI, Yamato. *The Washington Conference and After.* Stanford, Cal., 1928.

1424 KENNEDY, Thomas C. "Beard vs. F.D.R. on National Defense and Re-armament." *Mid-Am*, L (1968), 22-41.

1425 KENNEDY, Thomas C. "Charles A. Beard and the 'Big Navy Boys.'" *Mil Aff*, XXI (1967), 65-73.

1426 KLATCHKO, Mary. "Anglo-American Naval Competition." See 1061-A.

1427 KLEIN, Ira. "Whitehall, Washington and the Anglo-Japanese Alliance." See 1127.

1428 MILLION, Paul E., Jr. "The Influence of the Washington Naval Conference upon American Sea Power." Doctoral dissertation, Georgetown University, 1956.

1429 O'CONNOR, Raymond G. *Perilous Equilibrium: The United States and the London Naval Conference of 1930.* Lawrence, Kans., 1962.

1430 O'CONNOR, Raymond G. "The 'Yardstick' and Naval Disarmament in the 1920's." *Miss Val Hist Rev*, XLV (1958), 441-463.

1431 OYOS, Lynwood E. "The Navy and the United States Far Eastern Policy, 1930-1939." Doctoral dissertation, University of Nebraska, 1958.

1432 PELZ, Stephen Ernest. "Race to Pearl Harbor: The Failure of the Second London Naval Conference and the Coming of World War II." Doctoral dissertation, Harvard University, 1971.

1433 ROOD, Harold W. "Strategy Out of Silence: American Military Policy and the Preparation for War, 1919 to 1940." Doctoral dissertation, University of California, Berkeley, 1960.

1434 ROSKILL, Stephen. *Naval Policy Between the Wars.* Vol. I: *The Period of Anglo-American Antagonism, 1919-1929.* New York, 1968.

1435 SPINKS, Charles N. "The Termination of the Anglo-Japanese Alliance." *Pac Hist Rev*, VI (1937), 321-340.

1436 SPROUT, Harold, and Margaret SPROUT. *Toward a New Order of Sea Power.* Princeton, N.J., 1940.

1437 SULLIVAN, Mark. *The Great Adventure in Washington: The Story of the Conference.* New York, 1922.

1438 TATE, Merze, and Fidele FOY. "More Light on the Abrogation of the Anglo-Japanese Alliance." *Pol Sci Q*, LXXIV (1959), 532-554.

1438-A TRANI, Eugene P. "Secretary Denby Takes a Trip." *Michigan History*, LI (1967), 277-297. The U.S. Navy in the Far East.

1439 TULEJA, Thaddeus V. *Statesmen and Admirals: Quest for a Far Eastern Naval Policy.* New York, 1963.

1440 VINSON, John Chalmers. "The Imperial Conference of 1921 and the Anglo-Japanese Alliance." *Pac Hist Rev*, XXXI (1962), 257-266.

1441 VINSON, John Chalmers. "Military Force and American Policy, 1919-1939." *Isolation and Security.* See 72.

1442 VINSON, John Chalmers. *The Parchment Peace: The United States Senate and the Washington Conference, 1921-22.* Athens, Ga., 1955.

1443 WHEELER, Gerald E. *Prelude to Pearl Harbor: The United States Navy and the Far East, 1921-1931.* Columbia, Mo., 1963.

1444 WHEELER-BENNETT, John W. *The Pipe Dream of Peace: The Story of the Collapse of Disarmament.* New York, 1935.

1445 WILSON, Hugh R., Jr. *Disarmament and the Cold War in the Thirties.* New York, 1963.

1446 WINKLER, Fred H. "Disarmament and Security: The American Policy at Geneva, 1926-1935." *North Dakota Quarterly*, XXXIX (1971), No. 4, 21-33.

1447 WINKLER, Fred H. "The War Department and Disarmament, 1926-1935." *Historian*, XXVIII (1966), 426-446.

3. The Kellogg-Briand Pact

1448 COOPER, Russell M. *American Consultation in World Affairs for the Preservation of Peace.* New York, 1934. The Kellogg pact and after.

1449 CURRENT, Richard N. "Consequences of the Kellogg Pact." *Issues and Conflicts.* See 50.

1450 DE BENEDETTI, Charles. "Borah and the Kellogg-Briand Pact." *Pacific Northwest Quarterly*, LXIII (1972), 22-29.

1451 FERRELL, Robert H. *Peace in Their Time: The Origins of the Kellogg-Briand Pact.* New Haven, Conn., 1952.

1452 HEFLEY, J. Theodore. "War Outlawed: *The Christian Century* and the Kellogg Peace Pact." *Jour Q*, XLVIII (1971), 26-32.

1453 KNEESHAW, Stephen John. "The Kellogg-Briand Pact: The American Reaction." Doctoral dissertation, University of Colorado, 1971. 1928-1929 reactions to the pact.

1454 MEIBURGER, Sister Anne Vincent. *Efforts of Raymond Robins Toward . . . the Outlawry of War.* See 1166.

1455 MILLER, David Hunter. *The Peace Pact of Paris.* New York, 1928.

1456 SHOTWELL, James T. *War as an Instrument of National Policy and Its Renunciation in the Pact of Paris.* New York, 1929.

1457 STONER, John E. *S. O. Levinson and the Pact of Paris.* Chicago, 1943.

1458 VINSON, John Chalmers. *William E. Borah and the Outlawry of War.* Athens, Ga., 1957.

4. Relations with Canada and Great Britain

1459 BORCHARD, Edwin M. "The Neutrality Claims Against Great Britain." *Am J Int Law,* XXI (1927), 764-768.

1460 CHRISTY, Florence Jean. "Anglo-American Diplomacy." See 1117.

1461 DAWES, Charles G. *Journal as Ambassador to Great Britain.* New York, 1939. Dawes was ambassador during the Hoover administration.

1462 DIZIKES, John. "Britain, Roosevelt and the New Deal—1932-1938." Doctoral dissertation, Harvard University, 1964.

1463 FRIEDLANDER, Robert A. "New Light on the Anglo-American Reaction to the Ethiopian War, 1935-1936." *Mid-Am,* XLV (1963), 115-125.

1464 FRY, Michael G. *North Atlantic Diplomacy.* See 1120.

1465 HECHT, Robert A. "Great Britain and the Stimson Note of January 7, 1932." *Pac Hist Rev,* XXXVIII (1969), 177-191.

1466 HENDERSON, Gordon Grant. "International Law in American Foreign Policy: A Study of the Role of International Law in the Making of National Policy in Ten Disputes Between the United States and Great Britain in the Period 1919-1930." Doctoral dissertation, Columbia University, 1962.

1467 HENSON, Edward Lee, Jr. "Britain, America, and the European Crisis, 1937-1938." Doctoral dissertation, University of Virginia, 1969.

1468 KIMBALL, Warren F. "Lend-Lease . . . the Temptation of British Opulence." See 1833.

1469 KOTTMAN, Richard N. *Reciprocity and the North Atlantic Triangle, 1932-1938.* Ithaca, N.Y., 1968. American-Canadian-British relations.

1470 KOTTMAN, Richard N. "Volstead Violated: Prohibition as a Factor in Canadian-American Relations." *Can Hist Rev,* XLIII (1962), 106-126.

1471 LEUTZE, James Richard. "If Britain Should Fall: Roosevelt and British-American Naval Relations: 1938-1940." Doctoral dissertation, Duke University, 1970.

1472   MANNOCK, James Harold. "Anglo-American Relations, 1921-1928." Doctoral dissertation, Princeton University, 1962.

1473   PRATT, Lawrence. "The Anglo-American Naval Conversations on the Far East of January 1938." *Int Aff*, XLVII (1971), 745-763.

1474   WATT, Donald. "Roosevelt and Neville Chamberlain: Two Appeasers." *Int Jour*, XXVIII (1973), 185-204.

5. Relations with Europe and Russia

1475   AMBROSIUS, Lloyd E. "The United States and the Weimar Republic." See 1133.

1476   BAKER, James Franklin. "The United States and the Czechoslovak Crisis, 1938-1939." Doctoral dissertation, Tulane University, 1971.

1477   BAUER, Wolfred. "The Shipment of American Strategic Raw Materials to Nazi Germany: A Study in United States Economic Foreign Policy, 1933-1939." Doctoral dissertation, University of Washington, 1964.

1478   BELL, Leland V. "The Failure of Nazism in America: The German American Bund, 1936-1941." *Pol Sci Q*, LXXXV (1970), 585-599.

1479   BENNETT, Edward M. *Recognition of Russia: An American Foreign Policy Dilemma*. Waltham, Mass., 1970.†

1480   BERUTTI, John Morris. "Italo-American Diplomatic Relations, 1922-28." Doctoral dissertation, Stanford University, 1960.

1481   BISHOP, Donald G. *The Roosevelt-Litvinov Agreements: The American View*. Syracuse, N.Y., 1965.

1482   BLACK, Henry Wendell. "William C. Bullitt and the World Crisis, 1936-1943." Doctoral dissertation, University of Southern Mississippi, 1972. Bullitt was U.S. ambassador to France, 1936-1940.

1483   BOLLER, Paul F., Jr. "The 'Great Conspiracy' of 1933: A Study in Short Memories." *Southwest Review*, XXXIX (1954), 97-112. Concerns recognition of the U.S.S.R.

1484   BOSWELL, George Timothy. "Buddha Bill: The Roller-Coaster Career of William C. Bullitt, 1936-1940." Doctoral dissertation, Texas Christian University, 1972. Bullitt was U.S. ambassador to France.

1485   BOWERS, Claude G. *My Mission to Spain: Watching the Rehearsal for World War II*. New York, 1954.

1486   BOWERS, Robert E. "American Diplomacy, the 1933 Wheat Conference, and Recognition of the Soviet Union." *Ag Hist*, XL (1966), 39-52.

1487   BOWERS, Robert E. "Hull, Russian Subversion in Cuba, and Recognition of the U.S.S.R." *J Am Hist*, LIII (1966), 542-554.

1488   BRADDICK, Henderson B. "A New Look at American Policy During the Italo-Ethiopian Crisis, 1935-1936." *J Mod Hist*, XXXIV (1962), 64-73.

1489   BROWDER, Robert Paul. *The Origins of Soviet-American Diplomacy.* Princeton, N.J., 1953.†

1490   BROWDER, Robert Paul. "Soviet Far Eastern Policy and American Recognition, 1932-1934." *Pac Hist Rev*, XXI (1952), 263-273.

1491   BULLITT, Orville H., ed. *For the President—Personal and Secret: Correspondence between Franklin D. Roosevelt and William C. Bullitt.* Boston, 1972. Bullitt was ambassador to Russia 1933-1936, to France 1936-1940.

1492   BURKE, Bernard V. "American Economic Diplomacy and the Weimar Republic." *Mid-Am*, LIV (1972), 211-233.

1493   BURKS, David D. "The United States and the Geneva Protocol of 1924: 'A New Holy Alliance'?" *Am Hist Rev*, LXIV (1959), 891-905.

1494   CANNISTRARO, Philip V., and Theodore P. KOVALEFF. "Father Coughlin and Mussolini: Impossible Allies." *Journal of Church & State*, XIII (1971), 427-443.

1495   DALLEK, Robert. "Beyond Tradition: The Diplomatic Careers of William E. Dodd and George S. Messersmith, 1933-1938." *S Atl Q*, LXVI (1967), 233-244.

1496   DALLEK, Robert. *Democrat and Diplomat: The Life of William E. Dodd.* New York, 1968. Dodd was F.D.R.'s ambassador to Germany.

1497   DAVIES, Joseph E. *Mission to Moscow.* New York, 1941.

1498   DESANTI, Louis Aldo. "U.S. Relations with Italy Under Mussolini, 1922-1941." Doctoral dissertation, Columbia University, 1951.

1499   DIAMOND, Sander A. "Germany and the Bund Movement in the United States, 1923-1938." Doctoral dissertation, S.U.N.Y., Binghamton, 1971.

1500   DIGGINS, John P. "The Italo-American Anti-Fascist Opposition." *J Am Hist*, LIV (1967), 579-598.

1501   DIGGINS, John P. "Mussolini and America: Hero-Worship, Charisma, and the 'Vulgar Talent.' " *Historian*, XXVIII (1966), 559-585.

1502   DIGGINS, John P. *Mussolini and Fascism: The View from America.* Princeton, N.J., 1972.

1503   DODD, William E., Jr., and Martha DODD. *Ambassador Dodd's Diary, 1933-1938.* New York, 1941.

1504   ETZOLD, Thomas Herman. "Fair Play: American Principles and Practice in Relations with Germany 1933-1939." Doctoral dissertation, Yale University, 1970.

1505   FARNSWORTH, Beatrice. *Bullitt.* See 1142.

1506   FEINGOLD, Henry L. *The Politics of Rescue: The Roosevelt Administration and the Holocaust, 1938-1945* New Brunswick, N.J., 1970. About persecution of the Jews.

1507   FITHIAN, Floyd James. "Soviet-American Economic Relations, 1918-1933: American Business in Russia During the Period of Nonrecognition." Doctoral dissertation, University of Nebraska, 1964.

1508 FORD, Franklin. "Three Observers in Berlin: Rumbold, Dodd, and François-Poncet." *The Diplomats*. See 68.

1509 GUTTMAN, Allen. *The Wound in the Heart: America and the Spanish Civil War*. New York, 1962.

1510 HAIGHT, John McV., Jr., "France and the Aftermath of Roosevelt's 'Quarantine' Speech." *Wor Pol*, XIV (1962), 281-306.

1511 HAIGHT, John McV., Jr. "France, the United States and the Munich Crisis." *J Mod Hist*, XXXII (1960), 340-358.

1512 HAIGHT, John McV., Jr. "Roosevelt as Friend of France." *For Aff*, XLIV (1966), 518-526. On military aid in 1938.

1513 HARRIS, Brice, Jr. *The United States and the Italo-Ethiopian Crisis*. Stanford, Cal., 1964.

1514 HENRIKSON, Alan Keith. " 'World Appeasement': The American Road to Munich." Doctoral dissertation, Harvard University, 1970.

1515 JOHNSON, Niel M. *Viereck*. See 1154.

1516 JONAS, Manfred. "Prophet Without Honor: Hans Heinrich Dieckhoff's Reports from Washington." *Mid-Am*, XLVII (1965), 222-233. Dieckhoff was German ambassador to the U.S., 1938-1941.

1517 JORDAN, Laylon Wayne. "America's Mussolini: The United States and Italy." See 1155.

1518 KENNAN, George F. *From Prague After Munich: Diplomatic Papers 1938-1940*. Princeton, N.J., 1968.

1519 KENNAN, George F. *Memoirs*. See 2163.

1520 KIMBALL, Warren F. "Dieckhoff and America: A German's View of German-American Relations, 1937-1941." *Historian*, XXVII (1965), 218-243.

1521 KIPPHAN, Klaus. *Deutsche Propaganda in den Vereinigten Staaten, 1933-1941*. Heidelberg, 1971.

1522 KOLKO, Gabriel. "American Business and Germany, 1930-1941." *W Pol Q*, XV (1962), 713-728.

1523 LEFFLER, Melvyn Paul. "The Struggle for Stability: American Policy Toward France, 1921-1933." Doctoral dissertation, Ohio State University, 1972.

1524 LUBEK, Sister M. Evangela. "An Inquiry into United States-Czechoslovakian Relations Between 1918 and 1948 with Special Reference to the Munich Crisis and the Slovak Question." Doctoral dissertation, Georgetown University, 1969.

1525 MADDUX, Thomas Roth. "American Relations with the Soviet Union, 1933-1941." Doctoral dissertation, University of Michigan, 1969.

1526 MEIBURGER, Sister Anne Vincent. *Efforts of Raymond Robins Toward the Recognition of Soviet Russia*. See 1166.

1527   MILLSAP, Mary Ruth. "Mussolini and the United States: Italo-American Relations, 1935-1941." Doctoral dissertation, University of California, Los Angeles, 1972.

1528   NORMAN, John. "Influence of Pro-Fascist Propaganda on American Neutrality, 1935-1936." *Essays . . . Blakeslee.* See 90.

1529   OFFNER, Arnold A. *American Appeasement: United States Foreign Policy and Germany, 1933-1938.* Cambridge, Mass., 1968.

1530   OFFNER, Arnold A. "William E. Dodd: Romantic Historian and Diplomatic Cassandra." *Historian*, XXIV (1962), 451-469.

1531   PHILLIPS, William. *Ventures.* See 924.

1532   RHODES, Benjamin D. "The Origins of Finnish-American Friendship, 1919-1941." *Mid-Am*, LIV (1972), 3-19.

1533   ST. JOHN, Jacqueline D. "John F. Stevens: American Assistance to Russian and Siberian Railroads." See 1174.

1534   SCHUMAN, Frederick L. *Russia.* See 1176.

1535   SPEAR, Sheldon. "The United States and the Persecution of Jews in Germany, 1933-1939." *Jewish Social Studies*, XXX (1968), 215-242.

1536   SPENCER, Frank. "The United States and Germany in the Aftermath of War." *Int Aff*, XLIII (1967), 693-703. Spans the period 1918-1929.

1537   SZAJKOWSKI, Zosa. "Relief for German Jewry: Problems of American Involvement." *American Jewish Historical Quarterly*, LXII (1972), 111-145. Covers the mid-thirties.

1538   TAYLOR, F. Jay. *The United States and the Spanish Civil War, 1936-1939.* New York. 1956.

1539   TRAINA, Richard P. *American Diplomacy and the Spanish Civil War.* Bloomington, Ind., 1968.

1540   TREFOUSSE, Hans L. "Failure of German Intelligence in the United States, 1935-1945." *Miss Val Hist Rev*, XLII (1955), 84-100.

1541   ULLMAN, Richard H. "The Davies Mission and United States-Soviet Relations, 1937-1941." *Wor Pol*, IX (1957), 220-239.

1542   VALAIK, J. David. "Catholics, Neutrality, and the Spanish Embargo, 1937-1939." *J Am Hist*, LIV (1967), 73-85.

1543   VALAIK, J. David. "In the Days Before Ecumenism: American Catholics, Anti-Semitism, and the Spanish Civil War." *Journal of Church & State*, XIII (1971), 465-477.

1544   VAN EVEREN, Brooks. "Franklin D. Roosevelt and the German Problem 1914-1945." Doctoral dissertation, University of Colorado, 1970.

1545   WELTER, Barbara Ann. "The United States and Weimar Germany, 1919-1929." Doctoral dissertation, University of Wisconsin, 1960.

1546   WILLIAMS, William A. "A Note on American Foreign Policy in Europe in the Nineteen Twenties." *Sci Soc*, XXII (1958), 1-20.

1547   WILSON, Hugh R., Jr. *For Want of a Nail: The Failure of the League of Nations in Ethiopia.* New York, 1959.

1548   WITTGENS, Herman Joseph. "The German Foreign Office Campaign Against the Versailles Treaty: An Examination of the Activities of the *Kriegsschuldreferat* in the United States." Doctoral dissertation, University of Washington, 1970.

1549   WYMAN, David S. *Paper Walls: America and the Refugee Crisis, 1938-1941.* Amherst, Mass., 1968.

6. Relations with the Middle East and Africa

1550   BRYSON, Thomas A. "The Armenia-America Society." See 1199.

1551   DANIEL, Robert L. "American-Turkish Relations." See 1201.

1552   EVANS, Laurence. *Turkey.* See 1202.

1553   MCKINLEY, Edward Harvey. "American Relations with Tropical Africa." See 1207.

1554   NORRIS, Parthenia Emily. "United States and Liberia: The Slavery Crisis, 1929-1935." Doctoral dissertation, Indiana University, 1961.

1555   TRASK, Roger R. "Joseph C. Grew and Turco-American Rapprochement 1927-1932." *Studies on Asia*, VIII (1967), 139-170.

1556   TRASK, Roger R. "The 'Terrible Turk' and Turkish-American Relations in the Interwar Years." *Historian*, XXXIII (1970), 40-53.

1557   TRASK, Roger R. *United States Response to Turkish Nationalism.* See 181.

1558   TRASK, Roger R. "The United States and Turkish Nationalism: Investments and Technical Aid During the Ataturk Era." *Bus Hist Rev*, XXXVIII (1964), 58-77.

1559   WEISBORD, Robert G. "Black America and the Italian-Ethiopian Crisis: An Episode in Pan-Negroism." *Historian*, XXXIV (1972), 230-241.

7. Relations with Asia and the Pacific

1560   BALLANTINE, Joseph W. "Mukden to Pearl Harbor: The Foreign Policies of Japan." *For Aff*, XXVII (1949), 651-664.

1561   BASSETT, Reginald. *Democracy and Foreign Policy, a Case History: The Sino-Japanese Dispute, 1931-1933.* New York, 1952.

1562   BORG, Dorothy. *American Policy and the Chinese Revolution, 1925-1928*. New York, 1947.

1563   BORG, Dorothy. "Notes on Roosevelt's 'Quarantine' Speech." *Pol Sci Q*, LXXII (1957), 405-433.

1564   BORG, Dorothy. *The United States and the Far Eastern Crisis of 1933-1938*. Cambridge, Mass., 1964.

1565   BORG, Dorothy, and Shumpei OKAMOTO, eds. *Pearl Harbor as History: Japanese-American Relations 1931-1941*. New York, 1973. Essays by specialists.

1566   BRAISTED, William R. "China, the United States Navy, and the Bethlehem Steel Company." See 689.

1567   BUHITE, Russell D. "Nelson Johnson and American Policy Toward China, 1925-1928." *Pac Hist Rev*, XXXV (1966), 451-465.

1568   BUHITE, Russell D. *Nelson T. Johnson and American Policy Toward China, 1925-1941*. East Lansing, Mich., 1968.

1569   BURKE, Robert Louis. "Franklin D. Roosevelt and the Far East: 1913-1941." Doctoral dissertation, Michigan State University, 1969.

1570   CLAUSS, Errol MacGregor. "The Roosevelt Administration and Manchukuo, 1933-1941." *Historian*, XXXII (1970), 595-611.

1571   CLYDE, Paul H. "The Diplomacy of 'Playing No Favorites': Secretary Stimson and Manchuria, 1931." *Miss Val Hist Rev*, XXXV (1948), 187-202.

1572   COHEN, Warren I. "The Development of Chinese Communist Policy Toward the United States, 1922-1933." *Orbis*, XI (1967), 219-237.

1573   COHEN, Warren I. "The Development of Chinese Communist Policy Toward the United States, 1934-1945." *Orbis*, XI (1967), 551-569.

1574   CURRENT, Richard N. "The Stimson Doctrine and the Hoover Doctrine." *Am Hist Rev*, LIX (1954), 513-542.

1575   DAVIS, Clarence Baldwin. "Defensive Diplomacy . . . Japan and the United States." See 1220.

1576   ESTHUS, Raymond A. *From Enmity to Alliance: U.S.-Australian Relations, 1931-1941*. Seattle, 1964.

1577   FERRELL, Robert H. "The Mukden Incident: September 18-19, 1931." *J Mod Hist*, XXVII (1955), 66-72.

1578   FIFIELD, Russell H. "Secretary Hughes and the Shantung Question." *Pac Hist Rev*, XXIII (1954), 373-385.

1579   FITHIAN, Floyd James. "Dollars Without the Flag." See 1697.

1580   FRIEND, Theodore. *Between Two Empires: The Ordeal of the Philippines, 1929-1946*. New Haven, Conn., 1965.

1581   GREW, Joseph C. *Ten Years in Japan*. New York, 1944.

1582   GREW, Joseph C. *Turbulent Era*. See 466.

1583   HAIGHT, John M., Jr. "Franklin D. Roosevelt and a Naval Quarantine of Japan." *Pac Hist Rev*, XL (1971), 203-226.

1584   HECHT, Robert A. "Britain and America Face Japan, 1931-1933: A Study of Anglo-American Far Eastern Diplomacy During the Manchurian and Shanghai Crises." Doctoral dissertation, C.U.N.Y., 1970.

1585   HEINRICHS, Waldo H., Jr. *Grew*. See 470.

1586   HOLLINGSWORTH, James Lewis. "William R. Castle and Japanese-American Relations 1929-1933." Doctoral dissertation, Texas Christian University, 1971. Castle was adviser to President Hoover.

1587   HOYT, Frederick Bernard. "Americans in China and the Formation of American Policy, 1925-1937." Doctoral dissertation, University of Wisconsin, 1971.

1588   IRIYE, Akira. *After Imperialism: The Search for a New Order in the Far East, 1921-1931*. Cambridge, Mass., 1965.

1589   KOGINOS, Manny T. *The Panay Incident: Prelude to War*. Lafayette, Ind., 1967.

1590   LIBBY, Justin Harris. "The Irresolute Years: American Congressional Opinion Towards Japan, 1937-1941." Doctoral dissertation, Michigan State University, 1971.

1591   MCCARTY, Kenneth Graham, Jr. "Stanley K. Hornbeck and the Far East, 1931-1941." Doctoral dissertation, Duke University, 1970.

1592   MCCARTY, Kenneth G. "Stanley K. Hornbeck and the Manchurian Crisis." *Southern Quarterly*, X (1972), 305-324.

1593   MASLAND, John W. "Commercial Influences upon American Far Eastern Policy, 1937-1941." *Pac Hist Rev*, XI (1942), 281-299.

1594   MASLAND, John W. "Missionary Influence upon American Far Eastern Policy." *Pac Hist Rev*, X (1941), 279-296.

1595   NEUMANN, William L. "Franklin D. Roosevelt and Japan, 1913-1933." *Pac Hist Rev*, XXII (1953), 143-153.

1596   PAUL, Rodman W. *The Abrogation of the Gentleman's Agreement*. Cambridge, Mass., 1936.

1597   PERKINS, Ernest R. "The Non-Application of Sanctions Against Japan, 1931-1932." *Essays . . . Blakeslee*. See 90.

1598   PERRY, Hamilton Darby. *The Panay Incident: Prelude to Pearl Harbor*. New York, 1969.

1599   RAPPAPORT, Armin. *Henry L. Stimson and Japan, 1931-1933*. Chicago, 1963.

1600   SHEWMAKER, Kenneth E. *Americans and Chinese Communists, 1927-1945: A Persuading Encounter*. Ithaca, N.Y., 1971.

1601   SMITH, Sara R. *The Manchurian Crisis, 1931-1932: A Tragedy in International Relations*. New York, 1948.

1602 STERNSHER, Bernard. "The Stimson Doctrine: F.D.R. *versus* Moley and Tugwell." *Pac Hist Rev*, XXXI (1962), 281-289.

1603 STIMSON, Henry L. *The Far Eastern Crisis: Recollections and Observations.* New York, 1936.

1604 THOMSON, James C., Jr. *While China Faced West: American Reformers in Nationalist China, 1928-1937.* Cambridge, Mass., 1969.

1605 THORNE, Christopher. *The Limits of Foreign Policy: The West, the League and the Far Eastern Crisis of 1931-1933.* New York, 1973.

1606 TOLAND, John. *The Rising Sun: The Decline and Fall of the Japanese Empire, 1936-1945.* New York, 1970.

1607 TOZER, Warren Wilson. "Response to Nationalism and Disunity: United States Relations with the Chinese Nationalists, 1925-1938." Doctoral dissertation, University of Oregon, 1972.

1608 UTLEY, Jonathan Garrick. "The Department of State and the Far East, 1937-1941: A Study of the Ideas Behind Its Diplomacy." Doctoral dissertation, University of Illinois, 1970.

1609 VARG, Paul A. *The Closing of the Door: Sino-American Relations, 1936-1946.* East Lansing, Mich., 1973.

1610 WEST, Philip. "Yenching University and American-Chinese Relations." See 1241.

1611 WHEELER, Gerald E. "Isolated Japan: Anglo-American Diplomatic Cooperation, 1927-1936." *Pac Hist Rev*, XXX (1961), 165-178.

1612 WHEELER, Gerald E. *Prelude to Pearl Harbor.* See 1443.

1613 WHEELER, Gerald E. "Republican Philippine Policy, 1921-1933." *Pac Hist Rev*, XXVIII (1959), 377-390.

1614 WILLIAMS, William A. "China and Japan: A Challenge and a Choice of the Nineteen Twenties." *Pac Hist Rev*, XXVI (1957), 259-279.

1615 WILLOUGHBY, Westel W. *Foreign Rights and Interests in China.* 2 vols. Baltimore, 1927.

1616 YOUNG, Arthur N. *China and the Helping Hand, 1937-1945.* Cambridge, Mass., 1963. By an American financial adviser to the Chiang government.

8. Relations with Latin America

1617 BALDRIDGE, Donald Carl. "Mexican Petroleum and United States-Mexican Relations." See 1249.

1618 BAYLEN, Joseph O. "Sandino: Death and Aftermath." *Mid-Am*, XXXVI (1954), 116-139. About the Nicaraguan problem.

1619   BRADEN, Spruille. *Diplomats and Demagogues: The Memoirs of Spruille Braden.* New Rochelle, N.Y., 1971. Braden was active in bringing the Chaco War to an end in 1938.

1620   BUSHNELL, David. *Eduardo Santos and the Good Neighbor, 1938-1942.* Gainesville, Fla., 1967. The United States and Colombia.

1621   CHAPMAN, Charles E. "Intervention in Haiti." See 1253.

1622   CLARK, J. Reuben. *Memorandum on the Monroe Doctrine.* Washington, 1930.

1623   COOPER, Donald B. "The Withdrawal of the United States from Haiti, 1928-1934." *J Interam Stud,* V (1963), 83-101.

1624   COOPER, William Grant. "New Light on the Good Neighbor Policy: The United States and Argentina, 1933-1939." Doctoral dissertation, University of Pennsylvania, 1972.

1625   CRONON, E. David. "American Catholics and Mexican Anticlericalism, 1933-1936." *Miss Val Hist Rev,* XLV (1958), 201-230.

1626   CRONON, E. David. "Interpreting the New Good Neighbor Policy: The Cuban Crisis of 1933." *His Am Hist Rev,* XXXIX (1959), 538-567.

1627   CRONON, E. David. *Josephus Daniels in Mexico.* Madison, Wis., 1960.

1628   CURRY, Earl Ray. "The United States and the Dominican Republic, 1924-1933: Dilemma in the Caribbean." Doctoral dissertation, University of Minnesota, 1966.

1629   DANIELS, Josephus. *Shirtsleeves Diplomat.* Chapel Hill, N.C., 1947.

1630   DAVIS, Mollie C. "American Religious and Religiose Reaction to Mexico's Church-State Conflict, 1926-1927: Background to the Morrow Mission." *Journal of Church & State,* XIII (1971), 79-96.

1631   DECONDE, Alexander. *Herbert Hoover's Latin American Policy.* Stanford, Cal., 1951.

1632   DENNY, Harold N. *Dollars for Bullets: The Story of American Rule in Nicaragua.* New York, 1929.

1633   ELLIS, L. Ethan. "Dwight Morrow and the Church-State Controversy in Mexico." *His Am Hist Rev,* XXXVIII (1958), 482-505.

1634   FALKUS, M. E. "United States Economic Policy and the 'Dollar Gap' of the 1920's." *Econ Hist Rev,* XXIV (1971), 599-623.

1635   FERRELL, Robert H. "Repudiation of a Repudiation." *J Am Hist,* LI (1965), 669-673. On the Clark Memorandum and the Roosevelt Corollary.

1636   FRYE, Alton. *Nazi Germany and the American Hemisphere 1933-1941.* New Haven, Conn., 1967.

1637   GAYLOR, Sylvia Katz. "The Abrogation of the Platt Amendment: A Case Study in United States-Cuban Relations, with Special Emphasis on Public Opinion." Doctoral dissertation, New York University, 1971.

1638   GELLMAN, Irwin Frederick. "Good Neighbor Diplomacy and the Rise of Batista, 1933-1945." Doctoral dissertation, Indiana University, 1970.

1639   GELLMAN, Irwin F. "Prelude to Reciprocity: The Abortive United States-Colombian Treaty of 1933." *Historian,* XXXII (1969), 52-68.

1640   GIFFIN, Donald Warren. "The Normal Years: Brazilian-American Relations, 1930-1939." Doctoral dissertation, Vanderbilt University, 1962.

1641   GOLDWERT, Marvin. *The Constabulary in the Dominican Republic and Nicaragua: Progeny and Legacy of United States Intervention.* Gainesville, Fla., 1962.

1642   GREEN, David. *The Containment of Latin America: A History of the Myths and Realities of the Good Neighbor Policy.* Chicago, 1971. F.D.R.'s and Truman's policies.

1643   GRIEB, Kenneth J. "The United States and the Rise of General Maximiliano Hernández Martínez." *J Latin Am Stud,* III (1971), 151-172. Hernández Martínez came to power in El Salvador in 1931.

1644   GRIEB, Kenneth J. "Warren G. Harding and the Dominican Republic: U.S. Withdrawal, 1921-1923." *J Interam Stud,* XI (1969), 425-440.

1645   GUERRANT, Edward O. *Roosevelt's Good Neighbor Policy.* Albuquerque, N. Mex., 1950.

1646   GUGGENHEIM, Harry F. *The United States and Cuba.* New York, 1934. Written by Hoover's ambassador to Cuba.

1647   HAUPTMAN, Laurence Marc. "To the Good Neighbor: A Study of the Senate's Role in American Foreign Policy." Doctoral dissertation, New York University, 1972. Deals with the 1920's.

1648   HINDMAN, Ewell James. "The United States and Alvaro Obregon: Diplomacy by Proxy." Doctoral dissertation, Texas Tech University, 1972. About Mexico.

1649   HORN, James John. "Diplomacy by Ultimatum: Ambassador Sheffield and Mexican-American Relations, 1924-1927." Doctoral dissertation, S.U.N.Y., Buffalo, 1969.

1650   IGNASIAS, C. Dennis. "Propaganda and Public Opinion in Harding's Foreign Affairs: The Case for Mexican Recognition." *Jour Q,* XLVIII (1971), 41-52.

1651   JONES, Chester Lloyd. "Loan Controls in the Caribbean." *His Am Hist Rev,* XIV (1934), 141-162.

1652   JUÁREZ, Joseph Robert. "United States Withdrawal from Santo Domingo." *His Am Hist Rev,* XLII (1962), 152-190.

1653   KAMMAN, William. *A Search for Stability: United States Diplomacy Toward Nicaragua, 1925-1933.* Notre Dame, Ind., 1968.

1654   KANE, Nathaniel Stephen. "Charles Evans Hughes and Mexican-American Relations, 1921-1924." Doctoral dissertation, University of Colorado, 1970.

1655   LANGLEY, Lester D. "Negotiating New Treaties with Panama: 1936." *His Am Hist Rev,* XLVIII (1968), 220-233.

1656   MACAULAY, Neill. *The Sandino Affair*. Chicago, 1967. The U.S. marines in Nicaragua.

1657   MACHADO, Manuel A., Jr. "Aftosa and the Mexican-United States Sanitary Convention of 1928." *Ag Hist*, XXXIX (1965), 240-245.

1658   MACHADO, Manuel A., Jr. "The United States and the De la Huerta Rebellion." *Southwestern Historical Quarterly*, LXXV (1972), 303-324.

1659   MEYER, Lorenzo. *México y Estados Unidos en el Conflicto Petrolero (1917-1942)*. Mexico City, 1968.

1660   MILLSPAUGH, Arthur C. *Haiti*. See 1276.

1661   MINOR, Van Lieu. "A Brief Classified Bibliography Relating to United States Intervention in Nicaragua." *His Am Hist Rev*, XI (1931), 261-277.

1662   MUNRO, Dana G. "The American Withdrawal from Haiti, 1929-1934." *His Am Hist Rev*, XLIX (1969), 1-26.

1663   NEWTON, Wesley Phillips. "Aviation in the Relations of the United States and Latin America, 1916-1929." Doctoral dissertation, University of Alabama, 1964.

1664   NICOLSON, Harold G. *Dwight Morrow*. New York, 1935.

1665   PAGE, A. Nayland. "United States Diplomacy in the Tacna-Arica Dispute, 1884-1929." Doctoral dissertation, University of Oklahoma, 1958.

1666   PARKER, James R., and Terry G. SUMMONS. "The Rise and Fall of the Good Neighbor Policy: The North American View." *Maryland Historian*, I (1970), 31-44. A survey of historical writings.

1667   RANDALL, Stephen James. "Colombia, the United States, and Interamerican Aviation Rivalry, 1927-1940." *J Interam Stud*, XIV (1972), 297-324.

1668   RICE, Sister M. Elizabeth. *The Diplomatic Relations Between the United States and Mexico as Affected by the Struggle for Religious Liberty in Mexico, 1925-1929*. Washington, 1959.

1669   RIPPY, J. Fred *Latin America and the Industrial Age*. 2d ed. New York, 1947.

1670   ROSS, Stanley R. "Dwight Morrow and the Mexican Revolution." *His Am Hist Rev*, XXXVIII (1958), 506-528.

1671   ROTBERG, Robert I. *Haiti*. See 1283.

1672   SCHMIDT, Hans. *The United States Occupation of Haiti*. See 1286.

1673   SEIDEL, Robert N. "American Reformers Abroad." See 1713.

1674   SMITH, Robert Freeman. *The United States and Revolutionary Nationalism in Mexico*. See 1290.

1675   SNYDER, J. Richard. "William S. Culbertson in Chile: Opening the Door to a Good Neighbor, 1928-1933." *Int-Am Econ Aff*, XXVI (1972), No. 1, 81-96.

1675-A STEGMAIER, Harry Ignatius, Jr. "From Confrontation to Cooperation: The United States and Mexico, 1938-1945." Doctoral dissertation, University of Michigan, 1970.

1676   STEWARD, Dick Houston. "In Search of Markets: The New Deal, Latin America, and Reciprocal Trade." Doctoral dissertation, University of Missouri, 1969.

1677   SWEET, Dana Royden. "History of United States-Argentine Commercial Relations, 1918-1933." See 1291.

1677-A SWERCZEK, Ronald Emil. "The Diplomatic Career of Hugh Gibson, 1908-1938." Doctoral dissertation, University of Iowa, 1972. Gibson was ambassador to Brazil, 1933-1938, after numerous earlier assignments. See 1150.

1678   TIERNEY, John H., Jr. "U.S. Intervention in Nicaragua, 1927-1933: Lessons for Today." *Orbis,* XIV (1971), 1012-1028.

1679   TRANI, Eugene P. "Charles Evans Hughes: The First Good Neighbor." *Northwest Ohio Quarterly,* XL (1968), No. 4, 138-152.

1680   TRANI, Eugene P. "The Harding Administration and Recognition of Mexico." *Ohio History,* LXXV (1966), Nos. 2 and 3, 137-148.

1681   TULCHIN, Joseph S. *Policy Toward Latin America.* See 1296.

1682   WILLIAMS, William A. "Latin America: Laboratory of American Foreign Policy in the Nineteen-Twenties." *Int-Am Econ Aff,* XI (1957), No. 2, 3-30.

1683   WINKLER, Max. *Investments of United States Capital in Latin America.* Boston, 1928.

1684   WOOD, Bryce. *The Making of the Good Neighbor Policy.* New York, 1961.

1685   WOOD, Bryce. *The United States and Latin American Wars., 1932-1942.* New York, 1966.

1686   WOODS, Kenneth F. " 'Imperialistic America': A Landmark in the Development of U.S. Policy Toward Latin America." *Int-Am Econ Aff,* XXI (1967), No. 3, 55-72. Discusses the influence of a 1924 magazine article upon U.S. policy.

9. Economic Matters

1687   ALLEN, William R. "Cordell Hull and the Defense of the Trade Agreements Program, 1934-1940." *Isolation and Security.* See 72.

1688   ALLEN, William R. "The International Trade Philosophy of Cordell Hull, 1907-1933." *Am Econ Rev,* XLIII (1953), 101-116.

1689   BECKETT, Grace. *The Reciprocal Trade Agreements Program.* New York, 1941.

1690   BRANDES, Joseph. *Herbert Hoover and Economic Diplomacy: Department of Commerce Policy, 1921-1928.* Pittsburgh, 1962.

1691   COSTIGLIOLA, Frank. "The Other Side of Isolationism: The Establishment of the First World Bank, 1929-1930." *J Am Hist,* LIX (1973), 602-620.

1692   CULBERTSON, William S. *Reciprocity: A National Policy for Foreign Trade*. New York, 1937.

1693   DAWES, Charles G. *A Journal of Reparations*. New York, 1939.

1694   FEIS, Herbert. *1933: Characters in Crisis*. Boston, 1966. About the London economic conference.

1695   FEIS, Herbert. *Diplomacy of the Dollar: First Era, 1919-1932*. Baltimore, 1950.†

1696   FEIS, Herbert. *Seen from E. A*. New York, 1947.†

1697   FITHIAN, Floyd J. "Dollars Without the Flag: The Case of Sinclair and Sakhalin Oil." *Pac Hist Rev*, XXXIX (1970), 205-222.

1698   FURDELL, William J. "Cordell Hull and the London Economic Conference of 1933." Doctoral dissertation, Kent State University, 1970.

1699   GARDNER, Lloyd C. *Economic Aspects of New Deal Diplomacy*. Madison, Wis., 1964.†

1700   HOFFER, Peter C. "American Businessmen and the Japan Trade, 1931-1941: A Case Study of Attitude Formation." *Pac Hist Rev*, XLI (1972), 189-205.

1701   HUGHES, Brady Alexander. "Owen D. Young and American Foreign Policy, 1919-1929." Doctoral dissertation, University of Wisconsin, 1969. Wall Street diplomacy.

1702   ISRAEL, Fred L. "The Fulfillment of Bryan's Dream: Key Pittman and Silver Politics, 1918-1933." *Pac Hist Rev*, XXX (1961), 359-380.

1703   JONES, Joseph Marion. *Tariff Retaliation: Repercussions of the Hawley-Smoot Bill*. Philadelphia, 1934.

1704   KOLKO, Gabriel. "American Business and Germany." See 1522.

1705   LEFFLER, Melvyn. "The Origins of Republican War Debt Policy, 1921-1923: A Case Study in the Applicability of the Open Door Interpretation." *J Am Hist*, LIX (1973), 585-601.

1706   MCHALE, James Michael. "The New Deal and the Origins of Public Lending for Foreign Economic Development, 1933-1945." Doctoral dissertation, University of Wisconsin, 1970.

1707   MEYER, Richard Hemmig. *Bankers' Diplomacy: Monetary Stabilization in the Twenties*. New York, 1970.

1708   MOORE, James Ray. "A History of the World Economic Conference, London, 1933." Doctoral dissertation, S.U.N.Y., Stony Brook, 1972.

1709   MOULTON, Harold G., and Leo PASVOLSKY. *War Debts and World Prosperity*. Washington, 1932.

1710   NICHOLS, Jeannette P. "Roosevelt's Monetary Diplomacy in 1933." *Am Hist Rev*, LVI (1951), 295-317.

1711   PARRINI, Carl P. *Heir to Empire*. See 1304.

1712 RHODES, Benjamin D. "Reassessing 'Uncle Shylock': The United States and the French War Debt, 1917-1929." *J Am Hist*, LV (1969), 787-803.

1713 SEIDEL, Robert N. "American Reformers Abroad: The Kemmerer Missions in South America, 1923-1931." *J Econ Hist*, XXXII (1972), 520-545. Edwin Walter Kemmerer was economic adviser to five Andean countries.

1714 STROMBERG, Roland N. "American Business and the Approach of War, 1935-1941." *J Econ Hist*, XIII (1953), 58-78.

1715 TASCA, Henry J. *The Reciprocal Trade Policy of the United States*. Philadelphia, 1938.

1716 VAN METER, Robert Hardin, Jr. "United States and European Recovery." See 1307.

1717 WEINRICH, William Arthur. "Business and Foreign Affairs: The Roosevelt Defense Program, 1937-1941." Doctoral dissertation, University of Oklahoma, 1971.

1718 WHEELER-BENNETT, J. W. *The Wreck of Reparations*. New York, 1933.

1719 WILSON, Joan Hoff. *American Business and Foreign Policy, 1920-1933*. Lexington, Ky., 1971.

V. The Second World War

1. General

1720 AMBROSE, Stephen E. *Rise to Globalism*. See 49.

1721 BARNES, Harry Elmer, ed. *Perpetual War for Perpetual Peace; A Critical Examination of the Foreign Policy of Franklin Delano Roosevelt and Its Aftermath*. Caldwell, Idaho, 1953.

1722 BATEMAN, Herman E. "Observations on President Roosevelt's Health During World War II." *Miss Val Hist Rev*, XLIII (1956), 82-102.

1723 BLAND, Larry Irvin. "W. Averell Harriman: Businessman and Diplomat, 1891-1945." Doctoral dissertation, University of Wisconsin, 1972.

1724 BLUM, John M. *From the Morgenthau Diaries*. Vol. 2: *Years of Urgency, 1938-1941*. Vol. 3: *Years of War, 1941-1945*. Boston, 1965-1967.

1725 BRUENN, Howard G. "Clinical Notes on the Illness and Death of President Franklin D. Roosevelt." *Annals of Internal Medicine*, LXXII (1970), 579-591. Written by F.D.R.'s physician.

1726 BRYNIARSKI, Joan Lee. "Against the Tide: Senate Opposition to the Internationalist Foreign Policy of Presidents Franklin D. Roosevelt and Harry S. Truman, 1943-1949." Doctoral dissertation, University of Maryland, 1972.

1727 BUCHANAN, A. Russell. *The United States and World War II.* 2 vols. New York, 1964.†

1728 BUCHANAN, A. Russell, ed. *The United States and World War II: Military and Diplomatic Documents.* Columbia, S.C., 1972.†

1729 BURNS, James MacGregor. *Roosevelt: The Soldier of Freedom.* New York, 1970.† F.D.R. as war leader.

1730 CANTRIL, Hadley. *Public Opinion.* See 1322.

1731 CHURCHILL, Winston S. *The Second World War.* 6 vols. Boston, 1948-1953.

1732 CURRENT, Richard N. *Stimson.* See 1328.

1733 DALLEK, Robert. "Franklin Roosevelt as World Leader: A Review Article." *Am Hist Rev,* LXXVI (1971), 1503-1513.

1734 DIVINE, Robert A. *Roosevelt and World War II.* Baltimore, 1969.†

1735 DULLES, Foster Rhea, and Gerald E. RIDINGER. "The Anti-Colonial Policies of Franklin D. Roosevelt." *Pol Sci Q,* LXX (1955), 1-18.

1736 FEIS, Herbert. *Churchill, Roosevelt, Stalin: The War They Waged and the Peace They Sought.* Princeton, N.J.,1957.†

1737 FERRELL, Robert H. "The Price of Isolation." See 1343.

1738 FLYNN, George Q. "Franklin Roosevelt and the Vatican: The Myron Taylor Appointment." *Cath Hist Rev,* LVIII (1972), 171-194. The appointment was made in December 1939.

1739 GADDIS, John Lewis. *The United States and the Origins of the Cold War.* See 2045.

1740 GARDNER, Lloyd C. *Architects of Illusion; Men and Ideas in American Foreign Policy, 1941-1949.* Chicago, 1970.†

1741 GRAFF, Frank Warren. "Strategy of Involvement . . . Sumner Welles." See 1347.

1742 GREW, Joseph C. *Turbulent Era.* See 466.

1743 HEINRICHS, Waldo H., Jr. *Grew.* See 470.

1744 HOOKER, Nancy. *Moffat Papers.* See 1352.

1745 HULL, Cordell. *Memoirs.* See 1354.

1746 ISRAEL, Fred L., ed. *The War Diary of Breckinridge Long.* Lincoln, Neb., 1966. The diary of an Assistant Secretary of State.

1747 KENNAN, George F. *Memoirs.* See 2163.

1748 LEAHY, William D. *I Was There.* New York, 1950.

1749   LINDBERGH, Charles A. *The Wartime Journals of Charles A. Lindbergh.* New York, 1970.

1750   MACARTHUR, Douglas. *Reminiscences.* New York, 1964.

1751   MCNEAL, Robert H. "Roosevelt Through Stalin's Spectacles." *Int Jour,* XVIII (1963), 194-206.

1752   MORISON, Elting E. *Stimson.* See 1372.

1753   MORTON, Louis. "Sources for the History of World War II." *Wor Pol,* XIII (1961), 435-453.

1754   MURPHY, Robert. *Diplomat Among Warriors.* Garden City, N.Y., 1964.†

1755   NEUMANN, William L. "Allied Diplomacy in World War II: A Bibliographical Survey." *U S Naval Institute Proceedings,* LXXXI (1955), 829-834.

1756   PHILIPOSE, Thomas. "The 'Loyal Opposition': Republican Leaders and Foreign Policy, 1943-1946." Doctoral dissertation, University of Denver, 1972.

1757   PHILLIPS, William. *Ventures.* See 490.

1758   PRATT, Julius W. *Hull.* See 1383.

1759   RANGE, Willard. *Franklin D. Roosevelt's World Order.* Athens, Ga., 1959.

1760   RENOUVIN, Pierre. *World War II and Its Origins: International Relations, 1929-1945.* New York, 1969.

1761   ROOSEVELT, Elliott. *Personal Letters.* See 1387.

1762   RUETTEN, Richard T. "Harry Elmer Barnes and the 'Historical' Blackout." *Historian,* XXXIII (1971), 202-214. World War II historiographical controversy.

1763   SCHAPSMEIER, Edward L., and Frederick H. SCHAPSMEIER. *Prophet in Politics: Henry A. Wallace and the War Years, 1940-1965.* Ames, Iowa, 1971.

1764   SHERWOOD, Robert. *Roosevelt and Hopkins: An Intimate History.* New York, 1948.†

1765   SMITH, Gaddis. *American Diplomacy During the Second World War.* New York, 1965.†

1766   SMITH, R. Harris. *OSS: The Secret History of America's First Central Intelligence Agency.* Berkeley, Cal., 1972.

1767   SMITH, Robert Freeman. "American Foreign Relations 1920-1942." See 1392.

1768   SNELL, John L. *Illusion and Necessity: The Diplomacy of Global War, 1939-1945.* Boston, 1963.†

1769   STIMSON, Henry L., and McGeorge BUNDY. *On Active Service.* See 1393.

1770   TOMPKINS, C. David. *Senator Arthur H. Vandenberg: The Evolution of a Modern Republican, 1884-1945.* Lansing, Mich., 1970.

1771   TRASK, David F. "Consultation Among Allies." See 1043.

1772   VAN EVEREN, Brooks. "FDR and the German Problem." See 1544.

1773   WEDEMEYER, Albert C. *Wedemeyer Reports.* New York, 1958.

1774   WELLES, Sumner. *Seven Decisions That Shaped History.* New York, 1951.

1775   WELLES, Sumner. *The Time for Decision.* New York, 1944.

1776   WESTERFIELD, H. Bradford. *Foreign Policy and Party Politics from Pearl Harbor to Korea.* New Haven, Conn., 1955.

1777   WHITNEY, Courtney. *MacArthur: His Rendezvous with History.* New York, 1956.

1778   WILLOUGHBY, C. A., and John R. CHAMBERLAIN. *MacArthur, 1941-1951.* New York, 1954.

1779   WOODWARD, Sir Llewellyn. *British Foreign Policy in the Second World War.* London, 1962.

1780   WRIGHT, Gordon. *The Ordeal of Total War, 1939-1945.* New York, 1969.†

1781   YOUNG, Lowell Thomas. "Franklin D. Roosevelt and Imperialism." Doctoral dissertation, University of Virginia, 1970.

2. From Nominal Neutrality to the Pearl Harbor Attack

1782   ADAMS, Frederick C. "The Road to Pearl Harbor: A Reexamination of American Far Eastern Policy, July 1937-December 1938." *J Am Hist,* LVIII (1971), 73-92.

1783   ADLER, Selig. *Uncertain Giant.* See 1309.

1784   BAKER, Leonard. *Roosevelt and Pearl Harbor: A Great President in a Time of Crisis.* New York, 1970.

1785   BEATTY, David Pierce. "The Canada-United States Permanent Joint Board on Defense." Doctoral dissertation, Michigan State University, 1969. The board was created in 1940.

1786   BJERK, Roger C. W. "Kennedy at the Court of St. James: The Diplomatic Career of Joseph P. Kennedy, 1938-1940." Doctoral dissertation, Washington State University, 1971.

1787   BLACK, Henry Wendell. "William C. Bullitt." See 1482.

1788   BORG, Dorothy, and Shumpei OKAMOTO. *Pearl Harbor as History.* See 1565.

1789   BOSWELL, George Timothy. "Buddha Bill . . . Bullitt." See 1484.

1790   BOYLE, John H. "The Drought-Walsh Mission to Japan." *Pac Hist Rev,* XXXIV (1965), 141-161.

1791   BULLITT, Orville H. *For the President—Personal and Secret*. See 1491.

1792   BURKE, Robert Louis. "F.D.R. and the Far East." See 1569.

1793   BUTOW, R. J. C. "Backdoor Diplomacy in the Pacific: The Proposal for a Konoye-Roosevelt Meeting, 1941." *J Am Hist*, LIX (1972), 48-72.

1794   BUTOW, R. J. C. "The Hull-Nomura Conversations: A Fundamental Misconception." *Am Hist Rev*, LXV (1960), 822-836.

1795   BUTOW, R. J. C. *Tojo and the Coming of the War*. Princeton, N. J., 1961.

1796   CHADWIN, Mark Lincoln. *The Hawks of World War II*. Chapel Hill, N.C., 1968. About ardent interventionists.

1797   COLE, Wayne S. *America First: The Battle Against Intervention, 1940-1941*. Madison, Wis., 1953.

1798   COLE, Wayne S. "America First and the South, 1940-1941." *J S Hist*, XXII (1956), 36-47.

1799   COLE, Wayne S. "American Entry into World War II: A Historiographical Appraisal." *Miss Val Hist Rev*, XLIII (1957), 595-617.

1800   COMPTON, James V. *The Swastika and the Eagle: Hitler, the United States, and the Origins of World War II*. Boston, 1967.

1801   CONROY, Hilary. "The Strange Diplomacy of Admiral Nomura." *Proc Am Phil Soc*, CXIV (1970), 205-216. The eve of Pearl Harbor.

1802   CULBERT, David Holbrook. "Tantalus' Dilemma: Public Opinion, Six Radio Commentators, and Foreign Affairs, 1935-1941." Doctoral dissertation, Northwestern University, 1970.

1803   CURRENT, Richard N. "How Stimson Meant to 'Maneuver' the Japanese." *Miss Val Hist Rev*, XL (1953), 67-74.

1804   DAVIS, Forrest, and Ernest K. LINDLEY. *How War Came: An American White Paper from the Fall of France to Pearl Harbor*. New York, 1942.

1805   DAWSON, Raymond H. *The Decision to Aid Russia, 1941: Foreign and Domestic Politics*. Chapel Hill, N.C., 1959,

1806   DEWITT, Howard Arthur. "Hiram W. Johnson." See 899.

1807   DIVINE, Robert A. *The Reluctant Belligerent: American Entry into World War II*. New York, 1965.†

1808   DRUMMOND, Dwight F. *The Passing of American Neutrality, 1937-1941*. Ann Arbor, Mich., 1955.

1809   ESTHUS, Raymond A. "President Roosevelt's Commitment to Britain to Intervene in a Pacific War." *Miss Val Hist Rev*, L (1963), 28-38.

1810   ESTHUS, Raymond A. *U.S.-Australian Relations*. See 1576.

1811   FARAGO, Ladislas. *The Broken Seal: "Operation Magic" and the Secret Road to Pearl Harbor*. New York, 1967.

1812   FEHRENBACH, T. R. *F.D.R.'s Undeclared War, 1939 to 1941*. New York, 1967.

1813   FEIS, Herbert. *The Road to Pearl Harbor*. Princeton, N.J., 1950.†

1814   FEIS, Herbert. "War Came at Pearl Harbor: Suspicions Reconsidered." *Yale Review*, LXV (1956), 378-390.

1815   FERRELL, Robert H. "Pearl Harbor and the Revisionists." *Historian*, XVII (1955), 215-233.

1816   FRIEDLANDER, Saul. *Prelude to Downfall: Hitler and the United States, 1939-1941*. Trans. Aline B. and Alexander Werth. New York, 1967.

1817   FRIEDMAN, Donald J. *The Road from Isolation: The Campaign of the American Committee for Non-Participation in Japanese Aggression, 1938-1941*. Cambridge, Mass., 1968.

1818   GOODHART, Philip. *Fifty Ships That Saved the World: The Foundation of the Anglo-American Alliance*. Garden City, N.Y., 1965. About the destroyer-bases deal.

1819   GOTTLIEB, Moshe. "In the Shadow of War: The American Anti-Nazi Boycott Movement in 1939-1941." *American Jewish Historical Quarterly*, LXII (1972), 146-161.

1820   HAIGHT, John M., Jr. *American Aid to France, 1938-1940*. New York, 1970.

1820-A HERRING, George C., Jr. *Aid to Russia, 1941-1946: Strategy, Diplomacy, and the Origins of the Cold War*. New York, 1973.

1821   HERWIG, Holger H. "Prelude to *Weltblitzkrieg*: Germany's Naval Policy Toward the United States of America, 1939-1941." *J Mod Hist*, 43 (1971), 649-668.

1822   HERZOG, James H. "Influence of the United States Navy in the Embargo of Oil to Japan, 1940-1941." *Pac Hist Rev*, XXXV (1966), 317-328.

1823   HILTON, Stanley E. "The Welles Mission to Europe, February-March 1940: Illusion or Realism?" *J Am Hist*, LVIII (1971), 93-120.

1824   HOLBROOK, Francis Xavier. "United States Defense." See 1422.

1825   HSU, Immanuel C. Y. "Kurusu's Mission to the United States and the Abortive Modus Vivendi." *J Mod Hist*, XXIV (1952), 301-307.

1826   IKE, Nobutaka, trans. and ed. *Japan's Decision for War: Records of the 1941 Policy Conferences*. Stanford, Cal., 1967.

1826-A JOHNSON, Niel M. *Viereck*. See 1154.

1827   JONAS, Manfred. *Isolationism*. See 1360.

1827-A JONAS, Manfred. "Pro-Axis Sentiment and American Isolationism." *Historian*, XXIX (1967), 221-237.

1828   JONES, Alfred Haworth. "The Making of an Interventionist on the Air: Elmer Davis and CBS News, 1939-1941." *Pac Hist Rev*, XLII (1973), 74-93.

1829   JONES, Robert H. *The Roads to Russia: United States Lend-Lease to the Soviet Union*. Norman, Okla., 1969.

1830 KEMP, Arthur. "Summit Conferences During World War II as Instruments of American Diplomacy." *Issues and Conflicts*. See 50.

1831 KIMBALL, Warren F. " 'Beggar My Neighbor': America and the British Interim Finance Crisis, 1940-1941." *J Econ Hist*, XXIX (1969), 758-772.

1832 KIMBALL, Warren F. "Dieckhoff and America." See 1520.

1833 KIMBALL, Warren F. "Lend-Lease and the Open Door: The Temptation of British Opulence, 1937-1942." *Pol Sci Q*, LXXVI (1971), 232-259.

1834 KIMBALL, Warren F. *The Most Unsordid Act: Lend-Lease, 1939-1941*. Baltimore, 1969.

1835 KIPPHAN, Klaus. *Deutsche Propaganda*. See 1521.

1836 LANE, Peter Barry. "The United States and the Balkan Crisis of 1940-1941." Doctoral dissertation, University of Washington, 1972.

1837 LANGER, William L., and S. Everett GLEASON. *Challenge to Isolation*. See 1364.

1838 LANGER, William L., and S. Everett GLEASON. *The Undeclared War, 1940-1941*. New York, 1953.

1839 LEUTZE, James Richard. "If Britain Should Fall: Roosevelt and Churchill." See 1471.

1840 LEUTZE, James, ed. *The London Journal of General Raymond E. Lee 1940-1941*. Boston, 1971. Lee was military attaché at the U.S. embassy.

1841 LIBBY, Justin Harris. "Irresolute Years: American Congressional Opinion Towards Japan." See 1590.

1842 LU, David J. *From the Marco Polo Bridge to Pearl Harbor: Japan's Entry into World War II*. Washington, 1961.

1843 MCCARTY, Kenneth Graham, Jr. "Stanley K. Hornbeck and the Far East." See 1591.

1844 McCOY, Donald R. "Republican Opposition During War-time, 1941-1945." *Mid-Am*, XLIX (1967), 174-189.

1845 MADDUX, Thomas Roth. "American Relations with the Soviet Union." See 1525.

1846 MASLAND, John W. "Commercial Influences upon American Far Eastern Policy." See 1593.

1847 MASLAND, John W. "Missionary Influence upon American Far Eastern Policy." See 1594.

1848 MAY, Ernest R. *American Intervention: 1917 and 1941*. Washington, 1960. Bibliographical pamphlet.

1849 MAY, Ernest R. "Nazi Germany and the United States: A Review Essay." *J Mod Hist*, XLI (1969), 207-214.

1850 MILLSAP, Mary Ruth. "Mussolini and the United States." See 1527.

1851 MORTON, Louis. "The Japanese Decision for War." *U S Naval Institute Proceedings*, LXXX (1954), 1325-1335.

1852 MORTON, Louis. "Pearl Harbor in Perspective: A Bibliographical Survey." *U S Naval Institute Proceedings*, LXXXI (1955), 461-468.

1853 NEUMANN, William L. "How American Policy Toward Japan Contributed to War in the Pacific." *Perpetual War*. See 1721.

1854 ØRVIK, Nils. *Neutrality*. See 989.

1855 POGUE, Forrest C. *George C. Marshall: Ordeal and Hope, 1939-1942*. New York, 1966.

1856 POTTER, John Dean. *Yamamoto: The Man Who Menaced America*. New York, 1965. About the Pearl Harbor attack plan.

1857 RUSSETT, Bruce M. *No Clear and Present Danger: A Skeptical View of the United States Entry into World War II*. New York, 1972.†

1858 RYANT, Carl G. "From Isolation to Intervention: The *Saturday Evening Post*, 1939-42." *Jour Q*, XLVIII (1971), 679-687.

1859 SCHROEDER, Paul W. *The Axis Alliance and Japanese-American Relations, 1941*. Ithaca, N.Y., 1958.

1860 SCHWARTZ, Andrew J. *America and the Russo-Finnish War*. Washington, 1960.

1861 SMITH, Geoffrey S. *To Save a Nation; American Counter-Subversives, the New Deal, and the Coming of World War II*. New York, 1973. Focuses on eccentric isolationists.

1862 SOBEL, Robert. *The Origins of Interventionism: The United States and the Russo-Finnish War*. New York, 1960.

1863 STEELE, Richard W. "Political Aspects of American Military Planning, 1941-1942." *Mil Aff*, XXXV (1971), 68-74.

1864 STROMBERG, Roland N. "American Business and the Approach of War." See 1714.

1865 TREFOUSSE, Hans L. *Germany and American Neutrality, 1939-1941*. New York, 1951.

1866 TREFOUSSE, Hans L. "Germany and Pearl Harbor." *Far Eastern Quarterly*, XI (1951), 35-50.

1867 TUTTLE, William M., Jr. "Aid-to-the-Allies Short-of-War Versus American Intervention, 1940: A Reappraisal of William Allen White's Leadership." *J Am Hist*, LVI (1970), 840-858.

1868 United States Congress (79th Congress, 2d session). *Report of the Joint Committee on the Investigation of the Pearl Harbor Attack: Including the Minority Report*. Doc. 244. Washington, 1946. Reprint, New York, 1972.

1869 UTLEY, Jonathan Garrick. "Department of State and the Far East." See 1608.

1870   WALKER, Samuel. "Communists and Isolationism: The American Peace Mobilization, 1940-1941." *Maryland Historian*, IV (1973), 1-12.

1871   WARD, Robert E. "The Inside Story of the Pearl Harbor Plan." *U S Naval Institute Proceedings*, LXXVII (1951), 1270-1283.

1872   WATSON, Mark S. *Chief of Staff: Prewar Plans and Preparations*. Washington, 1950. The Army's official history.

1873   WEINBERG, Gerhard L. "Hitler's Image of the United States." *Am Hist Rev*, LXIX (1964), 1006-1021.

1874   WILSON, Theodore A. *The First Summit: Roosevelt and Churchill at Placentia Bay 1941*. Boston, 1941.

1875   WOHLSTETTER, Roberta. *Pearl Harbor: Warning and Decision*. Stanford, Cal., 1962.†

1876   WYMAN, David S. *Paper Walls: America and the Refugee Crisis*. See 1549.

3. Coalition War-Making

Overall Strategy

1876-A ARMSTRONG, Anne. *Unconditional Surrender: The Impact of the Casablanca Policy upon World War II*. New Brunswick, N.J., 1961.

1877   BALDWIN, Hanson W. *Great Mistakes of the War*. New York, 1950.

1878   CRAVEN, Wesley F., and James L. CATE, eds. *The Army Air Forces in World War II*. 7 vols. Washington, 1948-1958.

1879   EMERSON, William. "Franklin D. Roosevelt as Commander-in-Chief in World War II." *Mil Aff*, XXII (1958), 181-207.

1880   GREENFIELD, Kent Roberts. *American Strategy in World War II: A Reconsideration*. Baltimore, 1970.†

1881   GREENFIELD, Kent Roberts, ed. *Command Decisions*. New York, 1959.

1882   KECSKEMETI, Paul. *Strategic Surrender: The Politics of Victory and Defeat*. Stanford, Cal., 1958.†

1883   KOLKO, Gabriel. *The Politics of War: The World and United States Foreign Policy, 1943-1945*. New York, 1968.†

1884   MCNEILL, William Hardy. *America, Britain and Russia: Their Cooperation and Conflict, 1941-1946*. New ed. New York, 1970.†

1885   MASTNY, Vojtech. "Stalin and the Prospects of a Separate Peace in World War II." *Am Hist Rev*, LXXVII (1972), 1365-1388.

1886   MATLOFF, Maurice, and Edwin M. SNELL. *Strategic Planning for Coalition Warfare, 1941-1942*. Washington, 1953.

1887   MATLOFF, Maurice. *Strategic Planning for Coalition Warfare, 1943-1944*. Washington, 1959.

1888   MORISON, Samuel Eliot. *Strategy and Compromise*. Boston, 1958.

1889   MORISON, Samuel Eliot. *The Two-Ocean War*. Boston, 1963. A digest of his fourteen-volume official history of the U.S. Navy in World War II.

1890   O'CONNOR, Raymond G. *Diplomacy for Victory: FDR and Unconditional Surrender*. New York, 1971.

1891   POGUE, Forrest C. *George C. Marshall*. 3 vols. New York, 1963-1973.

1892   SMITH, Gaddis. *American Diplomacy During the Second World War*. See 1765.

The Front in Asia and the Pacific

1893   BUHITE, Russell D. *Patrick J. Hurley and American Foreign Policy*. Ithaca, N.Y., 1973. Hurley was ambassador to China, 1944-1945.

1894   BUHITE, Russell D. *Policy Toward China*. See 1568.

1895   BUTOW, Robert J. C. *Japan's Decision to Surrender*. Stanford, Cal., 1954.†

1896   CALDWELL, Oliver J. *A Secret War: Americans in China, 1944-1945*. Carbondale, Ill., 1972. An account by an "old China hand."

1897   CAMERON, Allan W., ed. *Viet-Nam Crisis: A Documentary History*. Vol. 1: *1940-1956*. Ithaca, N.Y., 1971.

1898   CHENNAULT, Claire Lee. *Way of a Fighter: The Memoirs of Claire Lee Chennault*. Ed. Robert Hotz. New York, 1949. The war in China.

1899   COHEN, Warren I. "American Observers and the Sino-Soviet Friendship Treaty of August, 1945." *Pac Hist Rev*, XXXV (1966), 347-349.

1900   COHEN, Warren I. "Chinese Communist Policy Toward U.S." See 1573.

1901   COLLIER, Basil. *The War in the Far East 1941-1945: A Military History*. New York, 1969.

1902   DRACHMAN, Edward R. *United States Policy Toward Viet-nam, 1940-1945*. Rutherford, N.J., 1970.

1903   DURRENCE, James Larry. "Ambassador Clarence E. Gauss and United States Relations with China, 1941-1944." Doctoral dissertation, University of Georgia, 1971.

1904   FEIS, Herbert. *China Tangle: The American Effort in China from Pearl Harbor to the Marshall Mission*. Princeton, N.J., 1953.†

1905   FETZER, James Alan. "Congress and China, 1941-1950." Doctoral dissertation, Michigan State University, 1969.

1906   FINE, Herbert A. "The Liquidation of World War II in Thailand." *Pac Hist Rev*, XXXIV (1965), 65-82. American influence on the Anglo-Thai peace settlement.

1907   FRIEND, Theodore. *Philippines*. See 1580.

1908   GARLOCK, Peter David. "The United States and the Indian Crisis, 1941-1943: The Limits of Anti-Colonialism." Doctoral dissertation, Yale University, 1972.

1909   HESS, Gary R. *America Encounters India, 1941-1947*. Baltimore, 1971.

1910   HESS, Gary R. "Franklin Roosevelt and Indochina." *J Am Hist*, LIX (1972), 353-368.

1911   HOPE, A. Guy. *America and Swaraj: The U.S. Role in Indian Independence*. Washington, 1968.

1912   JAUHRI, R. C. *American Diplomacy and Independence for India*. Bombay, 1970. Treats the years 1941-1947.

1913   JONES, F. C., *et al. The Far East, 1942-46*. London, 1955.

1914   JONES, F. C. *Japan's New Order in East Asia: Its Rise and Fall, 1937-1945*. London, 1954.

1915   KAWAI, Kazuo. *"Mokusatsu*, Japan's Response to the Potsdam Declaration." *Pac Hist Rev*, XIX (1950), 409-414.

1916   LIANG, Chin-tung. *General Stilwell in China, 1942-1944: The Full Story*. New York, 1972. The first study to draw on the private papers of Chiang Kai-shek.

1917   MAY, Ernest R. "The United States, the Soviet Union, and the Far Eastern War, 1941-1945." *Pac Hist Rev*, XXIV (1955), 153-174.

1918   MILES, Vice Admiral Milton E. *A Different Kind of War*. Garden City, N.Y., 1967. The war in China.

1919   MINEAR, Richard H. *Victors' Justice: The Tokyo War Crimes Trial*. Princeton, N.J., 1971.

1920   MORTON, Louis. "Soviet Intervention in the War with Japan." *For Aff*, XL (1962), 563-662.

1921   MULCH, Barbara E. G. "A Chinese Puzzle: Patrick J. Hurley and the Foreign Service Officer Controversy." Doctoral dissertation, University of Kansas, 1972.

1922   PECK, Jim. "America and the Chinese Revolution, 1942-1946: An Interpretation." *America's Asia: Dissenting Essays on American-East Asian Relations*. Ed. Edward Friedman and Mark Selden. New York, 1971.

1923   REED, John Jay. "American Diplomatic Relations with Australia during the Second World War." Doctoral dissertation, University of Southern California, 1969.

1924   ROMANUS, Charles F., and Riley SUNDERLAND. *The United States Army in World War II: The China-Burma-India Theater*. 3 vols. Washington, 1953-1960.

1925   SERVICE, John S. *The Amerasia Papers: Some Problems in the History of US-China Relations*. Berkeley, Cal., 1971. See 1935.

1926   SHEWMAKER, Kenneth E. *Americans and Chinese Communists*. See 1600.

1927 STILWELL, Joseph W. *The Stilwell Papers*. Ed. Theodore H. White. New York, 1948.†

1928 TOLAND, John. *The Rising Sun*. See 1606.

1929 TOZER, Warren W. "The Foreign Correspondents' Visit to Yenan in 1944: A Reassessment." *Pac Hist Rev*, XLI (1972), 207-224.

1930 TSOU, Tang. "The American Political Tradition and the American Image of Chinese Communism." *Pol Sci Q*, LXXVII (1962), 570-600.

1931 TSOU, Tang. *America's Failure in China 1941-50*. Chicago, 1963.

1932 TUCHMAN, Barbara W. "If Mao Had Come to Washington: An Essay in Alternatives." *For Aff*, 51 (1972-1973), 44-64. Discusses the apparent readiness of Mao to collaborate with the U.S. in 1945.

1933 TUCHMAN, Barbara W. *Stilwell and the American Experience in China, 1911-45*. New York, 1971.†

1934 United States Department of State. *China . . . 1944-1949*. See 2755.

1935 United States Senate (91st Congress, 1st Session), Committee on the Judiciary, Internal Security Subcommittee. *Amerasia Papers: A Clue to the Catastrophe of China*. Intro. by Anthony Kubek. Washington, 1970. Controversial version of U.S.-China relations during the war. See 1925.

1936 VARG, Paul A. *Closing of the Door: Sino-American Relations*. See 1609.

1937 WALTER, Austin Frederic. "Australia's Relations with the United States: 1941-1949." Doctoral dissertation, University of Michigan, 1954.

1938 WHITE, Theodore, and Annalee JACOBS. *Thunder Out of China*. New York, 1946.

1939 YOUNG, Arthur N. *China and the Helping Hand*. See 1616.

The Front in Europe, North Africa, and the Middle East

1940 AMBROSE, Stephen E. *Eisenhower and Berlin, 1945: The Decision to Halt at the Elbe*. New York, 1967.†

1941 AMBROSE, Stephen E. *The Supreme Commander: The War Years of General Dwight D. Eisenhower*. Garden City, N.Y., 1970.

1942 ANGLIN, Douglas G. *The St. Pierre and Miquelon Affair of 1941: A Study of Diplomacy in the North Atlantic Triangle*. Toronto, 1966.

1943 BAILEY, John Albert, Jr. "Lion, Eagle, and Crescent: The Western Allies and Turkey in 1943; A Study of British and American Diplomacy in a Critical Year of the War." Doctoral dissertation, Georgetown University, 1969.

1944 BARRETT, John William. "A Study of British and American Foreign Relations with Spain, 1942-1945." Doctoral dissertation, Georgetown University, 1970.

1945 BEITZELL, Robert. *The Uneasy Alliance: America, Britain, and Russia, 1941-1943*. New York, 1972.

1946   BLAIR, Leon Borden. *Western Window in the Arab World*. Austin, Tex., 1970. U.S.-Moroccan relations, 1942 to the 1960's.

1947   BLAYNEY, Michael Steward. "Diplomat and Humanist: The Diplomatic Career of Herbert Claiborne Pell." Doctoral dissertation, Washington State University, 1973. Pell was minister to Portugal, 1937-1941, and an advocate of the Nuremberg trials.

1948   BOSCH, William J. *Judgment on Nuremberg: American Attitudes Toward the Major German War-Crime Trials*. Chapel Hill, N.C., 1970.

1949   CABLE, John Nathanial. "The United States and the Polish Question, 1939-1948." Doctoral dissertation, Vanderbilt University, 1972.

1950   CALVOCARESSI, Peter. *Nuremberg: The Facts, the Law, and the Consequences*. London, 1947.

1951   CHANDLER, Alfred D., Jr., *et al.*, eds. *The Papers of Dwight David Eisenhower: The War Years*. 5 vols. Baltimore, 1970.

1952   CHASE, John L. "Unconditional Surrender Reconsidered." *Pol Sci Q*, LXX (1955), 258-279.

1953   CLARK, Mark W. *Calculated Risk*. New York, 1950. The general's experiences in North Africa and at the Allied High Commission for Austria.

1954   DAVIDSON, Eugene. "The Nuremberg Trials and One World." *Issues and Conflicts*. See 50.

1955   DEANE, John R. *The Strange Alliance: The Story of Our Efforts at Wartime Cooperation with Russia*. New York, 1947.

1956   DE GAULLE, Charles. *War Memoirs*. 3 vols. New York, 1955-1960.†

1957   DULLES, Allen. *The Secret Surrender*. New York, 1966. The Italian surrender and the Soviet reaction.

1958   EDEN, Anthony. *The Reckoning: The Memoirs of Anthony Eden, Earl of Avon*. Boston, 1965. This volume is for 1939-1945.

1959   EISENHOWER, Dwight D. *Crusade in Europe*. Garden City, N.Y., 1948.†

1960   EUBANKS, Richard Kay. "The Diplomacy of Postponement: The United States and Russia's Western Frontier Claims During World War II." Doctoral dissertation, University of Texas, 1971.

1961   FEINGOLD, Henry L. *The Roosevelt Administration and the Holocaust*. See 1506.

1962   FEIS, Herbert. *The Spanish Story*. New York, 1948. The war's spillover into neutral Spain.

1963   FUNK, Arthur L. *Charles de Gaulle: The Crucial Years, 1943-44*. Norman, Okla., 1959.

1964   GOTTSCHALK, Louis R. "Our Vichy Fumble." *J Mod Hist*, XX (1948), 47-56.

1965   HAMMERSMITH, Jack Leonard. "American Diplomacy and the Polish Question, 1943-1945." Doctoral dissertation, University of Virginia, 1970.

1966 HARRIS, Dennis Earl. "The Diplomacy of the Second Front: America, Britain, Russia and the Normandy Invasion." Doctoral dissertation, University of California, Santa Barbara, 1969.

1967 HAYES, Carlton J. H. *Wartime Mission to Spain, 1942-1945.* New York, 1945. Written by the American ambassador.

1968 HERRING, George C., Jr. *Aid to Russia.* See 1820-A.

1968-A HERRING, George C., Jr. "The United States and British Bankruptcy, 1944-1945: Responsibilities Deferred." *Pol Sci Q,* LXXXVI (1971), 260-280.

1969 HIGGINS, Trumbull. *Winston Churchill and the Second Front, 1940-1943.* New York, 1957.

1970 HUNT, John Joseph. "The United States Occupation of Iceland, 1941-1946." Doctoral dissertation, Georgetown University, 1966.

1971 JONES, Robert H. *The Roads to Russia: United States Lend-Lease to the Soviet Union.* Norman, Okla., 1969.

1972 KERTESZ, Stephen D. *East Central Europe.* See 2559.

1973 KIRK, George E. *The Middle East in the War.* New York, 1953.

1974 KOGAN, Norman. *Italy and the Allies.* Cambridge, Mass., 1956.

1975 LANGER, William L. *Our Vichy Gamble.* New York, 1947.†

1976 LEIGHTON, Richard M. "OVERLORD Revisited: An Interpretation of American Strategy in the European War, 1942-1944." *Am Hist Rev,* LXVIII (1963), 919-937.

1977 LINSENMEYER, William Stuart. "Allied Relations with Italy, 1943-1944." Doctoral dissertation, Vanderbilt University, 1972.

1978 MACMILLAN, Harold. *The Blast of War, 1939-1945.* New York, 1968. A memoir.

1979 MORSE, Arthur D. *While Six Million Died: A Chronicle of American Apathy.* New York, 1968.† Destruction of the Jews.

1980 PETERSON, Neal Henry. "Nor Call Too Loud on Freedom: The Department of State, General de Gaulle, and the Levant Crisis of 1945." Doctoral dissertation, Georgetown University, 1970.

1981 PIERRE, Andrew J. *Nuclear Politics: The British Experience with an Independent Strategic Force, 1939-1970.* New York, 1972. Discusses British-American collaboration.

1982 REBHORN, Marlette D. O. "De Gaulle's Rise to Power: The Failure of American Diplomacy, 1942-1944." Doctoral dissertation, University of Texas, 1971.

1983 ROSTOW, Eugene V. "Wartime Policies Toward Vichy and Franco." *Wor Pol,* I (1949), 381-394.

1984 SADLER, Charles Gill. "The Expendable Frontier: United States Policy on the Polish-German Frontier During the Second World War." Doctoral dissertation, Northwestern University, 1971.

1985   SMITH, Charles. "Lend-Lease to Great Britain 1941-1945." *Southern Quarterly*, X (1972), 195-208.

1986   SNELL, John L. *Wartime Origins of the East-West Dilemma over Germany.* New Orleans, 1959.

1987   STOLER, Mark Alan. "The Politics of the Second Front: American Military Planning and Diplomacy 1941-1944." Doctoral dissertation, University of Wisconsin, 1971.

1988   SWEENEY, J. K. "Portugal, the United States and Aviation, 1945." *Rocky Mtn Soc Sci J*, IX (1972), No. 2, 77-84.

1989   SWEENEY, Jerry K. "United States' Policy Toward Portugal During the Second World War." Doctoral dissertation, Kent State University, 1970.

1990   TREFOUSSE, Hans L. "Failure of German Intelligence." See 1540.

1991   VENKATARAMANI, M. S. *Undercurrents.* See 2233-A.

1992   VIORST, Milton. *Hostile Allies: FDR and Charles de Gaulle.* New York, 1965.

1993   WATSON, Bert Allan. "United States-Spanish Relations 1939-1946." Doctoral dissertation, George Washington University, 1971.

1994   WHITE, Dorothy Shipley. *Seeds of Discord: De Gaulle, Free France and the Allies.* Syracuse, N.Y., 1964.

1995   WILLSON, John Paul. "Carlton J. H. Hayes in Spain, 1942-1945." Doctoral dissertation, Syracuse University, 1969.

1996   WILLSON, John P. "Carlton J. H. Hayes, Spain, and the Refugee Crisis, 1942-1945." *American Jewish Historical Quarterly*, LXII (1972), 99-110.

1997   WILMOT, Chester. *The Struggle for Europe.* New York, 1952.†

1998   WOETZEL, Robert K. *The Nuremberg Trials in International Law.* London, 1960.

1999   ZAWODNY, J. K. *Death in the Forest.* Notre Dame, Ind., 1962. The Katyn massacre.

Yalta

2000   BUHITE, Russell D. "Patrick J. Hurley and the Yalta Far Eastern Agreement." *Pac Hist Rev*, XXXVII (1968), 343-353.

2001   CLEMENS, Diane Shaver. *Yalta: A Study in Soviet-American Relations.* New York, 1970.†

2002   FISCHER, Louis. *The Road to Yalta: Soviet Foreign Relations, 1941-1945.* New York, 1972.

2003   SNELL, John L., *et al. The Meaning of Yalta: Big Three Democracy and the Balance of Power.* Baton Rouge, La., 1956.†

2004   STETTINIUS, Edward R., Jr. *Roosevelt and the Russians: The Yalta Conference.* Ed. Walter Johnson. Garden City, N.Y., 1949.

2005 THEOHARIS, Athan. "James F. Byrnes: Unwitting Yalta Myth-Maker." *Pol Sci Q*, LXXXI (1966), 581-592.

2006 THEOHARIS, Athan. "Roosevelt and Truman on Yalta: The Origins of the Cold War." *Pol Sci Q*, LXXXVII (1972), 210-241.

2007 THEOHARIS, Athan G. *The Yalta Myths: An Issue in U. S. Politics, 1945-1955*. Columbia, Mo., 1970.

2008 WINNACKER, Rudolph A. "Yalta—Another Munich?" *Va Q Rev*, XXIV (1948), 521-537.

2009 XYDIS, Stephen G. "Greece and the Yalta Declaration." *American Slavic and East European Review*, XX (1961), 6-24.

The Atomic Bomb

2010 ALPEROVITZ, Gar. *Atomic Diplomacy: Hiroshima and Potsdam*. New York, 1965.†

2011 BATCHELDER, Robert C. *The Irreversible Decision, 1939-1950*. Boston, 1961.

2012 BURNS, Richard Dean. "Origins of the United States' Arms Inspection Policies." See 1409.

2013 FEIS, Herbert. *The Atomic Bomb and the End of World War II*. Princeton, 1966.† A revision of *Japan Subdued*.

2014 GIOVANNITTI, Len, and Fred FREED. *The Decision to Drop the Bomb*. New York, 1965.

2015 LIEBOW, Averill A. *Encounter with Disaster: A Medical Diary of Hiroshima, 1945*. New York, 1970.

2016 MADDOX, Robert James. "Atomic Diplomacy: A Study in Creative Writing." *J Am Hist*, LIX (1973), 925-934. Discusses Alperovitz's book (see 2010).

2017 MARX, Joseph Laurance. *Nagasaki: The Necessary Bomb?* New York, 1971. Examines Japan's readiness to surrender.

2018 MORTON, Louis. "The Decision to Use the Atomic Bomb." *For Aff*, XXXV (1957), 334-353.

2019 SCHOENBERGER, Walter Smith. *Decision of Destiny*. Athens, Ohio, 1969.

2020 SHERWIN, Martin Jay. "The Atomic Bomb, Scientists and American Diplomacy During the Second World War." Doctoral dissertation, University of California, Los Angeles, 1971.

2021 SHERWIN, Martin J. "The Atomic Bomb and the Origins of the Cold War: U.S. Atomic-Energy Policy and Diplomacy, 1941-45." *Am Hist Rev*, LXXVIII (1973), 945-968.

2022 SMITH, Alice Kimball. *A Peril and a Hope: The Scientists' Movement in America, 1945-1947*. Chicago, 1965.

2023 STIMSON, Henry L. "The Decision to Use the Atomic Bomb." *Harper's*, CLXLIV (1947), 97-107.

2024 YAVENDITTI, Michael John. "American Reactions to the Use of Atomic Bombs on Japan, 1945-1947." Doctoral dissertation, University of California, Berkeley, 1970.

4. Shaping the Future

Plans for the Peace

2025 ADAMS, Meredith B. L. "The Morgenthau Plan: A Study in Bureaucratic Depravity." 2 vols. Doctoral dissertation, University of Texas, 1971.

2026 CAMPBELL, Thomas M. "Nationalism in America's UN Policy, 1944-1945." *Int Organ*, XXVII (1973), 25-44.

2027 CHASE, John L. "The Development of the Morgenthau Plan Through the Quebec Conference." *J Pol*, XVI (1954), 324-359.

2028 DAVIS, Vincent. *Postwar Defense Policy and the U.S. Navy, 1943-1945*. Chapel Hill, N.C., 1966.

2029 DIVINE, Robert A. *Second Chance: The Triumph of Internationalism in America During World War II*. New York, 1967. On planning the U.N.

2030 DORN, Walter L. "The Debate over American Occupation Policy in Germany in 1944-45." *Pol Sci Q*, LXXII (1957), 481-501.

2031 GEORGE, James Herbert, Jr. "United States Postwar Relief Planning; The First Phase, 1940-1943." Doctoral dissertation, University of Wisconsin, 1970.

2032 GORDON, Leonard. "American Planning for Taiwan, 1942-1945." *Pac Hist Rev*, XXXVII (1968), 201-228.

2033 HOLBORN, Hajo. *American Military Government: Its Organization and Policies*. Washington, 1947.

2034 LOWE, Henry Jackson. "The Planning and Negotiation of U.S. Post-War Security, 1942-1943." Doctoral dissertation, University of Virginia, 1972.

2035 MILLER, John Andrew. "Air Diplomacy: The Chicago Civil Aviation Conference of 1944 in Anglo-American Wartime Relations and Post-war Planning." Doctoral dissertation, Yale University, 1971.

2036 NEUMANN, William L. *After Victory: Churchill, Roosevelt, Stalin and the Making of the Peace*. New York, 1967.†

2037 NEUMANN, William L. *Making the Peace, 1941-1945*. Washington, 1950.

2038 PENROSE, Ernest F. *Economic Planning for the Peace*. Princeton, N.J., 1953.

2039 PETROV, Vladimir. *Money and Conquest: Allied Occupation Currencies in World War II*. Baltimore, 1967.

2040 RIGGS, Robert E. "Overselling the UN Charter–Fact and Myth." *Int Organ*, XIV (1960), 277-90.

2041 ROBINS, Dorothy B. *Experiment in Democracy: The Story of U.S. Citizen Organizations in Forging the Charter of the United Nations.* New York, 1971.

2042 SMITH, Perry McCoy. *The Air Force Plans for Peace, 1943-1945.* Baltimore, 1970.

2043 WHEELER-BENNETT, John W., and Anthony NICHOLLS. *A Semblance of Peace: The Political Settlement After World War II.* New York, 1972.

2044 WOODBRIDGE, George. *UNRRA.* See 2331.

Seeds of the Cold War (See also 2246-2265)

2045 GADDIS, John Lewis. *The United States and the Origins of the Cold War, 1941-1947.* New York, 1972.†

2046 HERRING, George C., Jr. *Aid to Russia.* See 1820-A.

2046-A HERRING, George C., Jr. "Lend-Lease to Russia and the Origins of the Cold War, 1944-1945." *J Am Hist*, LVI (1969), 93-114.

2047 IRONS, Peter Hanlon. "America's Cold War Crusade: Domestic Politics and Foreign Policy, 1942-1948." Doctoral dissertation, Boston University, 1973.

2048 LAFEBER, Walter, ed. *The Origins of the Cold War, 1941-1947.* New York, 1971.† Documents and articles.

2049 LEVERING, Ralph Brooks. "Prelude to Cold War: American Attitudes Toward Russia During World War II." Doctoral dissertation, Princeton University, 1971.

2050 PATERSON, Thomas G. "The Abortive American Loan to Russia and the Origins of the Cold War, 1943-1946." *J Am Hist*, LVI (1969), 70-92.

2051 PATERSON, Thomas G. "Potsdam, the Atomic Bomb, and the Cold War: A Discussion with James F. Byrnes." *Pac Hist Rev*, XLI (1972), 225-230. Transcript by Warren Austin, August 1945.

2052 SNELL, John L. *Wartime Origins of the East-West Dilemma.* See 1986.

2053 STAROBIN, Joseph R. "Origins of the Cold War: The Communist Dimension." *For Aff*, 47 (1968-1969), 681-696.

5. Relations with Latin America

2054 BLASIER, Cole. "The United States, Germany, and the Bolivian Revolutionaries (1941-1946)." *His Am Hist Rev*, 52 (1972), 26-54.

2055 BOWERS, Claude G. *Chile Through Embassy Windows, 1939-1953.* New York, 1958.

2056 CLASH, Thomas Wood. "United States-Mexican Relations, 1940-1946: A Study of U.S. Interests and Policies." Doctoral dissertation, S.U.N.Y., Buffalo, 1972.

2057 CONN, Stetson, and Byron FAIRCHILD. *The Framework of Hemispheric Defense.* Washington, 1960. Official army history.

2058 FRYE, Alton. *Nazi Germany and the American Hemisphere.* See 1636.

2059 FURNISS, Edgar S., Jr. "American Wartime Objectives in Latin America." *Wor Pol*, II (1950), 373-389.

2060 GREEN, David. *Containment of Latin America.* See 1642.

2061 HINES, Calvin Warner. "United States Diplomacy in the Caribbean During World War II." Doctoral dissertation, University of Texas, 1968.

2062 HOLT, W. Stull. "The United States and the Defense of the Western Hemisphere, 1815-1940." *Pac Hist Rev*, X (1941), 29-38.

2063 McCAIN, Johnny Mac. "Contract Labor as a Factor in United States-Mexican Relations, 1942-1947." Doctoral dissertation, University of Texas, 1970.

2064 McCANN, Frank D., Jr. "Aviation Diplomacy: The United States and Brazil 1939-1941." *Int-Am Econ Aff*, XXI (1968), No. 4, 35-50.

2065 RUDGERS, David Frank. "Challenge to the Hemisphere: Argentina Confronts the United States, 1938-1947." Doctoral dissertation, George Washington University, 1972.

2066 SCRUGGS, Otey M. "The United States, Mexico, and the Wetbacks, 1942-1947." *Pac Hist Rev*, XXX (1960), 149-164.

2067 SMITH, O. Edmund, Jr. *Yankee Diplomacy: U.S. Intervention in Argentina.* Dallas, Tex., 1953.

2068 STEGMAIER, Harry Ignatius, Jr. "From Confrontation to Cooperation: The United States and Mexico." See 1675-A.

2069 WEATHERS, Bynum Edgar, Jr., "A Study of the Methods Employed in the Acquisition of Air Bases in Latin America for the Army Air Forces in World War II." Doctoral dissertation, University of Denver, 1971.

2070 WOODS, Randall Bennett. "United States' Policy Toward Argentina from Pearl Harbor to San Francisco." Doctoral dissertation, University of Texas, 1972.

6. Economic Questions

2071   BALDWIN, David A. *Economic Development*. See 2286.

2072   BLUM, John Morton. *Morgenthau*. See 1724.

2073   ECKES, Alfred Edward. "Bretton Woods: America's New Deal for an Open World." Doctoral dissertation, University of Texas, 1969.

2074   ECKES, Alfred E., Jr. "Open Door Expansionism Reconsidered: The World War II Experience." *J Am Hist*, LIX (1973), 909-924.

2075   FEIS, Herbert. *Seen from E. A.* See 1696.

2076   GARDNER, Lloyd C. *Economic Aspects*. See 1699.

2077   GARDNER, Richard N. *Sterling-Dollar Diplomacy*. Oxford, 1956.

2078   GUSTAFSON, Milton Odell. "Congress and Foreign Aid: The First Phase, UNRRA, 1943-1947." Doctoral dissertation, University of Nebraska, 1966.

2079   HERRING, George C., Jr. "Lend-Lease to Russia and the Origins of the Cold War." See 2046-A.

2080   HOFFER, Peter C. "American Businessmen and the Japan Trade." See 1700.

2081   MCHALE, James Michael. "The New Deal and . . . Foreign Economic Development." See 1706.

2082   PATERSON, Thomas G. "The Abortive Loan to Russia and the Origins of the Cold War." See 2050.

2083   PENROSE, Ernest F. *Economic Planning*. See 2038.

2084   STETTINIUS, Edward R., Jr. *Lend-Lease: Weapon for Victory*. New York, 1944.

2085   WEINRICH, William Arthur. "Business and Foreign Affairs." See 1717.

2086   YOUNG, Arthur N. *China's Wartime Finance and Inflation, 1937-1945*. Cambridge, Mass., 1965.

VI. The Era of the Cold War: Truman to Johnson

1. General

2087 ACHESON, Dean. *Present at the Creation: My Years in the State Department.* New York, 1969.†

2088 ADAMS, Sherman. *Firsthand Report: The Story of the Eisenhower Administration.* New York, 1961.

2089 ADLER, Les K., and Thomas G. PATERSON. "Red Fascism: The Merger of Nazi Germany and Soviet Russia in the American Image of Totalitarianism, 1930's-1950's." *Am Hist Rev,* LXXV (1970), 1046-1064.

2090 ALMOND, Gabriel A. *The American People and Foreign Policy.* Rev. ed. New York, 1960. Covers the years 1945 through 1960.

2091 ALPEROVITZ, Gar. *Cold War Essays.* Garden City, N.Y., 1970.†

2091-A AMBROSE, Stephen E. *Rise to Globalism.* See 49.

2092 ARMSTRONG, John P. "The Enigma of Senator Taft and American Foreign Policy." *Rev Pol,* XVII (1955), 206-231.

2093 BALL, George. *The Discipline of Power.* New York, 1968.

2094 BARUCH, Bernard M. *Public Years.* See 884.

2095 BEAL, John R. *John Foster Dulles: A Biography.* New York, 1959.

2096 BELL, Philip W. "Colonialism as a Problem in American Foreign Policy." *Wor Pol,* V (1952), 86-109.

2097 BERDING, Andrew H. *Dulles on Diplomacy.* Princeton, N.J., 1965.

2098 BERNSTEIN, Barton J., and Allen J. MATUSOW. *The Truman Administration: A Documentary History.* New York, 1966.†

2099 BOHLEN, Charles. *The Transformation of American Foreign Policy.* New York, 1969.†

2100 BRANDT-PELTIER, Louis. *Conceptions Américaines de Politique Etrangère; Kennan. Dulles.* Paris, 1953.

2101 BRANYAN, Robert L., and Lawrence H. LARSEN, eds. *The Eisenhower Administration 1953-1961: A Documentary History.* 2 vols. New York, 1971.

2102 BRIGGS, Ellis O. *Farewell to Foggy Bottom.* New York, 1964. Critique of American foreign policy.

2103 BROWN, Seyom. *The Faces of Power: Constancy and Change in United States Foreign Policy from Truman to Johnson.* New York, 1968.

2104   BRYNIARSKI, Joan Lee. "Against the Tide: Senate Opposition to Truman." See 1726.

2105   BRZEZINSKI, Zbigniew. "How the Cold War Was Played." *For Aff*, LI (1972-1973), 181-209. Categorizes the years 1947-1972 into periods of relative assertiveness by the U.S. or the U.S.S.R.

2106   BUNDY, McGeorge, comp. *The Pattern of Responsibility*. Boston, 1952. A collection of Dean Acheson's speeches.

2107   BYRNES, James F. *All in One Lifetime*. New York, 1958.

2108   BYRNES, James F. *Speaking Frankly*. New York, 1947.

2109   CARLETON, William G. *The Revolution in American Foreign Policy: Its Global Range*. New York, 1963.

2110   COCHRAN, Bert. *Harry Truman and the Crisis Presidency*. New York, 1973.

2111   COHEN, Bernard C. *Political Process*. See 2725.

2112   COHEN, Bernard C. *The Press and Foreign Policy*. Princeton, N.J., 1963.†

2113   CONNALLY, Tom (as told to Alfred Steinberg). *My Name Is Tom Connally*. New York, 1954. Connally was a member of the Senate Foreign Relations Committee.

2114   CRABB, Cecil V., Jr. "American Diplomatic Tactics and Neutralism." *Pol Sci Q*, LXXVIII (1964), 418-443.

2115   CRABB, Cecil V., Jr. *Bipartisan Foreign Policy: Myth or Reality?* Evanston, Ill., 1957.

2116   DEATON, Dorsey Milam. "The Protestant Crisis: Truman's Vatican Ambassador Controversy of 1951." Doctoral dissertation, Emory University, 1970.

2117   DIVINE, Robert A. "The Cold War and the Election of 1948." *J Am Hist*, LIX (1972-1973), 90-110.

2118   DONOVAN, Robert J. *Eisenhower: The Inside Story*. New York, 1956.

2119   DRUMMOND, Roscoe, and Gaston COBLENTZ. *Duel at the Brink: John Foster Dulles' Command of American Power*. Garden City, N.Y., 1960.

2120   DULLES, John Foster. *War or Peace*. New York, 1950.

2121   EISENHOWER, Dwight D. *The White House Years*. 2 vols. Garden City, N.Y., 1963.

2122   ELDER, Robert E. *The Policy Machine: The Department of State and American Foreign Policy*. Syracuse, N.Y., 1960.

2123   EVANS, Rowland, and Robert NOVAK. *Lyndon B. Johnson: The Exercise of Power*. New York, 1966.

2124   FAIRLIE, Henry. *The Kennedy Promise: The Politics of Expectation*. New York, 1973.

2125 FARNSWORTH, David N. *The Senate Committee on Foreign Relations.* Urbana, Ill., 1961.

2126 FERRELL, Robert H. *George C. Marshall.* New York, 1966. *Secretaries of State.* Vol. 15. See 79.

2127 FITZSIMONS, Louise. *The Kennedy Doctrine.* New York, 1972.

2128 FONTAINE, André. *A History of the Cold War: From the October Revolution to the Korean War, 1917-1960.* Trans. D. D. Paige. London, 1968.

2129 FREELAND, Richard M. *The Truman Doctrine and the Origins of McCarthyism: Foreign Policy, Domestic Politics, and Internal Security, 1946-1948.* New York, 1972.

2130 FULBRIGHT, J. William. *The Arrogance of Power.* New York, 1967.†

2131 FULBRIGHT, J. William. *Old Myths and New Realities.* New York, 1964.†

2132 GARDNER, Lloyd C. *Architects of Illusion.* See 1740.

2133 GERSON, Louis L. *John Foster Dulles.* New York, 1967. *Secretaries of State.* Vol. 17. See 79.

2134 GEYELIN, Philip L. *Lyndon B. Johnson and the World.* New York, 1966.

2135 GOLDMAN, Eric F. *The Tragedy of Lyndon Johnson: A Historian's Personal Interpretation.* New York, 1968.

2136 GOOD, Robert C. "The National Interest and Political Realism: Niebuhr's 'Debate' with Morgenthau and Kennan." *J Pol*, XXII (1960), 597-619.

2137 GOOD, Robert C. "The United States and the Colonial Debate." *Alliance Policy in the Cold War.* Ed. Arnold Wolfers. Baltimore, 1959.

2138 GOOLD-ADAMS, Richard. *John Foster Dulles: A Reappraisal.* New York, 1962.

2139 GRABER, Doris A. "The Truman and Eisenhower Doctrines in the Light of the Doctrine of Non-Intervention." *Pol Sci Q*, LXXIII (1958), 321-334.

2140 GRAEBNER, Norman A. *Cold War Diplomacy; American Foreign Policy, 1945-1960.* Princeton, N.J., 1962.†

2141 GRAFF, Henry F. *The Tuesday Cabinet: Deliberation and Decision on Peace and War Under Lyndon B. Johnson.* Englewood Cliffs, N.J., 1971. Firsthand observations.

2142 GRIFFIS, Stanton. *Lying in State.* Garden City, N.Y., 1952. Written by a U.S. ambassador to Poland, Egypt, Argentina, and Spain during the Truman years.

2143 GUHIN, Michael A. *John Foster Dulles: A Statesman and His Times.* New York, 1972.

2144 HALBERSTAM, David. *The Best and the Brightest.* New York, 1972.† Composite portrait of the policy-makers of the Kennedy and Johnson administrations.

2145 HAMMOND, Paul Y. *American Foreign Policy Since 1945.* New York, 1969.†

2146   HARR, John Ensor. *The Professional Diplomat*. Princeton, N.J., 1969. The foreign service since the Second World War.

2147   HARTMANN, Frederick H. *The New Age of American Foreign Policy*. New York, 1970.

2148   HARTMANN, Susan M. *Truman and the 80th Congress*. Columbia, Mo., 1971.

2149   HEREN, Louis. *No Hail, No Farewell*. New York, 1970. The Johnson administration.

2150   HILSMAN, Roger. *To Move a Nation: The Politics of Foreign Policy in the Administration of John F. Kennedy*. Garden City, N.Y., 1967.

2151   HILSMAN, Roger, and Robert C. GOOD, eds. *Foreign Policy in the Sixties: The Issues and the Instruments. Essays in Honor of Arnold Wolfers*. Baltimore, 1965.

2152   HOROWITZ, David, ed. *Containment and Revolution*. Boston, 1967.

2153   HOROWITZ, David. *Free World Colossus: A Critique of American Foreign Policy in the Cold War*. Rev. ed. New York, 1971.

2154   HUDSON, G. F. *The Hard and Bitter Peace*. New York, 1967.

2155   HUGHES, Emmet John. *The Ordeal of Power: A Political Memoir of the Eisenhower Years*. New York, 1963.

2156   INGRAM, Kenneth. *History of the Cold War*. London, 1955.

2157   JACKSON, Henry M., ed. *The Secretary of State and the Ambassador*. New York, 1964.† A contemporary assessment.

2158   JACOBSON, Harold Karan, ed. *America's Foreign Policy*. New York, 1960.

2159   JOHNSON, E. A. J. *American Imperialism in the Image of Peer Gynt: Memoirs of a Professor-Bureaucrat*. Minneapolis, 1971.

2160   JOHNSON, Haynes, and Bernard M. GWERTZMAN. *Fulbright: The Dissenter*. Garden City, N.Y., 1968.

2161   JOHNSON, Lyndon Baines. *The Vantage Point: Perspectives of the Presidency, 1963-1969*. New York, 1971. The memoir includes three chapters on Vietnam.

2162   KAPLAN, Lawrence S. *Recent American Foreign Policy: Conflicting Interpretations*. Homewood, Ill., 1972.† Readings.

2163   KENNAN, George F. *Memoirs*. Vol. 1, *1925-1950*. Vol. 2, *1950-1963*. Boston, 1967, 1972. See 2558.

2164   KENNAN, George F. *On Dealing with the Communist World*. New York, 1964.

2165   KENNAN, George F. *Realities of American Foreign Policy*. Princeton, N.J., 1954.

2166   KERTESZ, Stephen D., ed. *American Diplomacy in a New Era*. Notre Dame, Ind., 1961.

2167   KIERNAN, Bernard P. *The United States, Communism, and the Emergent World*. Bloomington, Ind., 1972.

2168 KISSINGER, Henry A. *The Necessity for Choice: Prospects of American Foreign Policy*. New York, 1961.

2169 KOLKO, Joyce, and Gabriel KOLKO. *The Limits of Power: The World and United States Foreign Policy, 1945-1954*. New York, 1972.†

2170 KUST, Matthew J. "The Great Dilemma of American Foreign Policy." *Va Q Rev*, XXXIV (1958), 224-239. About the "third world."

2171 LAFEBER, Walter. *America, Russia, and the Cold War, 1945-1971*. 2d ed. New York, 1972.†

2172 LARSON, Arthur. *Eisenhower: The President Nobody Knew*. New York, 1968.

2173 LASBY, Clarence G. *Project Paperclip: German Scientists and the Cold War*. New York, 1971. On the U.S. recruitment of brainpower.

2174 LEACACOS, John P. *Fires in the In-Basket: The ABC's of the State Department*. Cleveland, 1968.

2175 LERCHE, Charles O., Jr. *The Cold War . . . and After*. Englewood Cliffs, N.J., 1965.

2176 LERCHE, Charles O., Jr. "Southern Congressmen and the 'New Isolationism.'" *Pol Sci Q*, LXXV (1960), 321-337.

2177 LERCHE, Charles O., Jr. *The Uncertain South: Its Changing Patterns of Politics in Foreign Policy*. Chicago, 1964.

2178 LIPPMANN, Walter. *The Cold War: A Study in U.S. Foreign Policy*. New York, 1947.† Republished in 1973 with George F. Kennan's "The Sources of Soviet Conduct" and an Introduction by Ronald Steel.

2179 LIPPMANN, Walter. *Isolation and Alliances*. Boston, 1952.

2180 LODGE, Henry Cabot. *The Storm Has Many Eyes: A Personal Narrative*. New York, 1973. Lodge's diplomatic experiences at the U.N., in Vietnam, and at the Vatican.

2181 LUARD, Evan, ed. *The Cold War*. New York, 1964.

2182 LUKACS, John. *A New History of the Cold War*. Garden City, N.Y., 1966.

2183 MACARTHUR, Douglas. *Reminiscences*. See 1750.

2184 MCCAMY, James L. *Conduct of the New Diplomacy*. New York, 1964.

2185 MCLELLAN, David S. "The Role of Political Style: A Study of Dean Acheson." *Foreign Policy in the Sixties*. See 2151.

2186 MCPHERSON, Harry. *A Political Education: A Journal of Life with Senators, Generals, Cabinet Members and Presidents*. Boston, 1972. Written by President Johnson's special counsel, 1965-1969.

2187 MARSHALL, Charles Burton. *The Limits of Foreign Policy*. New York, 1954.

2188 MAY, Ernest R. "The Cold War." *The Comparative Approach to American History*. Ed. C. Vann Woodward. New York, 1968.†

2189   MILLIS, Walter, and Eugene S. DUFFIELD, eds. *The Forrestal Diaries.* New York, 1951.

2190   MORGENTHAU, Hans J. *Truth and Power.* New York, 1970. Essays on American foreign policy of the 1960's.

2191   NIXON, Richard. *Six Crises.* Garden City, N.Y., 1962.

2192   NOBLE, G. Bernard. *Christian A. Herter.* New York, 1970. *Secretaries of State.* Vol. 18. See 79.

2193   OGLESBY, Carl, and Richard SHAULL. *Containment and Change.* New York, 1967.

2194   O'NEILL, William L. *Coming Apart: An Informal History of America in the 1960's.* Chicago, 1971. Includes pointed assessments of foreign policy.

2195   OSGOOD, Robert E. *Alliances and American Foreign Policy.* Baltimore, 1968.

2196   OSGOOD, Robert E., *et al. America and the World: From the Truman Doctrine to Vietnam.* Baltimore, 1970.†

2197   PANZELLA, Emmett E. "The Atlantic Union Committee: A Study of a Pressure Group in Foreign Policy." Doctoral dissertation, Kent State University, 1969.

2198   PARENTI, Michael. *The Anti-Communist Impulse.* New York, 1970.

2199   PARMET, Herbert S. *Eisenhower and the American Crusades.* New York, 1972.

2200   PATERSON, Thomas G., ed. *Cold War Critics: Alternatives to American Foreign Policy in the Truman Years.* Chicago, 1971.†

2201   PATTERSON, James T. *Mr. Republican: A Biography of Robert A. Taft.* Boston, 1972.

2202   PAYNE, James L. *The American Threat: The Fear of War as an Instrument of Foreign Policy.* Chicago, 1970.† Analysis of the period since the Second World War.

2203   PERKINS, Dexter. *The Diplomacy of a New Age: Major Issues in U.S. Policy Since 1945.* Bloomington, Ind., 1967.†

2204   PHILLIPS, Cabell. *The Truman Presidency: The History of a Triumphant Succession.* New York, 1966.

2205   QUIGG, Philip W. *America the Dutiful: An Assessment of U.S. Foreign Policy.* New York, 1971. Covers the 1945-1970 period.

2206   REES, David. *The Age of Containment: The Cold War, 1945-1965.* New York, 1967.

2207   RESTON, James. *The Artillery of the Press: Its Influence on American Foreign Policy.* New York, 1967.

2208   ROSTOW, W. W. *The American Diplomatic Revolution.* Oxford, 1946. Pamphlet. A Harmsworth lecture.

2209 SCHAPSMEIER, Edward L., and Frederick H. SCHAPSMEIER. *Henry A. Wallace and the War Years.* See 1763.

2210 SCHUMAN, Frederick L. *The Cold War: Retrospect and Prospect.* Baton Rouge, La., 1962.

2211 SEABURY, Paul. *The Rise and Decline of the Cold War.* New York, 1967.

2212 SELLEN, Robert W. "Old Assumptions versus New Realities: Lyndon Johnson and Foreign Policy." *Int Jour,* XXVIII (1973), 205-229.

2213 SHULMAN, Marshall D. *Stalin's Foreign Policy Reappraised.* Cambridge, Mass., 1963.

2214 SIDEY, Hugh. *A Very Personal Presidency: Lyndon Johnson in the White House.* New York, 1968.

2215 SMITH, Gaddis. *Dean Acheson.* New York, 1972. *Secretaries of State.* Vol. 16. See 79.

2216 SNELL, John L. "The Cold War: Four Contemporary Appraisals." *Am Hist Rev,* LXVIII (1962), 69-75.

2217 SORENSEN, Theodore C. *Kennedy.* New York, 1965.

2217-A SPANIER, John W. *American Foreign Policy Since World War II.* 3d ed. New York, 1968.†

2218 SPENDER, Sir Percy. *Exercises in Diplomacy.* New York, 1970. Firsthand descriptions of ANZUS, the Colombo Plan, and J. F. Dulles.

2219 STEEL, Ronald. *Imperialists and Other Heroes: A Chronicle of the American Empire.* New York, 1971. Foreign policy from Truman through Nixon.

2220 STOESSINGER, John G. *Nations in Darkness: China, Russia, and America.* New York, 1971.

2221 STONE, I. F. *The Truman Era.* Intro. by Robert Sklar. New York, 1972.† Originally published in 1953.

2222 SYLWESTER, Harold J. "American Public Reaction to Communist Expansion: From Yalta to NATO." Doctoral dissertation, University of Kansas, 1970.

2223 SYMINGTON, James W. *The Stately Game.* New York, 1971. An account of author's experience as U.S. chief of protocol 1966-1968.

2224 TAYLOR, General Maxwell D. *Swords and Plowshares.* New York, 1972.

2225 THEOHARIS, Athan. "The Rhetoric of Politics: Foreign Policy, Internal Security, and Domestic Politics in the Truman Era, 1945-1950." *Politics and Policies of the Truman Administration.* Ed. Barton J. Bernstein. Chicago, 1970.

2226 THEOHARIS, Athan. *Seeds of Repression: Harry S. Truman and the Origins of McCarthyism.* Chicago, 1971.

2227 THEOHARIS, Athan. *The Yalta Myths.* See 2007.

2228 TRASK, David F. "The Imperial Republic; America in World Politics, 1945 to the Present." *The Unfinished Century.* See 96.

2229 TRIVERS, Howard. *Three Crises in American Foreign Affairs and a Continuing Revolution.* Carbondale, Ill., 1972. The Berlin wall, the Cuban missile crisis, Vietnam, and the scientific/technological revolution.

2230 TRUMAN, Harry S. *Memoirs.* 2 vols. Garden City, N.Y., 1955-1956.

2231 TRUMAN, Margaret. *Harry S. Truman.* New York, 1973.†

2232 TUGWELL, Rexford G. *Off Course: From Truman to Nixon.* New York, 1971.

2233 VANDENBERG, Arthur H., Jr., ed. *The Private Papers of Senator Vandenberg.* Boston, 1952.

2233-A VENKATARAMANI, M. S. *Undercurrents in American Foreign Relations.* New York, 1965. On India, the Suez crisis, and the U-2 affair.

2234 WALKER, Richard L., and George CURRY. *E. R. Stettinius, Jr.* [and] *James F. Byrnes.* New York, 1965. *Secretaries of State.* Vol. 14. See 79.

2235 WALTON, Richard J. *Cold War and Counterrevolution: The Foreign Policy of John F. Kennedy.* New York, 1972.†

2236 WALTZ, Kenneth N. *Foreign Policy and Democratic Politics: The American and British Experience.* Boston, 1967.

2237 WESTERFIELD, H. Bradford. *Foreign Policy and Party Politics.* See 1776.

2238 WHELAN, Joseph G. "George Kennan and His Influence on American Foreign Policy." *Va Q Rev*, XXXV (1959), 196-220.

2239 WHITE, William S. *The Responsibles: How Five American Leaders Coped with Crisis.* New York, 1972. The five are Robert Taft, Harry Truman, Dwight Eisenhower, John Kennedy, and Lyndon Johnson.

2240 WHITNEY, Courtney. *MacArthur.* See 1777.

2241 WILLOUGHBY, C. A., and John R. CHAMBERLAIN. *MacArthur.* See 1778.

2242 WOLF, Charles, Jr. *United States Policy and the Third World: Problems and Analysis.* Boston, 1967.

2243 WOULEY, Wesley T. "Abstinence and Reform: The Public Debate Regarding the Basic Principles of American Foreign Policy, 1945-1947." Doctoral dissertation, University of Chicago, 1971.

2244 WRIGHT, C. Ben. "George F. Kennan, Scholar-Diplomat: 1926-1946." Doctoral dissertation, University of Wisconsin, 1972.

2245 YOST, Charles. *The Conduct and Misconduct of Foreign Affairs: Reflections of U.S. Foreign Policy Since World War II.* New York, 1972. Written by a former ambassador to the U.N.

2. Studies Concerning the Origins of the Cold War (See also 2045-2053)

2246   BELL, Coral. *Negotiation from Strength.* New York, 1963.

2247   BERNSTEIN, Barton J. "American Foreign Policy and the Origins of the Cold War." *Politics and Policies of the Truman Administration.* Ed. Barton J. Bernstein. Chicago, 1970.

2248   COMPTON, James V., ed. *America and the Origins of the Cold War.* Boston, 1972.† Readings.

2249   FEIS, Herbert. *From Trust to Terror: The Onset of the Cold War, 1945-1950.* New York, 1970.

2250   GADDIS, John Lewis. *United States and the Origins of the Cold War.* See 2045.

2251   GAMSON, William A., and André MODIGLIANI. *Untangling the Cold War: A Strategy for Testing Rival Theories.* Boston, 1971.

2252   GARDNER, Lloyd C., Arthur SCHLESINGER, Jr., and Hans J. MORGENTHAU. *The Origins of the Cold War.* Waltham, Mass., 1970.†

2253   GRAEBNER, Norman A. "Cold War Origins and the Continuing Debate: A Review of Recent Literature." *J Confl Res*, XIII (1969), 123-132.

2253-A HERRING, George C., Jr. *Aid to Russia.* See 1820-A.

2254   HERZ, Martin F. *Beginnings of the Cold War.* Bloomington, Ind., 1966.

2255   IRONS, Peter Hanlon. "America's Cold War Crusade." See 2047.

2256   MADDOX, Robert James. *The New Left and the Origins of the Cold War.* Princeton, N.J., 1973.

2257   MAIER, Charles S. "Revisionism and the Interpretation of Cold War Origins." *Perspectives in American History*, IV (1970), 313-350.

2258   RICHARDSON, J. "Cold War Revisionism: A Critique." *Wor Pol*, XXIV (1972), 579-612.

2259   ROSE, Lisle A. *After Yalta: America and the Origins of the Cold War.* New York, 1973.

2260   SCHLESINGER, Arthur M., Jr. "Origins of the Cold War." *For Aff*, XLVI (1967), 22-52.

2261   SELLEN, Robert W. "Origins of the Cold War: An Historiographical Survey." *West Georgia College Studies in the Social Sciences*, IX (1970), 57-98.

2262   SHERWIN, Martin Jay. "The Atomic Bomb and the Origins of the Cold War." See 2021.

2263   SMITH, Daniel M. "The New Left and the Cold War." *Denver Quarterly*, IV (1970), 78-88.

2264   STOVER, Robert. "Responsibility for the Cold War—A Case Study in Historical Responsibility." *History and Theory*, XI (1972), 145-178.

2265   THEOHARIS, Athan. "Roosevelt and Truman on Yalta: The Origins of the Cold War." See 2006.

3. The U.S. in the U.N.

2266   BEICHMAN, Arnold. *The "Other" State Department: The United States Mission to the United Nations—Its Role in the Making of Foreign Policy.* New York, 1968.

2267   BLOOMFIELD, Lincoln P. *The United Nations and U.S. Foreign Policy.* Boston, 1960.

2268   CAMPBELL, Tom. *Masquerade Peace.* Gainesville, Fla., 1972. Focuses on Stettinius, the birth of the U.N., and the onset of the Cold War.

2269   EICHELBERGER, Clark M. *UN: The First Twenty-Five Years.* New York, 1970.

2270   GOODRICH, Leland M. *The United Nations.* New York, 1959.

2271   GROSS, Franz B., ed. *The United States and the United Nations.* Norman, Okla., 1964.

2272   HERO, Alfred O., Jr. "The American Public and the UN, 1954-1966." *J Confl Res*, X (1966), 436-475.

2273   HYDE, L. K., Jr. *The United States and the United Nations—Promoting the Public Welfare: Examples of American Co-operation, 1945-1955.* New York, 1960.

2274   LASH, Joseph P. *Eleanor: The Years Alone.* New York, 1972. Glimpses of Mrs. Roosevelt's participation in the early workings of the U.N.

2275   LIE, Trygve. *In the Cause of Peace: Seven Years with the United Nations.* New York, 1954.

2276   MAZUZAN, George Thaire. "Warren R. Austin: A Republican Internationalist and United States Foreign Policy." Doctoral dissertation, Kent State University, 1969. Austin was ambassador to the U.N., 1946-1952.

2277   PRATT, Virginia Anne. "The Influence of Domestic Controversy on American Participation in the United Nations Commission on Human Rights, 1946-1953." Doctoral dissertation, University of Minnesota, 1971.

2278   RIGGS, Robert E. *US/UN: Foreign Policy and International Organization.* New York, 1971.†

2279   RUBINSTEIN, Alvin Z., and George GINSBURGS, eds. *Soviet and American Policies in the United Nations: A Twenty-Five-Year Perspective.* New York, 1971.

2280   RUSSELL, Ruth B. *The United Nations and United States Security Policy*. Washington, 1968.

2281   URQUHART, Brian. *Hammarskjold*. New York, 1972. An account of Hammarskjold's eight years at the U.N.

2281-A WEILER, Lawrence D., and Anne Patricia SIMONS. *The United States and the United Nations*. New York, 1967.

2282   WILCOX, Francis O., and H. Field HAVILAND, Jr. *The United States and the United Nations*. Baltimore, 1961.

4. The Marshall Plan, Foreign Aid, and Other Economic Questions

2283   ADLER-KARLSSON, Gunnar. *Western Economic Warfare, 1947-1967: A Case Study in Foreign Economic Policy*. Stockholm, 1968.

2284   AMUZEGAR, Janangir. "Point Four: Performance and Prospect." *Pol Sci Q*, LXXIII (1958), 530-546.

2285   ARKES, Hadley. *Bureaucracy, the Marshall Plan, and the National Interest*. Princeton, N.J., 1972. How the Marshall Plan was executed.

2286   BALDWIN, David A. *Economic Development and American Foreign Policy, 1943-62*. Chicago, 1966.

2287   BAUER, Raymond A., *et al. American Business and Public Policy: The Politics of Foreign Trade*. New York, 1963.

2288   BINGHAM, Jonathan. *Shirt-Sleeve Diplomacy: Point-4 in Action*. New York, 1954.

2289   BLACK, Eugene R. *Diplomacy of Economic Development*. Cambridge, Mass., 1960.

2290   BROEHL, Wayne G. *United States Business Performance Abroad: The Case Study of the International Basic Economy Corporation*. Washington, 1968.† About a Rockefeller family enterprise.

2291   BROWN, William A., Jr., and Redvers OPIE. *American Foreign Assistance*. Washington, 1953.

2292   CLARK, Paul G. *American Aid for Development*. New York, 1972. An analysis of the record of the 1960's and a projection for the 1970's.

2293   CLAYTON, William L. "GATT, the Marshall Plan, and OECD." *Pol Sci Q*, LXXVIII (1963), 493-503.

2294   COHEN, Stephen D. *International Monetary Reform, 1964-1969: The Political Dimension*. New York, 1970.

2295   CURTIS, Thomas B., and John Robert VASTINE, Jr. *The Kennedy Round and the Future of American Trade*. New York, 1971. About trade talks that began in 1962.

2296   DIBACCO, Thomas V. "American Business and Foreign Aid: The Eisenhower Years." *Bus Hist Rev*, XLI (1967), 21-35.

2297   DOBNEY, Fredrick J., ed. *Selected Papers of Will Clayton*. Baltimore, 1971. Clayton advised President Truman on foreign economic policy.

2298   EVANS, John W. *The Kennedy Round in American Trade Policy: The Twilight of the GATT?* Cambridge, Mass., 1971.

2299   FEIS, Herbert. *Foreign Aid and Foreign Policy*. New York, 1964.

2300   FREIDELL, Theodore Donald. "Truman's Point Four: Legislative Enactment and Development in Latin America." Doctoral dissertation, University of Missouri, Kansas City, 1965.

2301   GARDNER, Richard N. *Sterling-Dollar Diplomacy*. See 2077.

2302   GARWOOD, Ellen Clayton. *Will Clayton: A Short Biography*. Austin, Tex., 1958.

2303   GLICK, Philip M. *The Administration of Technical Assistance: Growth in the Americas*. Chicago, 1957.

2304   HANSON, Simon G. "International Commodity Agreements: The 'Success' of the International Coffee Agreement: How the State Department Deceived the Congress." *Int-Am Econ Aff*, XXI (1967), No. 2, 55-79.

2305   HARVEY, Mose L. *East-West Trade and United States Policy*. New York, 1966.

2306   HAYTER, Teresa. *Aid as Imperialism*. Baltimore, 1971.† Criticizes the World Bank as agent of U.S. foreign policy.

2307   HITCHENS, Harold L. "Influences on the Congressional Decision to Pass the Marshall Plan." *W Pol Q*, XXI (1968), 51-68.

2308   HUMPHREY, Don Dougan. *The United States and the Common Market: A Background Study*. New York, 1962.

2309   JACOBY, Neil H. *Aid to Taiwan*. See 2738.

2310   JONES, Joseph M. *The Fifteen Weeks, February 21-June 5, 1947*. New York, 1955.† On the formulation of the Truman Doctrine and the Marshall Plan.

2311   JORDAN, Amos A., Jr. *Foreign Aid and the Defense of Southeast Asia*. New York, 1962.

2312   KAUFFMAN, Kenneth M., and Helena STALSON. "U.S. Assistance to Less Developed Countries, 1956-65." *For Aff*, XLV (1967), 715-725. Contains useful tabulations.

2313   KRAUSE, Lawrence B. *European Economic Integration and the United States*. Washington, 1968.

2314   MCCREARY, Edward A. *The Americanization of Europe: The Impact of Americans and American Business on the Uncommon Market*. Garden City, N.Y., 1964.

2315 MALLALIEU, William C. "The Origin of the Marshall Plan: A Study in Policy Formation and National Leadership." *Pol Sci Q*, LXXIII (1958), 481-504.

2316 MASON, Edward S. *Foreign Aid and Foreign Policy*. New York, 1964.

2317 MONTGOMERY, John D. *The Politics of Foreign Aid: American Experience in Southeast Asia*. New York, 1962.

2318 O'LEARY, Michael Kent. *The Politics of American Foreign Aid*. New York, 1967. Public, congressional and presidential attitudes.

2319 PATERSON, Thomas G. "The Economic Cold War: American Business and Economic Foreign Policy." Doctoral dissertation, University of California, Berkeley, 1968.

2320 PATERSON, Thomas G. "The Quest for Peace and Prosperity: International Trade, Communism, and the Marshall Plan." *Politics and Policies of the Truman Administration.* Ed. Barton J. Bernstein. Chicago, 1970.

2321 PREEG, Ernest H. *Traders and Diplomats*. Washington, 1970. A participant's account of the Kennedy Round.

2322 PRICE, Harry B. *The Marshall Plan and Its Meaning*. Ithaca, N.Y., 1955.

2323 PYE, Lucian W. "The Foreign Aid Instrument: Search for Reality." *Foreign Policy in the Sixties*. See 2151.

2324 PYE, Lucian W. "Soviet and American Styles in Foreign Aid." *Orbis*, IV (1960), 159-173.

2325 QUADE, Quentin L. "The Truman Administration and the Separation of Power: The Case of the Marshall Plan." *Rev Pol*, XXVII (1965), 58-77.

2326 RUBIN, Jacob A. *Your Hundred Billion Dollars: The Complete Story of American Foreign Aid*. Philadelphia, 1964.

2327 VERNON, Raymond. *America's Foreign Trade Policy and the GATT*. Princeton, N.J., 1957.

2328 WALTERS, Robert S. *American and Soviet Aid: A Comparative Analysis*. Pittsburgh, 1970.

2329 WARNE, William E. *Point 4*. See 2701.

2330 WOLF, Charles, Jr. *Foreign Aid: Theory and Practice in Southeast Asia*. Princeton, N.J., 1960.

2331 WOODBRIDGE, George, *et al. UNRRA: The History of the United Nations Relief and Rehabilitation Administration*. 3 vols. New York, 1950.

5. Military Alliances; Security and Intelligence; Nuclear Arms Control

2332   BADER, William B. *The United States and the Spread of Nuclear Weapons.* New York, 1968.

2333   BAINES, John M. "U.S. Military Assistance to Latin America: An Assessment." *J Interam Stud*, XIV (1972), 469-487. Assesses the 1960's.

2334   BECHHOEFFER, Bernhard G. *Postwar Negotiations for Arms Control.* Washington, 1961.

2335   BRENNAN, Donald G., ed. *Arms Control, Disarmament, and National Security.* New York, 1961.

2336   BRODIE, Bernard. *Escalation and the Nuclear Option.* Princeton, N.J., 1966.

2337   BRODIE, Bernard. *Strategy in the Missile Age.* Princeton, N.J., 1959.†

2338   BRODIE, Bernard. *War and Politics.* New York, 1973. On Korea, Vietnam, and nuclear strategy.

2339   BUCHAN, Alastair. *NATO in the 1960's.* Rev. ed. New York, 1963.

2340   COTTRELL, Alvin J., and James E. DOUGHERTY. *The Politics of the Atlantic Alliance.* New York, 1964.†

2341   DAVIS, Vincent. *The Admirals Lobby.* Chapel Hill, N.C., 1967.

2342   DAVIS, Vincent. *Postwar Defense Policy and the U.S. Navy.* See 2028.

2343   DEAN, Arthur H. *Test Ban and Disarmament: The Path of Negotiation.* New York, 1966.

2344   DULLES, Allen. *The Craft of Intelligence.* New York, 1963.

2345   DUNCAN, Francis. "Atomic Energy and Anglo-American Relations, 1946-1954." *Orbis*, XII (1968), 1188-1203.

2346   FALK, Stanley L. "The National Security Council Under Truman, Eisenhower, and Kennedy." *Pol Sci Q*, LXXIX (1964), 403-434.

2347   FOX, William T. R., and Annette Baker FOX. *NATO and the Range of American Choice.* New York, 1967. Contemporary commentary.

2348   FURNISS, Edgar S., Jr., ed. *American Military Policy: Strategic Aspects of World Political Geography.* New York, 1957.

2349   GOULDING, Phil G. *Confirm or Deny: Informing the People on National Security.* New York, 1970. The Pentagon's releases of information on Vietnam and other foreign affairs during the 1960's.

2350   HEWLETT, Richard G., and Francis DUNCAN. *Atomic Shield 1947/1952.* University Park, Pa., 1969. A volume in the official history of the Atomic Energy Commission.

2351 HOLBORN, Hajo. *American Military Government.* See 2033.

2352 HOOPES, Townsend. *Limits of Intervention.* See 2501.

2353 HOROWITZ, Irving Louis, ed. *The Rise and Fall of Project Camelot: Studies in the Relationship Between Social Science and Practical Politics.* Cambridge, Mass., 1967.† About a Pentagon project.

2354 HOVEY, Harold A. *United States Military Assistance: A Study of Policies and Practices.* New York, 1965.

2355 ISMAY, Lord. *NATO: The First Five Years, 1949-1954.* Paris, 1954.

2356 JACKSON, Henry M., ed. *The Atlantic Alliance.* New York, 1967. Testimony on NATO given before Senator Jackson's subcommittee.

2357 JACKSON, Henry M., ed. *The National Security Council.* New York, 1965.†

2358 JACOBSON, Harold Karan, and Eric STEIN. *Diplomats, Scientists, and Politicians: The United States and the Nuclear Test Ban Negotiations.* Ann Arbor, Mich., 1966.

2359 KAHN, Herman. *On Thermonuclear War.* Princeton, N.J., 1960.

2360 KAHN, Herman. *Thinking About the Unthinkable.* New York, 1964.†

2361 KANTER, Arnold. "Congress and the Defense Budget: 1960-1970." *Am Pol Sci Rev*, LXVI (1972), 129-143.

2362 KAPLAN, Lawrence S. "NATO and the Language of Isolationism." *S Atl Q*, LVII (1958), 204-215.

2363 KAPLAN, Lawrence S. "The United States and the Atlantic Alliance: The First Generation." *Twentieth-Century American Foreign Policy.* See 64. NATO through 1968.

2364 KAPLAN, Lawrence S. "The United States and the Origins of NATO, 1946-1949." *Rev Pol*, XXXI (1969), 210-222.

2365 KAUFMANN, William W. *The McNamara Strategy.* New York, 1964.

2366 KAUFMANN, William W., ed. *Military Policy and National Security.* Princeton, N.J., 1956.

2367 Keesing's Contemporary Archive. *Disarmament: Negotiations and Treaties, 1946-1971.* New York, 1972.

2368 KINTNER, William R., *et al. Forging a New Sword: A Study of the Department of Defense.* New York, 1958.

2369 KIRKPATRICK, Lyman B., Jr. *The Real CIA.* New York, 1968.

2370 KISSINGER, Henry A. *Nuclear Weapons and Foreign Policy.* New York, 1957.

2371 KISSINGER, Henry A. *Troubled Partnership.* New York, 1966.† On NATO.

2372 KNORR, Klaus, ed. *NATO and American Security.* Princeton, N.J., 1959.

2373 KNORR, Klaus. *On the Uses of Military Power in the Nuclear Age.* Princeton, N.J., 1966.

2374   KOLODZIEJ, Edward A. *The Uncommon Defense and Congress, 1945-1963.* Columbus, Ohio, 1966.

2375   LEVINE, Robert A. *The Arms Debate.* Cambridge, Mass., 1963.

2376   LIEBERMAN, Joseph I. *The Scorpion and the Tarantula: The Struggle to Control Atomic Weapons, 1945-1949.* Boston, 1970. The U.S.-U.S.S.R. disagreement.

2377   LILIENTHAL, David E. *The Journals of David E. Lilienthal.* Vol. 2: *The Atomic Energy Years.* New York, 1964.

2378   McGEEHAN, Robert. *The German Rearmament Question: American Diplomacy and European Defense After World War II.* Urbana, Ill., 1971.

2379   McNAMARA, Robert S. *The Essence of Security: Reflections in Office.* New York, 1968.

2380   MAY, Joseph Turner. "John Foster Dulles and the European Defense Community." Doctoral dissertation, Kent State University, 1969.

2381   MELMAN, Seymour, ed. *Disarmament: Its Politics and Economics.* Boston, 1962.

2382   MOSS, Norman. *Men Who Play God: The Story of the H-Bomb and How the World Came to Live with It.* New York, 1968.†

2383   MOULTON, Harland Buell. "American Strategic Power: Two Decades of Nuclear Strategy and Weapon Systems, 1945-1965." Doctoral dissertation, University of Minnesota, 1969.

2384   MOULTON, Harland B. *From Superiority to Parity: The United States and the Strategic Arms Race, 1961-1971.* Westport, Conn., 1972.

2385   MROZEK, Donald John. "Peace Through Strength: Strategic Air Power and the Mobilization of the United States for the Pursuit of Foreign Policy, 1945-1955." Doctoral dissertation, Rutgers University, 1972.

2386   NOGEE, Joseph L. *Soviet Policy Towards International Control of Atomic Energy.* Notre Dame, Ind., 1961.

2387   OSGOOD, Robert E. *Limited War: The Challenge to American Strategy.* Chicago, 1957.

2388   OSGOOD, Robert. *NATO: The Entangling Alliance.* Chicago, 1952.

2389   PIERRE, Andrew J. *Nuclear Politics.* See 1981.

2390   QUESTER, George H. *Nuclear Diplomacy: The First Twenty-Five Years.* New York, 1971. U.S.-Soviet nuclear diplomacy.

2391   RANSOM, Harry Howe. *The Intelligence Establishment.* Cambridge, Mass., 1970. Revision of a 1958 study, *Central Intelligence and National Security.*

2392   ROBERTS, Chalmers M. *The Nuclear Years: The Arms Race and Arms Control, 1945-1970.* New York, 1970.

2393   RUSSETT, Bruce M. *What Price Vigilance? The Burdens of National Defense.* New Haven, Conn., 1970.† Statistical analyses covering the recent past.

2394 SANDER, Alfred D. "Truman and the National Security Council: 1945-1947." *J Am Hist*, LIX (1972-1973), 369-388.

2395 SCHELLING, Thomas C., and Morton H. HALPERIN. *Strategy and Arms Control*. New York, 1961.

2396 SCHILLING, Warner R. "The H-Bomb Decision: How to Decide Without Actually Choosing." *Pol Sci Q*, LXXVI (1961), 24-46.

2397 SCHILLING, Warner R., Paul Y. HAMMOND, and Glenn H. SNYDER. *Strategy, Politics, and Defense Budgets*. New York, 1962.

2398 SCHWARZ, Urs. *American Strategy: A New Perspective. The Growth of Politico-Military Thinking in the United States*. Garden City, N.Y., 1966.†

2399 SMITH, Alice Kimball. *A Peril and a Hope: The Scientists' Movement in America, 1945-1947*. Chicago, 1965.

2400 SMITH, Mark E., Jr., and Claude J. R. JOHNS. *American Defense Policy*. 2d ed. Baltimore, 1968.

2401 SPANIER, John W., and Joseph L. NOGEE. *The Politics of Disarmament*. New York, 1962.

2402 STEIN, Harold, ed. *American Civil-Military Decisions: A Book of Case Studies*. Birmingham, Ala., 1963.

2403 STRAUSS, Lewis L. *Men and Decisions*. New York, 1962. Strauss was chairman of the AEC.

2404 TAYLOR, Maxwell D. *The Uncertain Trumpet*. New York, 1960.

2405 TERCHEK, Ronald J. *The Making of the Test Ban Treaty*. The Hague, 1970.

2406 THOMPSON, Robert. *Revolutionary War in World Strategy 1945-1969*. New York, 1970.

2407 TREWHITT, Henry L. *McNamara*. New York, 1971.

2408 WOLFERS, Arnold, ed. *Alliance Policy in the Cold War*. Baltimore, 1959.

2409 XYDIS, Stephen G. "The Genesis of the Sixth Fleet." *U S Naval Institute Proceedings*, LXXXIV (1958), No. 8, 41-50.

6. Flashpoints in the Cold War

The Problem of Germany

2410 AUSLAND, John C., and Col. Hugh F. RICHARDSON. "Crisis Management: Berlin, Cyprus, Laos." *For Aff*, XLIV (1966), 291-303.

2411 BALFOUR, Michael, and John MAIR. *Four-Power Control in Germany and Austria, 1945-1946*. London, 1956.

2412   CHARLES, Max. *Berlin Blockade*. London, 1959.

2413   CLAY, Lucius D. *Decision in Germany*. Garden City, N.Y., 1950.

2414   CONANT, James B. *My Several Lives: Memoirs of a Social Inventor*. New York, 1970. Conant was American high commissioner in occupied Germany.

2415   CRADDOCK, Walter R. "United States Diplomacy and the Saar Dispute, 1949-1955." *Orbis*, XII (1968), 247-267.

2416   DAVIDSON, Eugene. *The Death and Life of Germany: An Account of the American Occupation*. New York, 1959.

2417   DAVIS, Franklin M., Jr. *Come as a Conqueror: The United States Army's Occupation of Germany 1945-1949*. New York, 1967.

2418   DAVISON, W. Phillips. *The Berlin Blockade—A Study in Cold War Politics*. Princeton, N.J., 1958.

2419   FRANKLIN, William M. "Zonal Boundaries and Access to Berlin." *Wor Pol*, XVI (1963), 1-31.

2420   GARDNER, Lloyd C. "America and the German 'Problem,' 1945-1949." *Politics and Policies of the Truman Administration*. See 2247.

2421   GIMBEL, John. "Cold War: German Front." *Maryland Historian*, II (1971), 41-55. An historiographical essay.

2422   GOTTLIEB, Manuel. *The German Peace Settlement and the Berlin Crisis*. New York, 1960.

2423   JESSUP, Philip C. "The Berlin Blockade and the Use of the United Nations." *For Aff*, L (1971), 163-173.

2424   JESSUP, Philip C. "Park Avenue Diplomacy—Ending the Berlin Blockade." *Pol Sci Q*, LXXXVII (1972), 377-400.

2425   KUKLICK, Bruce. *American Policy and the Division of Germany; The Clash with Russia over Reparations*. Ithaca, N.Y., 1972.

2426   LITCHFIELD, Edward H., *et al. Governing Postwar Germany*. Ithaca, N.Y., 1950.

2427   MCGEEHAN, Robert. *German Rearmament*. See 2378.

2428   MCINNIS, Edgar W., *et al. The Shaping of Postwar Germany*. New York, 1960.

2428-A PLANCK, Charles R. *The Changing Status of German Reunification in Western Diplomacy, 1955-1966*. Baltimore, 1967.

2429   RATCHFORD, Benjamin U., and William D. ROSS. *Berlin Reparations Assignment*. Chapel Hill, N.C., 1947.

2430   SCHICK, Jack M. "American Diplomacy and the Berlin Negotiations." *W Pol Q*, XVIII (1965), 803-820.

2431   SCHICK, Jack M. *The Berlin Crisis 1958-1962*. Philadelphia, 1971.

2432   SCHICK, Jack M. "The Berlin Crisis of 1961 and U.S. Military Strategy." *Orbis*, III (1965), 816-831.

2433 SLUSSER, Robert M. *The Berlin Crisis of 1961; Soviet-American Relations and the Struggle for Power in the Kremlin, June-November 1961.* Baltimore, 1973.†

2434 SMITH, Jean Edward. *The Defense of Berlin.* Baltimore, 1963.

2435 SPENCER, Frank. "The United States and Germany in the Aftermath of War: II. The Second World War." *Int Aff,* XLIV (1968), 48-62.

2436 TRIVERS, Howard. *Three Crises.* See 2229.

2437 ZINK, Harold. *The United States in Germany, 1944-1955.* Princeton, N.J., 1957.

The Korean War

2438 BERGER, Carl. *The Korea Knot, a Military-Political History.* Rev. ed. Philadelphia, 1969.

2439 CARIDI, Ronald J. *The Korean War and American Politics: The Republican Party as a Case Study.* Philadelphia, 1969.

2440 CHO, Soon Sung. *Korea in World Politics, 1940-1950: An Evaluation of American Responsibility.* Berkeley, Cal., 1967.

2441 CLARK, Mark W. *From the Danube to the Yalu.* New York, 1954.

2442 CROFTS, Alfred. "The Start of the Korean War Reconsidered." *Rocky Mtn Soc Sci J,* VII (1970), 109-117.

2443 GARDNER, Lloyd C., ed. *The Korean War,* New York, 1972.† Articles from the *New York Times Magazine.*

2444 GEORGE, Alexander L. "American Policymaking and the North Korean Aggression." *Wor Pol,* VII (1955), 209-232.

2445 GOODRICH, Leland M. *Korea: A Study of U.S. Policy in the United Nations.* New York, 1956.

2446 GORDENKER, Leon. *The United Nations and the Peaceful Unification of Korea: The Politics of Field Operations, 1947-1950.* The Hague, 1959.

2447 HALPERIN, Morton H. "The Limiting Process in the Korean War." *Pol Sci Q,* LXXVIII (1963), 13-39.

2448 HIGGINS, Trumbull. *Korea and the Fall of MacArthur: A Precis in Limited War.* New York, 1960.

2449 HOYT, Edwin C. "The United States Reaction to the Korean Attack." *Am J Int Law,* LV (1961), 45-76.

2450 JOY, Admiral C. Turner. *How Communists Negotiate.* New York, 1955.

2451 LOFGREN, Charles A. "Mr. Truman's War: A Debate and Its Aftermath." *Rev Pol,* XXXI (1969), 223-241. Congress and the Korean War.

2452 MCLELLAN, David S. "Dean Acheson and the Korean War." *Pol Sci Q,* LXXXIII (1968), 16-39.

2453 MEADE, Edward G. *American Military Government in Korea.* New York, 1951.

2454   MODIGLIANI, André. "Hawks and Doves, Isolationism and Political Distrust: An Analysis of Public Opinion on Military Policy." *Am Pol Sci Rev*, LXVI (1972), 960-978. Relates to the Korean War.

2455   MUELLER, John E. "Trends in Popular Support for the Wars in Korea and Vietnam." *Am Pol Sci Rev*, LXV (1971), 358-375.

2456   NORMAN, John. "MacArthur's Blockade Proposals Against Red China." *Pac Hist Rev*, XXVI (1957), 161-174.

2457   PAIGE, Glenn D. *The Korean Decision: June 24-30, 1950*. New York, 1968.

2458   REES, David. *Korea: The Limited War*. New York, 1964.

2459   RIDGWAY, Matthew B. *The Korean War*. Garden City, N.Y., 1967.

2460   ROVERE, Richard H., and Arthur M. SCHLESINGER, Jr. *The General and the President*. New York, 1951.†

2461   SPANIER, John W. *The Truman-MacArthur Controversy and the Korean War*. Cambridge, Mass., 1959.†

2462   STONE, I. F. *The Hidden History of the Korean War*. 2d ed. New York, 1969.

2463   VATCHER, William H. *Panmunjon: The Story of the Korean Military Armistice Negotiations*. New York, 1958.

2464   WHITING, Allen S. *China Crosses the Yalu*. New York, 1960.

The Cuban Missile Crisis

2465   ABEL, Elie. *The Missile Crisis*. New York, 1966.†

2466   ALLISON, Graham T. *Essence of Decision: Explaining the Cuban Missile Crisis*. Boston, 1971.†

2467   DIVINE, Robert A., ed. *The Cuban Missile Crisis*. Chicago, 1971.†

2468   GREENE, Fred. "The Intelligence Arm: The Cuban Missile Crisis." *Foreign Policy in the Sixties*. See 2151.

2469   HORELICK, Arnold L. "The Cuban Missile Crisis: An Analysis of Soviet Calculations and Behavior." *Wor Pol*, XVI (1964), 363-389.

2470   KAHAN, Jerome H., and Anne K. LONG. "The Cuban Missile Crisis: A Study of Its Strategic Context." *Pol Sci Q*, LXXXVII (1972), 564-590.

2471   KENNEDY, Robert F. *Thirteen Days: A Memoir of the Cuban Missile Crisis*. Intro. by Robert S. McNamara and Harold Macmillan. New York, 1969.

2472   PACHTER, Henry M. *Collision Course: The Cuban Missile Crisis and Co-existence*. New York, 1963.

2473   TRIVERS, Howard. *Three Crises*. See 2229.

2474   WOHLSTETTER, Roberta. "Cuba and Pearl Harbor: Hindsight and Foresight." *For Aff*, XLIII (1965), 691-707. The missile crisis.

The Vietnam War

2475 AUSTIN, Anthony. *The President's War*. Philadelphia, 1971. An account of the Tonkin Gulf resolution.

2476 BAILEY, George A., and Lawrence W. LICHTY. "Rough Justice on a Saigon Street: A Gatekeeper Study of NBC's Tet Execution Film." *Jour Q*, XLIX (1972), 221-229, 238.

2477 BAIN, Chester A. *Vietnam: The Roots of Conflict*. Englewood Cliffs, N.J., 1967.

2478 BEISNER, Robert L. "1898 and 1968: The Anti-Imperialists and the Doves." See 609.

2479 BODARD, Lucien. *The Quicksand War: Prelude to Viet Nam*. Boston, 1967.

2480 BUTTINGER, Joseph. *Vietnam: A Dragon Embattled*. 2 vols. New York, 1967.

2481 CAMERON, Allan W. *Viet-Nam Crisis*. See 1897.

2482 CLIFFORD, Clark M. "A Viet Nam Reappraisal; The Personal History of One Man's View and How It Evolved." *For Aff*, XLVII (1969), 601-622. Clifford was Secretary of Defense in 1968-1969.

2483 COLE, Allen B., ed. *Conflict in Indochina and International Repercussions: A Documentary History*. New York, 1956.

2484 COOPER, Chester L. *The Lost Crusade: America in Vietnam*. New York, 1970.

2485 DEVILLERS, Philippe, and Jean LACOUTURE. *End of a War: Indochina, 1954*. New York, 1969. How the U.S. succeeded France in Indochina.

2486 ELLSBERG, Daniel. *Papers on the War*. New York, 1972.†

2487 FALK, Richard A., ed. *The Vietnam War and International Law*. 3 vols. to date. Princeton, N.J., 1968-1972.†

2488 FALL, Bernard. *Street Without Joy: Indochina at War, 1946-1954*. Harrisburg, Pa., 1961.

2489 FALL, Bernard B. *The Two Vietnams*. 2d ed. New York, 1966.

2490 FALL, Bernard. *Vietnam Witness 1953-66*. New York, 1966.

2491 FITZGERALD, Frances. *Fire in the Lake: The Vietnamese and the Americans in Vietnam*. Boston, 1972.

2492 GALLOWAY, John. *The Gulf of Tonkin Resolution*. Rutherford, N.J., 1970. Includes documents.

2493 GEORGE, Alexander L., David K. HALL, and William R. SIMONS. *The Limits of Coercive Diplomacy: Laos, Cuba, Vietnam*. Boston, 1971.†

2494 GORDON, Max. "The Pentagon Papers: Perception and Reality." *Sci Soc*, XXXVI (1972), 78-86.

2495   GOULDEN, Joseph C. *Truth Is the First Casualty: The Gulf of Tonkin Affair–Illusion and Reality*. Chicago, 1969.

2496   GOULDING, Phil G. *Confirm or Deny*. See 2349.

2497   GURTOV, Melvin. *The First Vietnam Crisis*. New York, 1967. Focuses on 1954.

2498   HALBERSTAM, David. *The Making of a Quagmire*. New York, 1965. Vietnam in the early 1960's.

2499   HAMMER, Ellen J. *The Struggle for Indochina, 1940-1955*. Rev. ed. Stanford, Cal., 1966.

2500   HAMMER, Ellen. *Vietnam: Yesterday and Today*. New York, 1966.

2501   HOOPES, Townsend. *The Limits of Intervention: An Inside Account of How the Johnson Policy of Escalation in Vietnam Was Reversed*. New York, 1969.†

2502   KAHIN, George, and John W. LEWIS. *The United States in Vietnam*. New York, 1967.†

2503   KRASLOW, David, and Stuart H. LOORY. *The Secret Search for Peace in Vietnam*. New York, 1968.†

2504   LACOUTURE, Jean. *Vietnam: Between Two Truces*. New York, 1966.

2505   LANCASTER, Donald. *The Emancipation of French Indo-China*. New York, 1961.

2506   LITTAUER, Raphael, and Norman UPHOFF, eds. *The Air War in Indochina*. Rev. ed. Boston, 1972.†

2507   MCALISTER, John T., Jr. *Viet Nam: The Origins of Revolution*. New York, 1969.

2508   MOORE, John Norton. *Law and the Indo-China War*. Princeton, N.J., 1972.†

2509   MORGENTHAU, Hans J. *Vietnam and the United States*. Washington, 1965.

2510   MUELLER, John E. "Trends in Popular Support for the Wars in Korea and Vietnam." See 2455.

2511   OBERDORFER, Don. *Tet!* Garden City, N.Y., 1971. The critical battle.

2512   PAGE, Benjamin I., and Richard A. BRODY. "Policy Voting and the Electoral Process: The Vietnam War Issue." *Am Pol Sci Rev*, LXVI (1972), 979-995. Concerns the 1968 election.

2513   RASKIN, Marcus G., and Bernard FALL, eds. *The Vietnam Reader*. New York, 1965.†

2514   ROSTOW, W. W. *The Diffusion of Power: An Essay in Recent History*. New York, 1972. A defense of U.S. Vietnam policy by L.B.J.'s adviser.

2515   SCHLESINGER, Arthur M., Jr. *The Bitter Heritage: Vietnam and American Democracy, 1941-1966*. Boston, 1967.

2516   SCOTT, Peter Dale. *The War Conspiracy: The Secret Road to the Second Indochina War.* Indianapolis, 1972.

2517   SHAPLEN, Robert. *The Lost Revolution: The U.S. in Vietnam, 1946-1966.* Rev. ed. New York, 1966.†

2518   SHAPLEN, Robert. *The Road from War: Vietnam 1965-1970.* New York, 1970. Reports from Vietnam.

2519   SHAPLEN, Robert. *Time Out of Hand: Revolution and Reaction in Southeast Asia.* New York, 1969.

2520   SHEEHAN, Neil, *et al. The Pentagon Papers: As Published by the New York Times.* New York, 1971.†

2521   STANDARD, William L. *Aggression: Our Asian Disaster.* New York, 1971. Argues that the U.S. violated domestic and international law in prosecuting the Vietnam war.

2522   STAVINS, Ralph, Richard J. BARNET, and Marcus G. RASKIN. *Washington Plans an Aggressive War.* New York, 1971.†

2523   TANHAM, George K., *et al. War Without Guns: American Civilians in Rural Vietnam.* New York, 1966.

2524   TAYLOR, Telford. *Nuremberg and Vietnam: An American Tragedy.* Chicago, 1970.

2525   TRAGER, Frank N. *Why Vietnam?* New York. 1966.

2526   TRIVERS, Howard. *Three Crises.* See 2229.

2527   *The Vietnam Hearings.* Intro. by J. William Fulbright. New York, 1966.† The February 1966 hearings before the Senate Foreign Relations Committee include statements of Dean Rusk, James M. Gavin, George F. Kennan, and Maxwell D. Taylor.

2528   WARNER, Geoffrey. "The United States and Vietnam 1945-65." *Int Aff,* XLVIII (1972), 379-394, 593-615.

2529   WINDCHY, Eugene C. *Tonkin Gulf.* Garden City, 1971. An account of the resolution passed by Congress.

2530   ZINN, Howard. *Vietnam: The Logic of Withdrawal.* Boston, 1967.

7. Relations with Russia and Europe (Including Britain)

2531   ABEL, Elie. *Missile Crisis.* See 2465.

2532   ACHESON, Dean. "The Illusion of Disengagement." *For Aff,* XXXVI (1958), 371-382.

2533   ALLEN, Harry C. *The Anglo-American Predicament: The British Commonwealth, the United States and European Unity.* New York, 1960.

2534 AUSLAND, John C., and Hugh F. RICHARDSON. "Crisis Management: . . . Cyprus." See 2410.

2535 BADER, William B. *Austria Between East and West, 1945-1955.* Stanford, Cal., 1966.

2536 BOHLEN, Charles E. *Witness to History 1929-1969.* New York, 1973. Important expert on Russia.

2537 BRZEZINSKI, Zbigniew, and Samuel P. HUNTINGTON. *Political Power: USA/USSR.* New York, 1964.†

2538 BYRNES, Robert F., ed. *The United States and Eastern Europe.* Englewood Cliffs, N.J., 1967.

2539 CABLE, John Nathanial. "United States and the Polish Question." See 1949.

2540 CAMPBELL, John C. *American Policy Toward Communist Eastern Europe.* Minneapolis, 1965.

2541 CAMPBELL, John C. *Tito's Separate Road: America and Yugoslavia in World Politics.* New York, 1967.

2542 CHASE, Harry Michael, Jr. "American-Yugoslav Relations, 1945-1956; A Study in the Motivation of U.S. Foreign Policy." Doctoral dissertation, Syracuse University, 1957.

2543 COULOMBIS, Theodore A. *Greek Political Reaction to American and NATO Influences.* New Haven, Conn., 1966.

2544 DAVIS, Paul C. "The New Diplomacy: The 1955 Geneva Summit Meeting." *Foreign Policy in the Sixties.* See 2151.

2545 DENNETT, Raymond, and Joseph E. JOHNSON. *Negotiating with the Russians.* Boston, 1951.

2546 DRUKS, Herbert. *Harry S. Truman and the Russians 1945-1953.* New York, 1967.

2547 DUNCAN, Francis. "Atomic Energy and Anglo-American Relations." See 2345.

2548 EDEN, Anthony. *Full Circle: the Memoirs of Anthony Eden.* Boston, 1960.

2549 EPSTEIN, Leon. *Britain—Uneasy Ally.* Chicago, 1954.

2550 FURNISS, Edgar S., Jr. *France, Troubled Ally: De Gaulle's Heritage and Prospects.* New York, 1960.

2551 GIMBEL, John. "On the Implementation of the Potsdam Agreement; An Essay on U.S. Postwar Policy." *Pol Sci Q*, LXXXVII (1972), 242-269.

2552 HAAS, Ernst B. *The Uniting of Europe.* Stanford, Cal., 1958.

2553 HAMBY, Alonzo L. "Henry A. Wallace, the Liberals, and Soviet-American Relations." *Rev Pol*, XXX (1968), 153-169.

2554 HOWLEY, Brig. General Frank L. *Berlin Command.* New York, 1950.

2555 JONES, Joseph M. *Fifteen Weeks.* See 2310.

2556   KATRIS, John A. *Eyewitness in Greece: The Colonels Come to Power*. St. Louis, 1971. A Greek journalist's statement on American involvement in the 1967 coup.

2557   KENNAN, George F. *Russia, the Atom, and the West*. New York, 1958.

2558   KENNAN, George F. "The Sources of Soviet Conduct." *For Aff*, XXV (1947), 566-582. Reprinted in 2163. The famous statement on "Containment."

2559   KERTESZ, Stephen D., ed. *The Fate of East Central Europe: Hopes and Failures of American Foreign Policy*. Notre Dame, Ind., 1956.

2560   KHRUSHCHEV, Nikita S. *Khrushchev Remembers*. Intro. by Edward Crankshaw. Trans. Strobe Talbott. Boston, 1970. An apparently authentic memoir.

2561   KLEIMAN, Robert. *Atlantic Crisis*. New York, 1964. About the Kennedy administration.

2562   KULSKI, W. W. *The Soviet Union in World Affairs: A Documented Analysis, 1964-1972*. Syracuse, N.Y., 1973.†

2563   LANE, Arthur Bliss. *I Saw Poland Betrayed*. Indianapolis, 1948. Bliss was U.S. ambassador to Poland, 1945-1947.

2564   LERNER, Daniel, and Raymond ARON, eds. *France Defeats EDC*. New York, 1957.

2565   MCINNIS, Edgar W. *The Atlantic Triangle and the Cold War*. Toronto, 1959. Concerns Canada, Britain, and the United States.

2566   MACMILLAN, Harold. *Pointing the Way, 1959-1961*. New York, 1972. A memoir.

2567   MACMILLAN, Harold. *Riding the Storm, 1956-1959*. New York, 1971.

2568   MACMILLAN, Harold. *Tides of Fortune, 1945-1955*. New York, 1969.

2569   MCNEILL, William Hardy. *America, Britain and Russia*. See 1884.

2570   MCNEILL, William Hardy. *Greece: American Aid in Action, 1947-1956*. New York, 1957.

2571   MCNEILL, William Hardy. *The Greek Dilemma: War and Aftermath*. Philadelphia, 1947.

2572   MALLALIEU, William C. *British Reconstruction and American Policy: 1945-1955*. New York, 1956.

2573   MONKMAN, C. A. *American Aid to Greece: A Report on the First Ten Years*. New York, 1958.

2574   MONTGOMERY, John D. *Forced to Be Free: The Artificial Revolution in Germany and Japan*. Chicago, 1958.

2575   MORGAN, Roger. "Washington and Bonn: A Case Study in Alliance Politics." *Int Aff*, XLVII (1971), 489-502.

2576   NEUSTADT, Richard E. *Alliance Politics*. New York, 1970. British-American relations during the Suez crisis (1956) and the Skybolt missile affair (1962).

2577   NEWHOUSE, John. *DeGaulle and the Anglo-Saxons*. New York, 1970.

2578   NUECHTERLEIN, Donald E. *Iceland: Reluctant Ally*. Ithaca, N.Y., 1961.

2579   NUNNERLY, David. *President Kennedy and Britain*. New York, 1972.

2580   OSGOOD, Robert E. "NATO: Problems of Security and Collaboration." *Am Pol Sci Rev*, LIV (1960), 106-129.

2581   PARKER, W. H. *The Superpowers: The United States and the Soviet Union Compared*. New York, 1972. A comparison of economic resources.

2582   PATERSON, Thomas G. "Eastern Europe and the Early Cold War: The Danube Controversy." *Historian*, XXXIII (1971), 237-247.

2583   PETROV, Vladimir. *Arthur Bliss Lane*. See 1381.

2584   PLISCHKE, Elmer. "Eisenhower's 'Correspondence Diplomacy' with the Kremlin: Case Study in Summit Politics." *J Pol*, XXX (1968), 137-159.

2585   PRICE, Harry B. *Marshall Plan and Its Meaning*. See 2322.

2586   RADVANYI, Janos. *Hungary and the Superpowers: The 1956 Revolution and Realpolitik*. Stanford, Cal., 1972.

2587   SMITH, Walter Bedell. *My Three Years in Moscow*. Philadelphia, 1950.

2588   STAVRIANOS, Leften S. "The United States and Greece: The Truman Doctrine in Historical Perspective." *Essays . . . Blakeslee*. See 90.

2589   ULAM, Adam B. *The Rivals: America and Russia Since World War II*. New York, 1971.†

2590   WELCH, William. *American Images of Soviet Foreign Policy: An Inquiry into Recent Appraisals from the Academic Community*. New Haven, Conn., 1970. Surveys the 1959-1968 period.

2591   WHITAKER, Arthur P. *Spain and Defense of the West: Ally and Liability*. New York, 1961.

2592   WHITE, Theodore. *Fire in the Ashes*. New York, 1953. Europe's recovery.

2593   WILLIS, F. Roy. *France, Germany, and the New Europe 1945-1963*. Stanford, Cal., 1965.

2594   WISE, David, and Thomas B. ROSS. *The U-2 Affair*. New York, 1962.

2595   XYDIS, Stephen G. "America, Britain, and the USSR in the Greek Arena, 1944-1947." *Pol Sci Q*, LXXVIII (1963), 581-596.

2596   XYDIS, Stephen G. *Greece and the Great Powers, 1944-1947: Prelude to the "Truman Doctrine."* Thessaloniki, 1963.

2597   ZINK, Harold. *United States in Germany*. See 2437.

8. *Relations with the Western Hemisphere (Including Canada)*

2598 ADAMS, Richard N., *et al. Social Change in Latin America Today: Its Implications for United States Policy*. New York, 1961.

2599 AITKEN, Hugh G. J., *et al. The American Economic Impact on Canada*. Durham, N.C., 1959.

2600 ALEXANDER, Robert J. *Communism in Latin America*. New Brunswick, N.J., 1957.

2601 ALLEN, Robert L. *Soviet Bloc Latin American Activities and Their Implications for United States Foreign Policy*. Washington, 1960.

2602 ATKINS, George Pope, and Larman C. WILSON. *United States and Trujillo*. See 223.

2603 BERLE, Beatrice Bishop, and Beal Jacobs TRAVIS. *From the Papers of Adolf A. Berle*. See 1052.

2604 BODE, Kenneth A. "An Aspect of United States Policy in Latin America: The Latin American Diplomats' View." *Pol Sci Q*, LXXV (1970), 471-491.

2605 BONSAL, Philip W. *Cuba, Castro, and the United States*. Pittsburgh, 1971. Written by a former U.S. ambassador to Cuba.

2606 BOWERS, Claude G. *Chile . . . Embassy*. See 2055.

2607 BRADSHAW, James Stanford. "The 'Lost' Conference: The Economic Issue in United States-Latin American Relations, 1945-1957." Doctoral dissertation, Michigan State University, 1972.

2608 BROWN, Lyle C., and James W. WILKIE. "Recent United States-Mexican Relations: Problems Old and New." *Twentieth-Century American Foreign Policy*. See 64.

2609 BURR, Robert N. *Our Troubled Hemisphere: Perspectives on United States-Latin American Relations*. Washington, 1967.

2610 COCHRANE, James D. "U.S. Policy Towards Recognition of Governments and Promotion of Democracy in Latin America Since 1963." *J Latin Am Stud*, IV (1972), 275-291.

2611 CONNELL-SMITH, Gordon. *The Inter-American System*. New York, 1966.

2612 DRAPER, Theodore. *Castroism, Theory and Practice*. New York, 1962.

2613 DRAPER, Theodore. *Castro's Revolution*. New York, 1962.†

2614 DRAPER, Theodore. "The Dominican Intervention Reconsidered." *Pol Sci Q*, LXXXVI (1971), 1-36.

2615 DRAPER, Theodore. *The Dominican Revolt: A Case Study in American Policy*. New York, 1968.

2616   DREIER, John C., ed. *The Alliance for Progress: Problems and Perspectives.* Baltimore, 1962. Lectures by five specialists.

2617   DREIER, John C. *The Organization of American States and the Hemisphere Crisis.* New York, 1962.

2618   DYER, John M. *United States-Latin American Trade and Financial Relations.* Coral Gables, Fla., 1961. Covers the post-World War II period.

2619   EISENHOWER, Milton S. *The Wine Is Bitter: The United States and Latin America.* New York, 1963.

2620   FRANCIS, Michael J. "The United States and the Act of Chapultepec." *Southwest Social Science Quarterly*, XLV (1964), 249-257.

2621   GEORGE, Alexander L., David K. HALL, and William R. SIMONS. *Limits of Coercive Diplomacy: Cuba.* See 2493.

2622   GILLIN, John, and K. H. SILVERT. "Ambiguities in Guatemala." *For Aff*, XXXIV (1956), 469-482.

2623   GORDON, Lincoln. *A New Deal for Latin America: The Alliance for Progress.* Cambridge, Mass., 1963.

2624   GORDON, Lincoln. "Punta del Este Revisited." *For Aff*, XLV (1967), 624-638. Review of the results of the 1961 conference.

2625   GORDON, Max. "A Case History of U.S. Subversion: Guatemala, 1954." *Sci Soc*, XXXV (1971), 129-155.

2626   GREEN, David. "The Cold War Comes to Latin America." *Politics and Policies of the Truman Administration.* See 2247.

2627   GREEN, David. *Containment of Latin America.* See 1642.

2628   GREGG, Robert W., ed. *International Organization in the Western Hemisphere.* Syracuse, N.Y., 1968.

2629   HALPERIN, Maurice. *The Rise and Decline of Fidel Castro.* Berkeley, Cal., 1972.

2630   HANSON, Simon G. *Dollar Diplomacy Modern Style: Chapters in the Failure of the Alliance for Progress.* Washington, 1970.

2631   HANSON, Simon G. "The End of the Good Neighbor Policy." *Int-Am Econ Aff*, VII (1953), No. 2., 3-49. Covers the initial months of the Eisenhower administration.

2632   HANSON, Simon G. *Five Years of the Alliance for Progress.* Washington, 1967.

2633   HOROWITZ, Irving Louis. *Project Camelot.* See 2353.

2634   JOHNSON, Leland L. "U.S. Business Interests in Cuba and the Rise of Castro." *Wor Pol*, XVII (1965), 440-459.

2635   KURZMAN, Dan. *Santo Domingo: Revolt of the Damned.* New York, 1965.

2636 LAZO, Mario. *Dagger in the Heart: American Policy Failures in Cuba.* New York, 1968.†

2637 LEVINSON, Jerome, and Juan DE ONÍS. *The Alliance That Lost Its Way: A Critical Report on the Alliance for Progress.* Chicago, 1970.†

2638 LIEUWEN, Edwin. *Arms and Politics in Latin America.* Rev. ed. New York, 1961.

2639 LLERAS CAMARGO, Alberto. "The Alliance for Progress: Aims, Distortions, Obstacles." *For Aff,* XLII (1963), 25-37.

2640 LOWENTHAL, Abraham F. *The Dominican Intervention.* Cambridge, Mass., 1972. Analysis of the 1965-1966 operation.

2641 MCDERMOTT, Louis M. "Guatemala, 1954: Intervention or Aggression?" *Rocky Mtn Soc Sci J,* IX (1972), No. 1, 79-88.

2642 MCINNIS, Edgar W. *Atlantic Triangle and the Cold War.* See 2565.

2643 MARTIN, John Bartlow. *Overtaken by Events: The Dominican Crisis from the Fall of Trujillo to the Civil War.* Garden City, N.Y., 1966.

2644 MARTZ, John D. *Central America: The Crisis and the Challenge.* Chapel Hill, N.C., 1959.

2645 MARTZ, John D. *Communist Infiltration in Guatemala.* New York, 1956.

2646 MAY, Ernest R. "The Alliance for Progress in Historical Perspective." *For Aff,* XLI (1963), 757-774.

2647 MEYER, Karl, and Tad SZULC. *The Cuban Invasion: The Chronicle of a Disaster.* New York, 1962.

2648 MORAN, Theodore H. "The Alliance for Progress and 'The Foreign Copper Companies and their Local Conservative Allies'. in Chile, 1955-1970." *Int-Am Econ Aff,* XXV (1972), No. 4, 3-24.

2649 MORRISON, DeLesseps S. *Latin American Mission: An Adventure in Hemisphere Diplomacy.* Ed. Gerold Frank. New York, 1965.

2650 PETRAS, James F., and Robert LAPORTE, Jr. *Cultivating Revolution: The United States and Agrarian Reform in Latin America.* New York, 1971. Case studies: Chile, Cuba, Peru.

2651 PIKE, Fredrick B. "Guatemala, the United States, and Communism in the Americas." *Rev Pol,* XVII (1955), 232-261.

2652 PLANK, John, ed. *Cuba and the United States.* Washington, 1967.

2653 RIPPY, J. Fred. *Globe and Hemisphere: Latin America's Place in the Postwar Foreign Relations of the United States.* Chicago, 1958.

2654 ROGERS, William D. *The Twilight Struggle: The Alliance for Progress and the Politics of Development in Latin America.* New York, 1967.

2655 SCHNEIDER, Ronald M. *Communism in Guatemala, 1944-1954.* New York, 1958.

2656   SLATER, Jerome. *Intervention and Negotiation: The United States and the Dominican Revolution.* New York, 1970. Deals with the intervention of 1965-1966.

2657   SLATER, Jerome. "The Limits of Legitimization in International Organizations: The Organization of American States and the Dominican Crisis." *Int Organ*, XXIII (1969), 48-72. About the 1965-1966 crisis.

2658   SLATER, Jerome. *The OAS and United States Foreign Policy.* Columbus, Ohio, 1967.

2659   SMETHERMAN, Bobbie B., and Robert M. SMETHERMAN. "The CEP Claims, U.S. Tuna Fishing and Inter-American Relations." *Orbis*, XIV (1970-1971), 951-972. CEP stands for Chile, Ecuador, and Peru. Period covered: the 1960's.

2660   SMITH, Earl E. T. *The Fourth Floor: An Account of the Castro Revolution.* New York, 1962.

2661   SMITH, O. Edmund, Jr. *U.S. Intervention in Argentina.* See 2067.

2662   SOWARD, F. H. "The Changing Relations of Canada and the United States Since the Second World War." *Pac Hist Rev*, XXII (1953), 155-168.

2663   SPECTOR, Stephen David. "United States Attempts at Regional Security and the Extension of the Good Neighbor Policy in Latin America, 1945-1952." Doctoral dissertation, New York University, 1970.

2664   SUÁREZ, Andrés. *Cuba: Castroism and Communism, 1959-1966.* Cambridge, Mass., 1967.

2665   SZULC, Tad. *Dominican Diary.* New York, 1965.

2666   SZULC, Tad. *The Winds of Revolution.* Rev. ed. New York, 1965.

2667   TAYLOR, Philip B., Jr. "The Guatemalan Affair: A Critique of United States Foreign Policy." *Am Pol Sci Rev*, L (1956), 787-806.

2668   THOMAS, Ann Van Wynen, and A. J. Thomas, Jr. *The Organization of American States.* Dallas, Tex., 1963.

2669   WAGNER, R. Harrison. *United States Policy Toward Latin America: A Study in Domestic and International Politics.* Stanford, Cal., 1970. Focuses on economic policies, 1945-1960.

2670   WILLIAMS, Edward J. *The Political Themes of Inter-American Relations.* Belmont, Cal., 1971. On intervention, the Cold War, and the third world.

2671   WILLIAMS, William A. *The U.S., Cuba, and Castro.* New York, 1962.

9. Relations with the Middle East

2672   AGWANI, M. S., ed. *The Lebanese Crisis, 1958: A Documentary Study.* New York, 1965.

2673 ALDRICH, Winthrop W. "The Suez Crisis: A Footnote to History." *For Aff*, XLV (1967), 541-552.

2674 ARCILESI, Salvatore Alfred. "Development of United States Foreign Policy in Iran, 1949-1960." Doctoral dissertation, University of Virginia, 1965.

2675 BLAIR, Leon Borden. *Western Window in the Arab World*. See 1946.

2676 CAMPBELL, John C. *Defense of the Middle East: Problems of American Policy*. Rev. ed. New York, 1960.

2677 COPELAND, Miles. *The Game of Nations: The Amorality of Power Politics*. New York, 1970. Concerns American agents and Nasser.

2678 DOUGHERTY, James E. "The Aswan Decision in Perspective." *Pol Sci Q*, LXXIV (1959), 21-45.

2679 ENGLER, Robert. *The Politics of Oil*. New York, 1961.

2680 FEIS, Herbert. *The Birth of Israel: The Tousled Diplomatic Bed*. New York, 1969. Includes some British-American disagreements.

2681 FERRELL, Robert H. "United States Policy in the Middle East." *American Diplomacy in a New Era*. See 2166.

2682 FINER, Herman. *Dulles over Suez; The Theory and Practice of His Diplomacy*. Chicago, 1964.

2683 FITZSIMONS, M. A. "The Suez Crisis and the Containment Policy." *Rev Pol*, XIX (1957), 419-445.

2684 GALLMAN, Waldeman J. *Iraq Under General Nuri: My Recollections of Nuri al Said, 1954-1958*. Baltimore, 1963. By the American ambassador to Iraq.

2684-A HARRIS, George S. *Troubled Alliance: Turkish-American Problems in Historical Perspective, 1945-1971*. Washington, 1972.†

2685 HAYKAL, Muhammad Hasanayn. *The Cairo Documents: The Inside Story of Nasser and His Relationship with World Leaders, Rebels, and Statesmen*. Intro. by Edward R. F. Sheehan. Garden City, N.Y., 1973.

2686 HOSKINS, Halford L. *The Middle East: Problem Area in World Politics*. New York, 1954.

2687 HUREWITZ, Jacob C. *Middle East Dilemmas: The Background of United States Policy*. New York, 1953.

2688 KIRK, George E. *The Middle East, 1945-1950*. New York, 1954.

2689 LENCZOWSKI, George. *The Middle East in World Affairs*. 3d ed. Ithaca, N.Y., 1962.

2690 LENCZOWSKI, George. *Oil and State in the Middle East*. Ithaca, N.Y., 1960.

2691 LILIENTHAL, Alfred M. *What Price Israel*. Chicago, 1953.

2692   MCDONALD, James G. *My Mission in Israel, 1948-1951*. New York, 1951.

2693   MIKESELL, Raymond F., and Hollis B. CHENERY. *Arabian Oil: America's Stake in the Middle East*. Chapel Hill, N.C., 1949.

2694   MILLSPAUGH, Arthur C. *Americans in Persia*. Washington, 1946.

2695   SMOLANSKY, O. M. "Moscow and the Suez Crisis, 1956: A Reappraisal." *Pol Sci Q*, LXXX (1965), 581-605.

2696   SNETSINGER, John Goodall. "Truman and the Creation of Israel." Doctoral dissertation, Stanford University, 1970.

2697   STEVENS, Georgiana G., ed. *The United States and the Middle East*. New York, 1964.

2698   STEVENS, Richard P. *American Zionism and U.S. Foreign Policy, 1942-1947*. New York, 1962.

2699   THOMAS, Hugh. *Suez*. New York, 1967.

2700   THORNBURG, Max W. *People and Policy in the Middle East: A Study of Social and Political Change as a Basis for United States Policy*. New York, 1964.

2701   WARNE, William E. *Mission for Peace: Point 4 in Iran*. Indianapolis, 1956. Written by the director of the program.

10. Relations with Africa

2702   ATTWOOD, William. *The Reds and the Blacks: A Personal Adventure*. New York, 1967. By the U.S. ambassador to Guinea and Kenya.

2703   EMERSON, Rupert. *Africa and United States Policy*. Englewood Cliffs, N.J., 1967.

2704   EMERSON, Rupert. "American Policy in Africa." *For Aff*, XL (1962), 303-315.

2705   GOLDSCHMIDT, Walter, ed. *The United States and Africa*. New York, 1963.

2706   GORDON, King. *The United Nations in the Congo: A Quest for Peace*. New York, 1962.

2707   HANCE, William A., ed. *Southern Africa and the United States*. New York, 1968.

2708   KINSEY, Winston Lee. "The United States and Ghana, 1951-1966." Doctoral dissertation, Texas Tech University, 1969.

2709   LEFEVER, Ernest W. "U.S. Policy, the UN and the Congo." *Orbis*, XI (1967), 394-413.

2710   LEFEVER, Ernest W. *Uncertain Mandate: Politics of the U.N. Congo Operation*. Baltimore, 1967.

2711 LIEBNOW, J. Gus. "United States Policy in Africa Below the Sahara." *American Diplomacy in a New Era*. See 2166.

2712 MCKAY, Vernon. *African Diplomacy*. New York, 1966.

2713 MCKAY, Vernon. *Africa in World Politics*. New York, 1963.

2714 MORGENTHAU, Hans J. "United States Policy Toward Africa." *Africa in the Modern World*. Ed. Calvin W. Stillman. Chicago, 1955.

2715 MORROW, John H. *First American Ambassador to Guinea*. New Brunswick, N.J., 1967.

2716 O'BRIEN, Conor Cruise. *To Katanga and Back: A U.N. Case History*. New York, 1963.

11. *Relations with Asia and the Pacific*

East Asia

2717 ADUARD, Baron E. J. van Lewe. *Japan from Surrender to Peace*. New York, 1954.

2718 APPLETON, Sheldon. *The Eternal Triangle? Communist China, the United States, and the United Nations*. East Lansing, Mich., 1961.

2719 BARNETT, A. Doak. *Communist China and Asia: Challenge to American Policy*. New York, 1960.

2720 BEAL, John Robinson. *Marshall in China*. Garden City, N.Y., 1970. Marshall's 1946 mission.

2721 BLUM, Robert. *The United States and China in World Affairs*. Ed. A. Doak Barnett. New York, 1966.

2722 BOYER, William W., and Neylan AKRA. "The United States and the Admission of Communist China: Imminence of Change." *Pol Sci Q*, LXXVI (1961), 332-353.

2723 CARY, James. *Japan Today: Reluctant Ally*. New York, 1962.

2724 CLUBB, O. Edmund. "Formosa and the Offshore Islands in American Policy, 1950-1955." *Pol Sci Q*, LXXIV (1959), 517-531.

2725 COHEN, Bernard C. *The Political Process and Foreign Policy: The Making of the Japanese Peace Settlement*. Princeton, N.J., 1957.

2726 DOWER, John W. "Occupied Japan and the American Lake, 1945-1950." *America's Asia: Dissenting Essays on Asian-American Relations*. Ed. Edward Friedman and Mark Selden. New York, 1971.

2727 DULLES, Foster Rhea. *American Policy Toward Communist China: The Historical Record, 1949-1969*. New York, 1972.

2728   DUNN, Frederick S. *Peace-Making and the Settlement with Japan.* Princeton, N.J., 1963.

2729   FAIRBANK, John K. *China: The People's Middle Kingdom and the U.S.A.* Cambridge, Mass., 1967.

2730   FEAREY, Robert A. *The Occupation of Japan: Second Phase, 1948-1950.* New York, 1950.

2731   FEIS, Herbert. *China Tangle.* See 1904.

2732   FEIS, Herbert. *Contest over Japan.* New York, 1967. On occupation policies.

2733   FETZER, James Alan. "Congress and China." See 1905.

2734   FRIEDMAN, Edward. "Problems in Dealing with an Irrational Power: America Declares War on China." *America's Asia: Dissenting Essays on Asian-American Relations.* Ed. Edward Friedman and Mark Selden. New York, 1971. Deals with the Korean War period.

2735   GREENE, Fred. *U.S. Policy and the Security of Asia.* New York, 1968.

2736   GUHIN, Michael A. "The United States and the Chinese People's Republic: The Non-Recognition Policy Revisited." *Int Aff,* XLV (1969), 44-63.

2737   HOHENBERG, John. *Between Two Worlds: Policy, Press, and Public Opinion in Asian-American Relations.* New York, 1967. Covers the years 1945-1966.

2738   JACOBY, Neil H. *U.S. Aid to Taiwan: A Study of Foreign Aid, Self-Help, and Development.* New York, 1967.

2739   KAWAI, Kazuo. *Japan's American Interlude.* Chicago, 1960.

2740   KEMP, Virginia May. "Congress and China, 1945-1959." Doctoral dissertation, University of Pittsburgh, 1966.

2741   MACFARQUHAR, Roderick, ed. *Sino-American Relations, 1949-1971.* New York, 1972. Documents and essays.

2742   MONTGOMERY, John D. *Artificial Revolution . . . Japan.* See 2574.

2743   MONTGOMERY, John D. *Foreign Aid.* See 2317.

2744   MORLEY, James W. *Japan and Korea: America's Allies in the Pacific.* New York, 1965.

2745   PACKARD, George R., III. *Protest in Tokyo: The Security Treaty Crisis of 1960.* Princeton, N.J., 1966.

2746   RANKIN, Karl Lott. *China Assignment.* Seattle, 1964. Written by the first American ambassador to Taiwan.

2747   REISCHAUER, Edwin O. *Beyond Vietnam: The United States and Asia.* New York, 1967.†

2748   SEBALD, William J., with Russell BAINES. *With MacArthur in Japan: A Personal History of the Occupation.* New York, 1965.

2749 SERVICE, John S. *The Amerasia Papers*. See 1925.

2750 STEELE, A. T. *The American People and China*. New York, 1966.

2751 STOPSKY, Fred Harold. "An Analysis of the Conflict Within the United States Federal Government in the Period 1949-1956 Concerning American Policy Toward China." Doctoral dissertation, New York University, 1969.

2752 STUART, John Leighton. *Fifty Years in China*. New York, 1954. Stuart was U.S. ambassador to China after World War II.

2753 TSOU, Tang. *America's Failure in China*. See 1931.

2754 TSOU, Tang. "Civil Strife and Armed Intervention: Marshall's China Policy." *Orbis*, VI (1962), 76-101.

2755 United States Department of State. *United States Relations with China: With Special Reference to the Period 1944-1949*. Washington, 1949. Reprinted, Stanford, Cal., 1967. The "China White Paper."

2756 WARD, Robert E. "The Origins of the Present Japanese Constitution." *Am Pol Sci Rev*, L (1956), 980-1010.

2757 WITTNER, Lawrence S. "MacArthur and the Missionaries: God and Man in Occupied Japan." *Pac Hist Rev*, XL (1971), 77-98.

2758 YOUNG, Kenneth T. *Negotiating with the Chinese Communists: The United States Experience, 1953-1967*. New York, 1968.†

2759 ZAGORIA, Donald S. *The Sino-Soviet Conflict*. New York, 1962.

South and Southeast Asia and the Pacific

2760 AUSLAND, John C., and Col. Hugh F. RICHARDSON. "Crisis Management: Laos." See 2410.

2761 BARNDS, William J. *India, Pakistan, and the Great Powers*. New York, 1972. Encompasses American policy in South Asia, 1947-1972.

2762 BOWLES, Chester. *Ambassador's Report*. New York, 1954. About India.

2763 BOWLES, Chester. *Promises to Keep: My Years in Public Life, 1941-1969*. New York, 1971. Bowles was U.S. ambassador to India 1951-1953 and 1963-1969.

2764 BRODKIN, E. I. "United States Aid to India and Pakistan: The Attitudes of the Fifties." *Int Aff*, XLIII (1967), 664-677.

2765 CLUBB, O. Edmund. *The United States and the Sino-Soviet Bloc in Southeast Asia*. Washington, 1962.

2766 COLBERT, Evelyn. "Reconsiderations; the Road Not Taken; Decolonization and Independence in Indonesia and Indochina." *For Aff*, LI (1972-1973), 608-628. Traces American involvement.

2767 COULTER, John W. *Pacific Dependencies of the United States*. New York, 1957.

2768   FALL, Bernard B. *Anatomy of a Crisis: The Laotian Crisis of 1960-1961.* Ed. Roger M. Smith. Garden City, N.Y., 1969.

2769   FIFIELD, Russell H. *The Diplomacy of Southeast Asia, 1945-1958.* New York, 1958.

2770   FIFIELD, Russell H. *Southeast Asia in United States Policy.* New York, 1963.

2771   GALBRAITH, John Kenneth. *Ambassador's Journal: A Personal Account of the Kennedy Years.* Boston, 1969. Galbraith was U.S. ambassador to India.

2772   GEORGE, Alexander L., David K. HALL, and William R. SIMONS. *Limits of Coercive Diplomacy: Laos.* See 2493.

2773   GOLAY, Frank H., ed. *The United States and the Philippines.* Englewood Cliffs, N.J., 1966.

2774   GOULD, James W. *The United States and Malaysia.* Cambridge, Mass., 1969.

2775   HAYES, Samuel P., ed. *The Beginning of American Aid to Southeast Asia.* Lexington, Mass., 1971.

2776   HESS, Gary R. *America Encounters India.* See 1909.

2777   HILL, Kenneth L. "President Kennedy and the Neutralization of Laos." *Rev Pol*, XXI (1969), 353-369.

2778   JAUHRI, R. C. *American Diplomacy and Independence for India.* See 1912.

2779   JONES, Howard Palfrey. *Indonesia: The Possible Dream.* New York, 1971. This account was written by the U.S. ambassador to Indonesia, 1958-1965.

2780   LANSDALE, Major General Edward Geary. *In the Midst of Wars: An American's Mission to Southeast Asia.* New York, 1972. A memoir about General Lansdale's work in Vietnam in the 1950's.

2781   McCOY, Alfred W., *et al. The Politics of Heroin in Southeast Asia.* New York, 1972.

2782   McLANE, Charles B. *Soviet Strategies in Southeast Asia.* Princeton, N.J., 1966.

2783   MIRSKY, Jonathan, and Stephen E. STONEFIELD. "The United States in Laos, 1945-1962." *America's Asia: Dissenting Essays on Asian-American Relations.* See 2726.

2784   NICHOLS, Jeannette P. "United States Aid to South and Southeast Asia, 1950-1960." *Pac Hist Rev*, XXXII (1963), 171-184.

2785   PALMER, Norman D. *South Asia and United States Policy.* Boston, 1966.

2786   PERITZ, René. "American-Malaysian Relations: Substance and Shadows." *Orbis*, XI (1967), 532-550.

2787   RANDLE, Robert F. *Geneva 1954: The Settlement of the Indochinese War.* Princeton, N.J., 1969.

2788   ROSINGER, Lawrence K. *India and the United States: Political and Economic Relations*. New York, 1950.

2789   STANTON, Edwin F. *Brief Authority: Excursions of a Common Man in an Uncommon World*. New York, 1965. Stanton was ambassador to Thailand, 1946-1953.

2790   STARKE, J. G. *The Anzus Treaty Alliance*. New York, 1965.

2791   STEVENSON, Charles A. *The End of Nowhere: American Policy Toward Laos Since 1954*. Boston, 1972.

2792   SUNG YONG KIM. *United States-Philippine Relations, 1946-1956*. Washington, 1968.

2793   TALBOT, Phillips, and S. L. POPLAI. *India and America*. New York, 1958.

2794   TAYLOR, Alastair M. *Indonesian Independence and the United Nations*. Ithaca, N.Y., 1960.

2795   TAYLOR, George E. *The Philippines and the United States: Problems of Partnership*. New York, 1964.

2795-A THEE, Marek [GDANSKI, Marek]. *Notes of a Witness: Laos and the Second Indochina War*. New York, 1973.† Written by a member of the International Control Commission.

2796   TRAGER, Frank N. "American Foreign Policy in Southeast Asia." *Studies on Asia*, VI (1965), 17-59. Covers the years 1945-1965.

2797   TRAGER, Frank N. "The United States and Pakistan: A Failure of Diplomacy." *Orbis*, IX (1965), 613-629.

2798   VANDENBOSCH, Amry, and Richard A. BUTWELL. *Southeast Asia Among the World Powers*. Lexington, Ky., 1957.

2799   VENKATARAMANI, M. S. *Undercurrents in American Foreign Relations*. See 2233-A.

2800   WALTER, Austin Frederic. "Australia's Relations with the United States: 1941-1949." See 1937.

2801   WARNER, Geoffrey. "The United States and Vietnam." See 2528.

2802   WEINER, Myron. "United States Policy in South and Southeast Asia." *American Diplomacy in a New Era*. See 2166.

2803   WILSON, David A. *The United States and the Future of Thailand*. New York, 1970. History of the U.S.-Thai alliance.

2804   WOLF, Charles, Jr. *Foreign Aid . . . in Southeast Asia*. See 2330.

12. Cultural and Information Programs

2805   ASHABRANNER, Brent. *A Moment in History*. Garden City, 1971. The first decade of the Peace Corps.

2806   CAREY, Robert G. *The Peace Corps*. New York, 1970.

2807   COOMBS, Philip H. *The Fourth Dimension of Foreign Policy: Educational and Cultural Affairs*. New York, 1964.

2808   DIZARD, W. P. *The Strategy of Truth: The Story of the U.S. Information Service*. Washington, 1961.

2809   ELDER, Robert E. *The Information Machine: The United States Information Agency and American Foreign Policy*. Syracuse, N.Y., 1968.

2810   FRANKEL, Charles. *The Neglected Aspect of Foreign Affairs*. Washington, 1966. Educational and cultural affairs.

2811   FUCHS, Lawrence H. *"Those Peculiar Americans": The Peace Corps and American National Character*. New York, 1967.

2812   HENDERSON, John W. *The United States Information Agency*. New York, 1969.

2813   JOHNSON, Walter, and Francis J. COLLIGAN. *The Fulbright Program: A History*. Chicago, 1965.

VII. Kissinger, the Nixon Doctrine, and Beyond

2814   *Asahi Shimbun* Staff. *The Pacific Rivals*. New York, 1972. Tokyo newsmen's view of recent U.S.-Japanese relations.

2815   BARBER, Hollis W. "The United States vs. the United Nations." *Int Organ* XXVII (1973), 139-163. Covers recent interactions.

2816   BARNDS, William J. *India, Pakistan, and the Great Powers*. See 2761.

2817   BEHRMAN, Jack N. *National Interests and the Multinational Enterprise: Tensions Among the North Atlantic Countries*. Englewood Cliffs, N.J., 1970. About contemporary relations between multinational corporations and governments.

2818   BINNING, William C. "The Nixon Foreign Aid Policy for Latin America." *Int-Am Econ Aff*, XXV (1971), No. 1, 31-45.

2819   BRANDON, Henry. *The Retreat of American Power*. Garden City, N.Y., 1973. A journalist's description of U.S. foreign policy under Nixon and Kissinger.

2820   BRZEZINSKI, Zbigniew. "How the Cold War Was Played." See 2105.

2821   BURCHETT, Wilfred G. *The Second Indochina War: Cambodia and Laos*. New York, 1970. Discusses the 1970 incursions by U.S. troops.

2822   CALLEO, David. *The Atlantic Fantasy: The U.S., NATO, and Europe*. Baltimore, 1970. A contemporary critique.

2823 CAMPBELL, John Franklin. *The Foreign Affairs Fudge Factory*. New York, 1971. A dissection of American foreign policy bureaucracy.

2824 CAMPS, Michael. "Sources of Strain in Trans-Atlantic Relations." *Int Aff*, XLVIII (1972), 559-578.

2825 CHAUDHRI, Mohammed Ahsen. *Pakistan and the Great Powers*. Karachi, 1970. A contemporary analysis of Pakistan's relations with the U.S., the U.S.S.R., and China.

2826 CHITTICK, William O. *State Department, Press and Pressure Groups: A Role Analysis*. New York, 1970.

2827 COCHRANE, James D. "U.S. Policy Towards . . . Latin America." See 2610.

2828 FOX, Annette Baker. "Domestic Pressures in North America to Withdraw Forces from Europe." *European Security and the Atlantic System*. See 2830.

2829 FOX, Annette Baker. "NATO and the American Nuclear Deterrent." *European Security and the Atlantic System*. See 2830.

2830 FOX, William T. R., and Warner R. SCHILLING, eds. *European Security and the Atlantic System*. New York, 1973. Current and recent American relationships to the European security arrangement.

2831 FULBRIGHT, J. William. *The Crippled Giant: American Foreign Policy and Its Domestic Consequences*. New York, 1972.† Essay by the chairman of the Senate Foreign Relations Committee.

2832 GALLOWAY, Jonathan F. *The Politics and Technology of Satellite Communications*. Lexington, Mass., 1972.

2833 GARDNER, Lloyd C., ed. *The Great Nixon Turnabout: America's New Foreign Policy in the Post-Liberal Era*. New York, 1973.† A collection of articles.

2834 GIRLING, J. L. S. "The Guam Doctrine." *Int Aff*, XLVI (1970), 48-62.

2835 GRANT, Jonathan S., *et al.*, comps. *Cambodia: The Widening War in Indochina*. New York, 1971. Selected documents.

2836 GRAUBARD, Stephen R. *Kissinger: Portrait of a Mind*. New York, 1973.

2837 GRAY, Colin S. "Of Bargaining Chips and Building Blocks: Arms Control and Defense Policy." *Int Jour*, XXVIII (1973), 266-296. On the SALT negotiations.

2838 HAHN, Walter F. "The Nixon Doctrine: Design and Dilemmas." *Orbis*, XVI (1972-1973), 361-376.

2839 HARRIS, George S. *Turkish-American Problems*. See 2684-A.

2840 HARTMANN, Frederick H. *New Age of American Foreign Policy*. See 2147.

2841 JANSEN, Michael E. *The United States and the Palestinian People*. Beirut, 1970.

2842 JENKINS, Roy. *Afternoon on the Potomac? A British View of America's Changing Position in the World.* New Haven, Conn., 1972. Lectures.

2843 KEOHANE, Robert O., and Joseph S. NYE, Jr., eds. *Transnational Relations and World Politics.* Cambridge, Mass., 1972.

2844 KIERNAN, Bernard P. *The United States, Communism, and the Emergent World.* Bloomington, Ind., 1972.

2845 KILDOW, Judith Tegger. *INTELSAT: Policy-Maker's Dilemma.* Lexington, Mass., 1973. The conflict between the State Department and private corporations over satellite communications.

2846 LANDAU, David. *Kissinger: The Uses of Power.* Boston, 1972.

2847 MANDEL, Ernest. *Europe vs. America: Contradictions of Imperialism.* New York, 1970.

2848 MAZLISH, Bruce. *In Search of Nixon; A Psychohistorical Inquiry.* New York, 1972.

2849 MOULTON, Harland B. *From Superiority to Parity . . . the Strategic Arms Race.* See 2384.

2850 NEWHOUSE, John. *Cold Dawn: The Story of SALT.* New York, 1973.

2851 NEWHOUSE, John, *et al. U.S. Troops in Europe: Issues, Costs, and Choices.* Washington, 1971.

2852 OSGOOD, Robert E., *et al. Retreat from Empire? The First Nixon Administration.* Baltimore, 1973.

2853 PAUL, Roland A. *American Military Commitments Abroad.* New Brunswick, N.J., 1973. Outlines the origins of current commitments.

2854 PUSEY, Merlo J. *The U.S.A. Astride the Globe.* Boston, 1971. The United States as world policeman.

2855 RAPOPORT, Anatol. *The Big Two: Soviet-American Perceptions of Foreign Policy.* Indianapolis, 1971.

2856 ROSTOW, Eugene V. *The Future of American Foreign Policy.* New York, 1972.

2857 SHARP, Daniel A., ed. *U.S. Foreign Policy and Peru.* Austin, Tex., 1972. Discusses the contemporary situation.

2858 STANLEY, Timothy W., and Darnell M. WHITT. *Detente Diplomacy: United States and European Security in the 1970's.* New York, 1970.

2859 STENNIS, John C., and J. William FULBRIGHT. *The Role of Congress in Foreign Policy.* Washington, 1971. Opinions of two senators.

2860 STRANGE, Susan. "The Dollar Crisis 1971." *Int Aff*, XLVIII (1972), 191-216.

2861 TRASK, David F. "The Imperial Republic." See 2228.

2862 TUCKER, Robert W. *A New Isolationism: Threat or Promise?* New York, 1972.†

2863 TUCKER, Robert W. *The Radical Left and American Foreign Policy*. Baltimore, 1971.†

2864 United States Department of State. *United States Foreign Policy, 1969/70: A Report of the Secretary of State*. Washington, 1971. A volume for 1971 appeared in 1972, and one for 1972 in 1973.

2865 United States President (Nixon). *U.S. Foreign Policy for the 1970's*. Washington, 1970-1973. Annual volumes.

2866 VAN DER LINDEN, Frank. *Nixon's Quest for Peace*. Washington, 1972.

2867 VERNON, Raymond. *Sovereignty at Bay: The Multi-national Spread of U.S. Enterprises*. New York, 1971.

2868 WEIL, Gordon L., and Ian DAVIDSON. *The Gold War: The Story of the World's Monetary Crisis*. New York, 1970.

2869 WENK, Edward, Jr. *The Politics of the Ocean*. Seattle, 1972.

2870 WILLS, Garry. *Nixon Agonistes: The Crisis of the Self-Made Man*. Boston, 1970.†

NOTES

INDEX

INDEX

INDEX

C

INDEX

INDEX

INDEX

INDEX

INDEX

INDEX

INDEX

INDEX

INDEX

INDEX

INDEX